To: Tara

Sharon Newton

John 10:10(b)
NLT, TLB

Sharon Newton does an outstanding job of capturing the story of the Exodus and the journey through the wilderness in a fresh, unique way. This book will inspire hope in every believer who walks through those seasons of difficulty and waiting we all face. You will be encouraged to discover that every wilderness experience is only preparing you for the destiny God has for you.

—Rev. Bryan Carter, Senior Pastor,
Concord Church, Dallas, Texas

Sharon Newton's spiritual lessons encouraged me from the very beginning of the book. She imaginatively infuses the biblical narrative into our own everyday lives. Enter into her dialogue and your heart will be enriched by spiritual discoveries for the rest of your life.

—Ramesh Richard PhD, ThD
President, Ramesh Richard Evangelism and Church Health
Professor, Global Theological Engagement and Pastoral Ministries,
Dallas Theological Seminary

BITTER CUP, SWEET AFTERTASTE

LESSONS FROM THE WILDERNESS

*with spiritual lessons in italics and corresponding
scriptures provided as footnotes*

SHARON NEWTON

WESTBOW
P R E S S®
A DIVISION OF THOMAS NELSON
& ZONDERVAN

Edited by Marilyn Bradford

**For access to the scripture versions cited in this book,
you may go to www.biblegateway.com**

Scripture taken from the Amplified Bible, copyright © 1954, 1958, 1962, 1964, 1965, 1987 by The Lockman Foundation. Used by permission.

Scripture taken from the Holy Bible, NEW INTERNATIONAL VERSION®. Copyright © 1973, 1978, 1984 by Biblica, Inc. All rights reserved worldwide. Used by permission. NEW INTERNATIONAL VERSION® and NIV® are registered trademarks of Biblica, Inc. Use of either trademark for the offering of goods or services requires the prior written consent of Biblica US, Inc.

Scripture quotations taken from the Holy Bible, New Living Translation, Copyright © 1996, 2004. Used by permission of Tyndale House Publishers, Inc., Wheaton, Illinois 60189. All rights reserved.

Scripture taken from The Living Bible copyright © 1971 by Tyndale House Foundation. Used by permission of Tyndale House Publishers Inc., Carol Stream, Illinois 60188. All rights reserved. The Living Bible, TLB, and the The Living Bible logo are registered trademarks of Tyndale House Publishers.

WestBow Press books may be ordered through booksellers or by contacting:

WestBow Press
A Division of Thomas Nelson & Zondervan
1663 Liberty Drive
Bloomington, IN 47403
www.westbowpress.com
1 (866) 928-1240

ISBN: 978-1-4908-8679-4 (sc)
ISBN: 978-1-4908-8680-0 (hc)
ISBN: 978-1-4908-8678-7 (e)

Library of Congress Control Number: 2015911171

Print information available on the last page.

WestBow Press rev. date: 01/11/2018

TABLE OF CONTENTS

CHAPTER 1

A HARD REALITY

It had been two years since God's chosen people left the clutches of slavery in Egypt. In the middle of the wilderness, millions, now free, lay sleeping in tents strewn across the desert as far as the eye could see. My husband Bezalel and I were among the chosen. While the camp was still cool and quiet, I instinctively woke up just before dawn, as I had every day since leaving Egypt. With my eyes still closed and my soul writhing in pain, I lay hoping that the dreadful events of yesterday were all just a dream. Overcome with hopelessness, I had no will to face the day, let alone the rest of my life. My circumstances were so emotionally overwhelming that they had begun to affect my physical body as well. As I sat up in bed, my head throbbed and my heart raced. Surmising that as long as I was alive, I had to eat, I managed to swing my stiff, aching legs over the side of the bed to begin the task of collecting manna for the household for the day. The reality that this drafty tent in this dry, barren, lifeless wilderness would be my home until the day I left this earth engulfed me.

With labored breath, I held my heavy head in my hands and sobbed uncontrollably with no regard for waking my sleeping family.

With his head still on the pillow, Bezalel reached over and gently stroked my shoulder without saying a word, even though he was in his own private hell. His touch, which usually soothed me, provided no comfort. But I turned and touched his hand, just to let him know that I cared that he cared.

"Talk to me, Chaya," he said softly, still holding my hand and caressing it as he did when he needed me to open up my soul to him.

I looked away for a few moments to collect my thoughts. Before I could clearly communicate my feelings to him, I first needed to understand for myself what was going on inside of me.

"I'm tired, and I'm not sure I can do this anymore," I said from a grief-filled heart as I turned and looked directly into his eyes. I exhaled, relieved to finally be able to say what I had been thinking for a long time. "I'm tired of this miserable, empty wilderness, tired of trying to do the right thing but having little to show for it, just tired of waiting on God to keep His promise to make our lives worth living."

Bezalel had not only been listening to my words, but also carefully studying my face and body language. I could tell that he wanted to thoroughly understand every nuance of what I thought and felt so that he could give me the wise counsel that I so desperately needed.

He reflected for a moment, carefully choosing his words. Then he said, "I know you better than anyone else on the face of this earth, and I know that you are a strong, resilient woman. With my own eyes, I have seen you weather far more adversity than the little bit of discomfort and the long wait that come with being in this wilderness. So I know you can do this. Am I right?"

I pondered his words and had to admit that he was right. He had seen me persevere through the emotionally painful miscarriage of our firstborn child, and his bout with adultery, which I knew he deeply regretted. And he had witnessed every other misfortune that I had overcome.

"Yes, you're right. You are always right," I told him, grateful for his helpful perspective. As I felt my shoulders relax, and my face soften, I leaned over and grazed his lips with a kiss to say "thank you." I was encouraged by his words of wisdom, which gave me the strength I needed to keep moving. With my newfound resolve, *I was determined not to be worn down and defeated by the wilderness but instead to make it work for me and my family. One way or another, I would make it produce good fruit for us,*[1] however long we lived.

My wise husband gave me one more crucial thought to consider. He said, "Don't give up on God yet. He may just have a plan to bring something magnificent out of this journey through the wilderness."

"Hmmm," I said to myself, wondering if this novel idea might have some merit.

Without speaking another word, we solemnly got up, roused the children, covered ourselves with cloaks, and headed off into the barely lit desert to gather food. Even after two years, we still could not emotionally come to terms with the harshness of the desert. Because we had lived in a land as abundantly fertile and green as Egypt for most of our lives, the desert's stark contrast was an insurmountable shock to us

---

[1] Hebrews 10:35–36 (NIV)

every single day. Instead of lush palm trees, vibrant crops, and an endless supply of fresh water from the Nile River, there was nothing but sand and rocks of the same dull color, spanning as far as the eye could see in every direction. Rather than the evening warmth that could be counted on to bring my days as a slave to a pleasant end, the cold desert nights numbed my fingers and toes and turned them blue. With no wind to provide even an occasional breeze, the heat was suffocating throughout most of the day. And except for the noise we made and the howling wind of an occasional sandstorm, the desert was eerily quiet, void of even a trace of life. It was obviously a place that was not originally designed for long-term human habitation, but merely a place to be passed through as one passes through a dark, foreboding valley in haste.

The four of us set off in different directions yet remained within the area allotted to our tribe. Thousands of people were already out, planning to finish the task before the sun came up over the horizon and melted the manna away. Gathering it was hard work. The white flakes contained a honey-like substance that made them sweet but sticky. Because they stuck slightly to the desert floor as they fell, some effort was required to collect them. They were small in size, so amassing enough of them to fulfill the daily requirement of two quarts per person was labor intensive and hard on our backs. But we learned the hard way that those who did not get up in time and gather diligently went hungry.

Few people spoke, as we were still too emotionally numb to talk. We merely nodded politely to acknowledge each other then went back to our own dismal introspection. As we bent down to pick up the flakes of manna and put them in clay jars, we all inwardly pondered how what started out so right went so terribly wrong. We wondered how we had come to face such a hard reality.

While mindlessly gathering sustenance for the day, I vividly recalled the excitement I felt just over forty days ago. The twelve tribes of Israel were finally on the outskirts of Canaan, the land God had promised to give us. It had been a long, grueling two-year journey from Egypt through a wilderness that our leader Moses accurately described as "that vast and dreadful desert." We had spent two years living in tents, wandering around like homeless nomads, breathing sand, eating only manna, and waiting with anticipation for the day when we would arrive at our new home in Canaan.

"For the first time in my life, I am truly happy," I told Bezalel one evening in our tent as I hugged him tightly and smiled with my head against his chest.

"Don't I make you happy?" he asked inquisitively as he looked down at me. "I do try."

"I know you do," I replied sincerely. "And you do make me happy. But I mean totally happy, and hopeful, about everything – like not having to work for anyone else for the rest of our lives, unless we want to. Both of us are talented. We can do things and make things that people will pay good money for." I stopped for a moment and pleasantly imagined us having our own businesses, before continuing. "Like having a home of our own that we can decorate with new furniture and nice things, and not having to live in slave quarters. Like having our own land and our own garden so we can eat whatever we want instead of what somebody else doesn't want. Like sending our children to school so they can have a future. You know what I mean, totally happy."

"I know exactly what you mean!" he exclaimed, smiling as he vividly envisioned such a life. "And we are going to be happy. I promise you," he said as he gave me that look that told me I could count on it.

But instead of just going in and taking the land of Canaan as we had all hoped, Moses assembled the people and told us that God had something He wanted us to do first.

"The Lord has given me the names of one man from each tribe who will go in ahead of the rest of us, explore the land, and report what the group finds. They are to see what the land is like, whether the people who live there are strong or weak, few or many. They'll find out what kind of land they live in. Is it good or bad? Are their towns open and exposed or walled and fortified? How is the soil? Is it fertile or poor? Are there trees on it or not? And since it's the season for the first ripe grapes, they will try to bring back some of the fruit of the land."

Then he called the men chosen for the mission, saying, "When I call your name, please step forward." Twelve men made their way through the crowd with pleased looks on their faces, proud to have been chosen to represent their tribes.

They were all leaders and brave men of character whom the people themselves would have chosen if asked whom they would personally recommend. One of them was Caleb, who was from our tribe of Judah. The Israelites prayed for the men and the success of their mission and sent them on their way.

The twelve men crossed the border and traveled for days inside the land, seeing mostly small, walled towns and picturesque countryside. Canaan was somehow better than Egypt, the only other place they had ever known. Perhaps it just seemed better because it would soon be ours and we would be free there. The sky appeared bluer, the grass greener, and the clouds fluffier. Even the bird sounds seemed crisper and more distinct. Instead of scorching heat, the bright sun provided a warmth that both soothed and nourished. The place appealed to the senses. It looked and felt good.

Once they were on the main road to the first major city called Hebron, long before they even saw the city gates, they were truly overwhelmed. On both sides of the road, farmland stretched out wide across the horizon. Lush, vibrant vegetable crops of all kinds grew everywhere. There were fruit and olive trees, vineyards, and wheat and barley fields in abundance. They stopped and gorged themselves on succulent figs, dates, pomegranates, and grapes, laughing hysterically as the juice ran down their chins. They hadn't eaten fruit since they left Egypt two years ago, and they couldn't get enough of it. They ate and rested and ate and rested again, savoring as much of the milk and honey of the land as they could before finally moving on. They were so enthralled by everything they saw and experienced as they traveled that before they knew it, the day was coming to an end.

They moved quickly in order to enter Hebron before the city closed the gates for the night at sundown. Because they were full and tired, there was little conversation. And then, as if on cue, they all looked up at the same time and saw the city in all of its splendor at the top of the hill. Even though they were grown men, they looked like children with their mouths and eyes open with amazement. The city walls were at least twenty feet high and ten feet deep. Elaborate reliefs of battle scenes, conquests, and victories covered the walls, all painted in vibrant colors. Rising above the wall was what could only have been the king's palace. While they had great expectations for their future home, nothing they heard had prepared them for what they saw and how impressive it was.

Suddenly they heard the sound of hoof beats and fearing that they could be in danger, they quickly hid themselves in the wheat fields adjacent to the road. From there they watched as a man who must have been the king rode by on his mount, flanked on all sides by his guards. He was regal in appearance and sat tall in his saddle with his head held high under his ornate crown. The battalion of one hundred well-armed soldiers that accompanied him was alert and undoubtedly ready to meet any threat, real or perceived. Strangely, the king and his guards seemed huge, significantly larger than most men. The twelve men remained in the fields, peering out until they saw them disappear inside the city gates. Then they set out for the same destination.

They arrived just in time. A farmer who had been selling his produce was leaving to return to his farm in the country. He was the last one out of the city, and they were the last ones in for the night. He was whistling merrily as he drove his empty wagon indicating that he'd had a successful day. The farmer nodded and tipped his hat as he passed, undoubtedly having seen them. Oddly, the gatekeeper almost walked into them, as though they were invisible to him.

Even though it was sundown, the paved, well-lit streets of the city bustled with activity. Shops were still open selling exotic goods of all kinds – beautiful clothing, fragrant spices, fresh meat and fish, aged cheeses, wines, and whatever else one had the money to buy. All of the people were dressed in exquisite clothing and wore solid gold jewelry – earrings, necklaces, nose rings, ankle bracelets and the like. The houses were large and spacious. Even the work animals were healthy looking thoroughbreds. If anyone poor lived there, they never crossed their paths. Everywhere they turned they saw only affluence.

The twelve men browsed in the shops throughout the city until most of the activity began to die down. But one in particular brimmed with customers until closing time. Reminiscent of the shops in Egypt, this one made the gods that the people worshiped, by hand. Gold and silver human crafted deities of all sizes and kinds (Baal, Chemosh, Ashteroth, etc.) lined the shelves. They were grouped by name with a banner above each section identifying them. Organizing the gods like this ensured that the buyer would get the one they believed would best meet their needs.

From where they stood, they could see a workshop in the back where the gods were made. Pretending to be interested in buying one, Ammiel was allowed to go into the workroom and observe the god-making process. Several men sat at several stations, each performing a specific work. Some carved the wood, others sanded it, and yet others covered it with gold or silver. Each task was performed with precision and great care. The process ultimately resulted in finished products in such demand that customers were lined up out the door to purchase them after dark.

The shop also sold intricately carved shrines that were custom made for each god. Customers needed only to take the god and the shrine home, set them up, and worship at a ready-made altar.

Having grown up in Egypt, the home of thousands of gods, the idol worship that the twelve men saw in Canaan did not surprise them. In fact, many of the Israelites left Egypt carrying some of their gods in their garments. But the Lord, the God who brought us up out of Egypt, strictly forbade us to worship any god but Him. In spite of some of the Israelite's actions, we well understood that no god was to be as important as, or more important than our God, I Am. Those among us who truly revered Him destroyed their worthless idols and set their hearts on Him only.

As the activity in the city waned, and its citizens settled in for the night, the twelve men left the shop. Wanting not to even run the risk of drawing any unnecessary attention to themselves, they passed several comfortable, inviting inns and chose instead to seek nightly sanctuary elsewhere.

An unused stall in an open stable served as their resting place for the night. The hay was clean and fresh, and they were grateful for the sparse accommodations. Perfectly grilled and delectably seasoned gazelle they had purchased earlier was their evening meal. It was so tender that it required minimal chewing, almost melting in their mouths. And it was so tasty that they licked their fingers when the meat was all gone to savor what was left of the delicacy.

Leaning back against the side of the stall, they spoke softly and seriously as the moonlight shining through a window lit up their small abode.

"So do you think you're going to like our new home?" Caleb asked the others, as his broad smile demonstrated that he definitely would.

Shammua responded first. "Like it? What's there not to like? This place is like paradise on earth. It really is the land of milk and honey. I want to know what we did to deserve this. And what did these people do to make God want to put them out of it?"

Ammiel, the quiet, deep-thinker who had been looking dazed spoke up. "I can hardly believe that this land is going to be ours. But I can see why God has chosen to take it from the Canaanites and give it to us. They don't believe in Him. They buy their man-made gods in shops, take them home, set up shrines for them and worship them. Their towns and cities are full of altars where they offer sacrifices to their false gods. And they have built elaborate temples for them to live in."

"Well, their loss is our gain," Joshua said enthusiastically. "This place is perfect! The climate is warm and comfortable. The soil is rich and fertile. Everything planted in it grows bountifully. Streams, pools, and wells are everywhere, so we have easy access to water for our animals and ourselves. The homes are large and spacious so our families can have room to spread out. I can't think of anything we need or want that isn't already here in abundance. This place is better than we could have ever imagined."

Gahdi raised his hand, eager to interject his opinion. "Yes, yes, everything you said is true. But you're forgetting the biggest problem. Those humongous people we heard about, the Nephilim, live here. All of them are giants. Like the king and his guards, the men are one and a half to two times our size. Even the women are as big as our biggest men. Yes, the land does flow with milk and honey. But we're not going to enjoy a minute of it because we're going to get killed trying to take it from these enormous people."

Caleb spoke up quickly. "Let's not talk ourselves out of what is ours to have. So what if the people are bigger than us. Our God is bigger than them and their gods. We saw with our own eyes what He can do. We were slaves in Egypt living miserable lives with no chance for freedom. We prayed to God day and night asking Him to rescue us, and He did. He sent Moses to tell Pharaoh to let us go. When Pharaoh said 'no,' God destroyed Egypt with nine plagues."

Nahbi nodded emphatically in agreement and eagerly continued the story. "Then he hit them where it really hurt with one last plague. He told us to take a perfect lamb from our flocks, one without a spot or a blemish. We slaughtered it, being careful not to break any of its bones, and took its blood and put it on the top and sides of the outside of the door frame. That night, God's death angel came through and killed every firstborn child in Egypt, except ours. The death angel passed over us when He saw the blood of the lamb."

"Let me finish the story," said Gueul, eager to help the others remember how mightily God moved on our behalf. "When Pharaoh saw that his firstborn son had died, that's all it took. He wanted us out of Egypt and told us to leave. So we marched out, heads held high, a free people, basking in victory. But by the time we got to the Red Sea, Pharaoh changed his mind and came after us with his entire army to take us back into slavery. We were horrified when we saw them coming. With the Red Sea in front of us and our enemy behind us, we were trapped with nowhere to go. But God had a plan. He opened up the Red Sea, and we walked through it on dry ground. Pharaoh's army followed us into the Red Sea. Then God let the water flow back and drowned them all."

"Well said!" exclaimed Caleb as he stood and clapped. *"If we will just remember how God has kept His word and led us and our ancestors to victory in the past, we will have the faith to believe that He will continue to help us. Don't ever contradict what God says. He promised to give us this land that flows with milk and honey. All we have to do is trust Him."*[2]

---

[2] Romans 4:18–21 (TLB)

"*Those giants are just a test,*" Joshua interjected encouragingly. "*God knew when He sent us to explore the land that we would see them. God gives victory to those who believe Him even if they can't see how He is going to do what He has promised.*[3] He made a promise to our ancestor Abraham when he was 75 years old that he would have a son by his wife, Sara. A long time passed and they became so old that their bodies were as good as dead, and they couldn't have children anymore. But they believed God anyway, and when Abraham was 100 years old, and Sarai was 90, she gave birth to Isaac. *God specializes in miracles. This is just a test! We can't let what we see cause us to doubt God and cancel out His good plans for us.*"

"I don't know," said Sethur slowly and skeptically as he ran his fingers through his dark, wavy hair. "I keep thinking of the king's soldiers that we saw guarding him on the road into the city. They were fierce, like the type that will fight to the death for what belongs to them. They have lived on this land for hundreds of years because they are stronger than anyone who has ever thought about or tried to take it from them."

"You've got a point," said Igal, who had been quietly reflecting on all that the others had to say. "These descendants of Anak the giant built this city of Hebron. They were the first people ever to live here. This place is like the Garden of Eden, and they are not giving it up without a real fight. And we don't have what it takes to give them one." He continued, holding up a finger as he made each of three points. "Their fighters are at least twice the size of ours, they are better trained, and they have better armor and weapons. We would be fools to take them on," he said with finality.

---

[3] John 20:29(b) (NIV)

The others who had not yet spoken chimed in and agreed with him. Even Nahbi and Gueul, who had been convinced that the Israelites would win, began to hesitate. The twelve heatedly debated the issue and decided to take a vote when they couldn't reach a consensus. One at a time, they stated their position. In the end, only Joshua and Caleb were still hopeful. The other ten were prepared to go back to the camp and report that their journey had been fruitless. They were ready to say that the Israelites should abandon the foolish notion of ever conquering and living in the land that flowed with milk and honey, and that we had come this far for nothing. They would reassure the others that it was better this way. If they chose not to fight, at least they would get to keep their lives. Joshua and Caleb knew then that the other ten would successfully convince the fickle Israelites that they were right.

None of the twelve men slept well that night, thinking only of their return home the next day. That sick, foreboding feeling in the pit of their stomachs was not just there because of the disappointment that their news would bring to their kinsmen. They were also sickened by the bleakness of their own future.

They rose early and set out while it was still dark. They were just in time to slip out of the city gates just after they opened, but before the farmers and merchants came in to peddle their wares. The twelve men walked in virtual silence, each consumed with his own thoughts, nursing his own heavy heart.

One day into the two-day walk back to their camp in the Desert of Paran, they passed a vineyard. Remembering that they had been commissioned to bring back some of the fruit of the land, they stopped and sampled some of the grapes in the vineyard. Indicative of the quality of produce that grew in the land of milk and honey, they were large and succulent and tasted as good as they looked. They cut off a single cluster of the grapes, tied it to a wooden branch, and two of them carried it on their shoulders.

When they were within one hour of arriving home, Joshua and Caleb tried one last time to persuade the other ten to change their minds.

"Listen," Caleb said seriously as he abruptly turned and faced the others who had been walking behind them, causing them to stop short. "The fate of all our people is in our hands right now. When we get home, we need to be positive about what we saw. If we encourage them to trust God, we will all win. If we discourage them and they lose heart, we will all lose."

"We can be honest about what we saw, about the fortified, walled cities and the giants," Joshua added. "But we have to also remind them of what we know. God, who miraculously brought us out of Egypt, promised to bring us into this exceptionally good land and give it to us. He proved Himself to us before, and He will do it again. We just need to give Him a chance."

"Now you two listen," Nahbi said defiantly. "I cannot pretend like I did not see what I saw, like somehow those walls are going to just fall over, and those giant people are going to drop dead. I will not let me or my family be killed chasing some dream." The other nine dissenters voiced their agreement with Nahbi through their silence and their fearful facial expressions.

"You are all missing the point," Caleb said in a raised voice that was atypical of his meek, controlled nature. "We are not saying that we expect to defeat them by ourselves," he continued as he nodded in Joshua's direction, indicating that they were of the same mind. "This is the Lord's battle. He is God enough to win it without our help. All we need to do is trust Him and follow whatever instructions He gives us."

"This discussion is over!" said Gueul. "You two can believe what you believe," he stated while motioning to Joshua and Caleb. "The rest of us will believe what we believe."

"I know what the problem is," Joshua said pointing accusingly at the ten. "Our God is not your God! That's why you don't trust Him. You're like those people we just left who worship handmade gods, mere things that have no life and no power."

"Don't you dare lecture us," Shammua shouted back. "Okay. So we do believe in other gods too. There. I said it. What has your God done for us anyway? We are much worse off now than we were as slaves in Egypt. There we lived in houses in a beautiful land along the Nile River surrounded by palm trees. We ate fresh melons and dates and onions and garlic and leeks." He smiled as he remembered the version he wanted to remember of his former life. "We ate fresh fish and meat of every kind, as much as we wanted. But for the last two years we have lived in small tents, always on the move, always hot, always tired, with gritty sand in our hair and clothes. And worst of all, we eat that disgusting manna every day." He then spat on the ground to emphasize his utter disdain for the wilderness experience.

Knowing that any argument he put forth at that point would be futile, Joshua threw up his hands in surrender and said, "Let's try to make it back to camp by midday." Since his two attempts to reason with them had been futile, he hoped that when they got there, our leader Moses could somehow get through to the ten rebels. It was obvious that their trust in God was limited at best.

CHAPTER 2

THE SENTENCING

It had been exactly 40 days since the twelve left the Desert of Paran to explore Canaan. In anticipation of their scheduled arrival, Moses and the entire congregation casually assembled in the area they had left and would return to, eagerly awaiting their report.

"I don't know about you, my boy," Moses said to Bezalel in a hearty voice as he patted him on the back. "But I'm ready to drink some milk and eat some honey."

"You and me both," Bezalel replied enthusiastically. Then he held out his hands and looking at them said, "I'm ready to get back to work. I don't feel right if I'm not using my hands to make something or to hold my woman." They both laughed because they both understood a man's need to be doing purposeful work and to have the companionship of a wife who made him a better man.

Moses liked Bezalel. He was a man of wisdom and integrity, one of the few people in the group with whom he felt he could be transparent. *As a wise leader, he knew that not everyone who wanted to befriend him had a pure motive.*[4] So he truly appreciated Bezalel's friendship.

"Just think," Moses said optimistically. "We could be in our new home in a few days."

"So what's the plan?" Bezalel asked, switching to a serious tone. He too was hopeful but also eager to find out what they had to do next. "Will we have to go to war with the Canaanites to take that land?"

"I'm praying about that very same question, and I am waiting for the answer," Moses told him plainly. "The Lord will let me know at just the right time."

"Doesn't that make you nervous sometimes?" Bezalel asked, genuinely curious. "I mean, being responsible for successfully leading all these people to this place and then going in and settling down, but not knowing what to do next until the very last minute?"

"Yes, it used to make me nervous," Moses admitted. "Sometimes I wondered what I would do if the Lord didn't come through in time. Or if I misunderstood what He said. I was worried about making a mess of things because I did what made sense to me instead of what God wanted me to do. And I didn't want anyone else to think I didn't know what I was doing. Even when I felt like I didn't know what I was doing. But I got past all of that. *I knew I couldn't wonder if I heard clearly from God because there was too much at stake. I had to know for sure. So I started spending more time with Him, cultivating a closer relationship, just the two of us, talking and listening. Now I understand exactly what He is saying.*[5] *And I trust Him*

---

[4] Proverbs 12:26(a) (NIV); 1 Timothy 5:22(a) (NIV)

[5] Isaiah 30:21 (NIV)

completely so I know beyond any doubt that He will always come through on time."[6]

Hearing Moses express his original fears made Bezalel appreciate him even more. It showed that he was a great leader but still an ordinary man just like himself. And he was even more impressed with Moses' determination to act only on the instructions he received from the Lord and not on his own ideas. To Bezalel, Moses set *the standard for a leader worth following, one whose thoughts and vision are of divine origin*[7] *and one who should be respected and supported.*

"We're fortunate to have you as a leader," Bezalel gratefully told Moses. "And I couldn't ask for a better friend." Moses humbly acknowledged the compliment with a smile.

Before long, the twelve came over the hill and into view. When the trumpeters saw them, they sounded their arrival. Many of the Israelites ran up and hugged them, happy that they had returned safely.

Moses led the twelve up a higher hill so that everyone would be able to see them when they addressed the people.

"Blessed children of our forefather Israel," Moses said with emotion, quieting the crowd. He was full of hope for the Israelite's future, eagerly wanting to hear what the men had to share. "The twelve explorers the Lord sent to survey the land that will be our new home are back, and they have much to tell us. Let's hear what they have to say."

The crowd immediately fell silent. Nahbi, the spokesperson for the ten rebels, spoke up first. "The land that we explored is exceptional – much better than we could have ever imagined. Look at some of the fruit we found there!" he said as they held out the massive cluster of grapes.

---

[6] Galatians 6:9 (AMP)

[7] 1 Corinthians 11:1 (AMP); 1 Corinthians 2:16 (AMP)

The large assembly clapped with elation, their eyes fixed on the fruit. We all knew it meant that the land was rich and fertile and would make an excellent home. This first sign was hopeful, and we were encouraged.

None of us could have foretold what would be said next. "But," Nahbi continued, "The land is full of Nephilim, the giant offspring of demonic spirits who mated with human beings hundreds of years ago. We heard about them back in Egypt and we thought they were a myth, but that's not true. They are very real. All of their cities have high, thick walls. And they are well-armed and well-trained. We have no chance of overpowering them. We're just going to get ourselves killed by trying. We need to head back to Egypt. The Egyptians will be glad to have us back."

The crowd was stunned by the bad news. The stupor on our faces expressed our disbelief and disappointment. We had such high hopes for a land we could finally call our own. Our ancestor Abraham had lived in Canaan as an alien and we lived as aliens and slaves in Egypt. Now our hopes had been dashed in an instant.

Caleb quickly moved to the front and silenced the people, hoping to control the damage the ten naysayers had potentially done. "We should go up and take possession of the land because we can definitely do it," he exclaimed confidently.

But the ten men who had gone up with him pleaded with the crowd. "Please listen to us. We can't attack those people. They are stronger than we are, and they would crush us!" They continued to spread a negative report among the Israelites about the land they had explored. They said, "All the people we saw there are those enormous descendants of that ancient race of people called the Nephilim. They are so tall we felt like grasshoppers next to them." And the people believed the negative voices of the ten naysayers instead of God, who had promised to give them the land.

All the Israelites cried aloud and wept bitterly, devastated that the dream they had cherished like a baby growing in their wombs had been aborted. Bezalel and I were no exception. We too had made the tragic mistake of entertaining the negative voices that caused us to doubt that we would ever receive the wonderful things the Lord had in store for us.

"This cannot be happening to us!" I exclaimed in disbelief. "I can't go back to Egypt. I just can't," I cried, having concluded that that was exactly what was about to happen. "I'm not going back," I defiantly exclaimed, vigorously shaking my head as tears the size of raindrops escaped my tightly closed eyes and streamed down my face uncontrollably. "I would rather die first."

As a natural-born survivor, I was trying desperately not to let myself believe that we had no other option, in spite of the devastating news we had just received. "Pharaoh hates us even more now than he did before because he thinks we are to blame for what happened to Egypt and his beloved son," I said. "If we go back, he will pay us back by working us to death rebuilding his country. There's nothing back there for us except more slavery and more misery!"

"You are right," Bezalel admitted, equally as dejected and deeply saddened that the situation had deteriorated to this point. "If we go crawling back Pharaoh will think the Lord deserted us and he can treat us however he wants to. But what choice do we have? The Promised Land is not going to happen for us, and if we stay here in the desert we will die."

With one voice, the other Israelites grumbled against Moses and Aaron, saying to them, "We wish we had died in Egypt or even here in this wilderness. Why is the Lord bringing us to this land only to get us killed? Then our wives and children will be taken as slaves. Wouldn't we be better off if we just went back to Egypt?" And as if they were sure they had no other options, they said to each other, "Let's choose a leader and go back to Egypt."

Dumbfounded, Moses and Aaron fell face downward on the ground in front of the entire Israelite assembly. They prayed fervently in fear of what God would do in response to the people's unbelief.

Joshua and Caleb tore their clothes as an expression of their pain and sorrow over what was transpiring before their very eyes. They knew that unless the people could be persuaded to abandon their determination to turn their backs on God, they would forfeit the magnificent life He had planned for them, and incur His judgment as well. In one last effort to save them all, they said to the entire Israelite assembly, "The land we traveled through and explored is exceptionally good. *If we obey the Lord, He will be pleased with us. Then He will lead us safely into the land He promised us that flows with milk and honey, and He will give it to us.*[8] But don't rebel against Him! That would be foolish. And do not be afraid of the people of the land, because we will devour them. The Lord is with us, so their protection is gone. Don't be afraid of them!"

But the whole assembly remained unconvinced and talked about stoning Joshua and Caleb. Then the glory of the Lord appeared in a cloud in front of all the Israelites. They heard the Lord say to Moses, "How long will these people despise me? How long will they refuse to believe in me, in spite of all

---

[8] Numbers 14:8 (NLT)

the miracles I have performed on their behalf? I will disinherit them and destroy them with a plague, but I will make you into a nation even greater and stronger than they."

Moses said to the Lord, "If you do that, what will the Egyptians think when they hear about it? They saw how you mightily rescued these people they had enslaved. And they have already told the inhabitants of this land, the Canaanites, about it. So the Canaanites know full well that you are with us and that you are seen face to face. They know that you stay with us in a pillar of cloud by day and a pillar of fire by night to guide and protect us. If you kill these people all at one time, leaving none alive, the Egyptians, the Canaanites and all the other surrounding nations who have heard about you will find out. They will say, 'The Lord had to kill them because He couldn't take care of them in the wilderness. He wasn't capable of bringing them into the land He promised to give them, so He slaughtered them in the desert.' Please don't do this. Your reputation and honor are at stake."

Moses continued his intercession with the Lord, desperately trying to spare the lives of the faithless, grumbling Israelites. "Remember when you were describing yourself to me. You said 'I, the Lord, am a merciful and gracious God, slow to anger, overflowing with love, and forgiving of sin and rebellion. But I do not let those who are guilty go unpunished. Instead, I punish the children for the sins of their parents down to their grandchildren and great-grandchildren.' Please let your actions be consistent with your character. Forgive the sins of these wayward, unruly people just as you have done from the time they left Egypt until now."

The Lord replied, "I have forgiven these wicked people who do nothing but grumble and complain against me, just like you asked. But I promise, as surely as I live, not one of those who saw the miracles I performed in Egypt and the wilderness, but who ten times refused to trust me and obey me – not one of them will ever see the land I promised to their ancestors. No one who has treated me with contempt will ever see it. *Don't they realize that I hear and scrutinize every word they say?*[9] So tell them I said this, 'As surely as I live I will do to you exactly what I heard you say. In this wilderness, every male twenty years old, or more who has grumbled and complained against me will die. Not even one of you will enter the land I promised to give you, except Caleb and Joshua, who both trust me and fully obey me. Your disobedience and lack of faith nullified my promise to you. As for your children, that you said would be taken as slaves, I will bring them in to enjoy the land you did not have the faith to enter and possess. But they will not go in right now. Your children will be wandering shepherds here in the desert for thirty-eight more years. They will spend a total of forty long, excruciating years, suffering for your lack of faith until the last of your bodies lies in the wilderness. For forty years – one year for each of the forty days you explored the land – you will suffer for your sins and know what it is like to have me against you. When I sent the men into the land to explore it, I was merely testing you by giving you another opportunity to trust me. But since you refused to do so, you will breathe your last breath in this wilderness. Here you will die. Now, since you are so afraid of the Canaanites, tomorrow you are to turn back and set out along the route to the Red Sea, back into the desert where you came from.'"

Moses did not have to repeat anything that the Lord had spoken to him since the Israelites had clearly heard every

---

[9] Psalm 33:13–15 (TLB)

word. And the Lord's words dealt an even heavier blow to them than the words of the ten naysayers because their words merely grieved them, but His words permanently sealed their fate. They were horrified that they had just been sentenced to spend the rest of their lives in the place they had come to hate with every fiber of their beings. So their eyes immediately turned to the ten men who were guilty of bringing nothing more than their negative opinions to them. The ten were still standing in the same spot where they had relayed the very news that led to the Israelite's demise.

"Kill them, kill all of them," the people shouted with rage as they gathered rocks in piles to stone them. They consoled themselves with the thought that they would make them pay dearly for the damage they had done. Some of the men moved toward the ten to indicate that it would serve no purpose for them to try to run. Desperate to try and save his life, Shammua, one of the ten, held up his hand and frantically said, "No, wait, it's not too late. We can still go and take possession of the land. I remember the way. I'll lead you." But having heard the finality in the Lord's voice when He issued their sentence, most of the people knew not to believe Shammua. They ignored him and returned to the task of gathering stones. Little did they know it, but at that very moment the Lord was in the process of exacting His own vengeance.

"Look," someone shouted, pointing to the ten. The people stopped what they were doing and looked up. All of a sudden, for no external reasons, the ten naysayers began to convulse and vomit. Their bodies shook violently for several seconds and then they dropped to the ground, utterly dead.

Everyone gasped in horror, immediately aware of the fact that it was God who had severely judged them for the role they played in dissuading the others from trusting Him. The Israelites were stricken with fear after watching the Lord make an example out of the ten. They were finally convinced that *even a loving God can run out of patience with those who interfere with His plans.* Some of them ran to and fro, frantically searching for family members, before retreating to the safety of their tents. Others gathered in groups, hoping to find solace in numbers.

In the pandemonium that ensued from the deaths, Bezalel and I were separated from each other. On my way to find him, I passed a group of men and women who were closely huddled together. I thought I heard them say something about going into Canaan, so I slowed down, alarmed and fearful of the very thought. I wondered how anyone in their right mind could possibly be thinking about disobeying the Lord after what we had just seen Him do to the ten. One of the women I knew in the group waved me over to join them. The woman was acutely aware that the conversation they were having could lead to serious trouble, but she was hoping to enlist another participant in their plan.

"Listen," whispered an older man who appeared to be their leader as he looked around to be sure that no one else was listening to them. "The way I see it, we have two choices. We can go back into the desert and stay there until we die. Or we can get together as big a group as we can and go in and take Canaan for ourselves, just like Shammua said. The Lord has told me that He will go with us and give us the victory." I watched as the others in the group beamed with hope as they listened to him. Desperate to hear what they wanted to believe, they seemed oblivious to the fact that his words contradicted what they heard the Lord say with their own ears less than an hour ago.

Greatly alarmed and without fear of any reprisal, I was compelled to speak up. "Why would the Lord tell you something different than He just told us?" I asked the leader of the group. All the others turned their eyes to him, awaiting an answer to what they knew was a valid question.

"These people know me," he said definitively, with the smooth tongue of a serpent, appalled that anyone dared to challenge him. "I have been a spiritual advisor to their tribe since most of them were born. And they know that I hear from God just like Moses does."

"Then you won't mind if Moses knows what you are planning?" I asked him, putting him on the spot. "If you hear from God just as he does, he will merely confirm what you heard. Then you will know that you all are going into Canaan with the Lord's blessing."

"That's true," one of the others said as the rest nodded in agreement. "We must be sure that the Lord will go with us and make our mission successful."

Knowing that the group could change their minds about going if Moses didn't agree, he acquiesced. "That's a good idea," the older leader said, feigning a smile.

From where I was standing I could see Moses talking to someone not far away. "There's Moses over there," I said, pointing in his direction. "I'll go get him and bring him here."

The group watched as I approached Moses and spoke to him. Though they couldn't hear us, they saw his demeanor change from cordiality to grave concern. Moses was shocked when he heard their presumptuous plan. When our short conversation ended, we both walked with a sense of urgency back to the group. The older man stepped to the front indicating that he was the one in charge and would be doing the speaking. Moses recognized him immediately. He was a known rebel, one who could be counted on to do the opposite of what should be done and to lead others to do the same.

"I understand that you are planning to lead a group of people into Canaan to take possession of it," Moses said to him.

"Yes, I am," the older man said defiantly. "The Lord has instructed me to lead the faithful few into the Promised Land and we will be heading out first thing in the morning."

"I see," said Moses. "So the Lord spoke to you and gave you a plan that will allow you to avoid His judgment, did He?"

The older man deliberately ignored the question and said what he and the others in his group wanted to believe. "God is a good God, and He does not want His children to suffer. We know we sinned, but now we are ready to go up to the land the Lord promised!"

Tired of listening to their foolishness, Moses told them unequivocally, "It's too late! You had your chance to go in and possess the land. You were right on the brink of receiving what God had for you, but you blew it. *That opportunity is no longer available. Don't you understand that God's promises are conditional, and they cannot be fulfilled at any time and under any circumstances?*[10] So why are you disobeying the Lord's orders to go back into the wilderness? This plan of yours to enter the land will not succeed because the Lord is not with you! The Canaanites will confront you there and defeat you. Because you have turned away from the Lord, He will not be with you."

---

[10] Hebrews 3:7–11 (NLT)

Still fuming, Moses walked away, and I went with him. The people in the group just stood there and watched us leave, left speechless by what they had just heard. When we were far enough away that we could no longer be seen, Moses turned to me and thanked me.

"You are a brave woman," he said. I appreciate you for bringing that folly to my attention. This is a big camp, and I need people like you to make me aware of what's going so I can know what to address and how to pray."

"Anytime," I said sincerely. "The only way we are going to make it is to stick together." Then I left him and headed for home.

Still rebellious and in spite of the warning they were given, the group rose early the next morning and set out for the Promised Land of Canaan. They went into the hill country anyway, even though neither Moses nor the Lord went with them to ensure their success. Then, exactly as they were told would happen, the Canaanites who lived there came down, attacked them, and beat them until they ran for their lives.

Dejected, defeated and having forfeited God's purpose for their lives, they, along with the other Israelites, headed back into the wilderness. They would all live out the remainder of their earthly days there, grieving over how *they were right on the verge of getting exactly what they wanted, but sinned and missed the opportunity.*

CHAPTER 3

THE WAILING

Awakened by the shrill scream of terror, I sat straight up in my bed. Wide-eyed and frightened to death, I listened intently, hoping to determine what it was and where it came from. Then, as if on cue, more screams came in rapid succession from near and from afar. Something terrible was happening – something that sounded like the presence of death.

Then all of a sudden, it came to me. I had heard those cries of anguish before. It was during our last night in Egypt when the death angel had come through and killed every firstborn. Infants, children, teenagers, adults, the aged, mothers, fathers, sisters, brothers – every Egyptian, who had been born first, no matter how long ago, was put to death.

And now, it was happening again. God was keeping His word. He had told us that every male twenty-years-old and older would die in the wilderness. Exactly seven days from the day that we had been told to go back into the desert, the killing process had begun.

Worried about my family, I quickly looked over at Bezalel. Alarmed that the noise hadn't awakened him, I found myself hoping that he wasn't dead. Seeing his chest move in and out as he breathed, I let out a sigh of relief. Then that same breath was sucked from my body with panic as I thought of my son, who had just turned twenty-one. I jumped out of bed and ran as fast as I could to the portion of the tent where he slept behind a curtain. He, too, was only sleeping.

Without hesitation, I dropped to my knees and begged God to spare them, to not kill them along with the first group. Through tears of pain and desperation, I petitioned Him, as a loving, caring matriarch and wife would do.

"Oh Lord," I pled. "Pleeease hear my cry. Have mercy on me and my family. Please don't take my husband and my son from me yet. Leave them with me a little while longer. Help me to be a better wife and a better mother. Forgive me for where I have failed and help me to do better. Give me more time, more time to love them, more time to enjoy them and more time to help prepare them for eternity."

My loud sobbing awakened my hard-sleeping family, even though the distant wailing had not. Greatly concerned, they came to me as I prayed almost prostrate on the floor.

"What is it, Chaya? What is it?" Bezalel asked anxiously, as he looked at me and listened to the screaming that he finally heard and understood. I rose from my knees, grabbed him and held him tightly. As I reached for my son, Shemaiah, he rushed into our embrace with a look of fear on his face that he picked up from the fear he saw on mine. I cried deeply, and they let me do so without saying another word, each with a deep feeling of concern for our future.

Our daughter, Mychal, stood nearby watching us and listening to the screaming that she heard outside. She was a young but intuitive fifteen-year-old, and she, too, knew immediately what was taking place.

Grateful that Mychal was not in danger, but needing to have my entire family close to me, I opened the circle and ushered her in. She melted into the comfort of our arms. She too had something to lose. One day soon, her father and brother would no longer be with her. Because we were a close-knit family, we bore each other's pain and found solace in each other.

Always thinking of others, Bezalel broke our silent embrace. "Someone out there needs our help," he said, confident that God was with his family enabling us to survive in spite of the mind-numbing reality we were facing. I knew that my concerned husband was right and that *the best way for us to deal with our pain is to help someone else in theirs.* So I grabbed his hand to unite with him as he prayed a simple prayer, asking God to use us to help our friends and neighbors as He saw fitly. Then together we left the tent and ventured into the night.

The wailing sounds of grief and anguish were coming from everywhere. Before we had gotten even as far as two tents from our own, we ran into Moses.

"Bezalel!" Moses exclaimed as he embraced him, obviously relieved to see that he was still alive. "I was just coming to look for you. You don't know how happy I am to see that you are still with us."

"I am even happier than you are," Bezalel said with all sincerity. "Did you need me to help you do something?"

"Yes," Moses began solemnly. By now you know what's going on. I need you and Chaya to spread out and help me by providing some comfort and encouragement to the relatives of the dead men within your tribe. The people knew this was going to happen, but they weren't emotionally prepared for it. We have to help them get through this."

"That's just what we were on our way to do," Bezalel told him. "We're glad to help out."

"I knew I could count on my two friends," Moses said, gratefully. He squeezed my hand to let me know that he appreciated me too. Then he left us and moved on to solicit the help of some others.

Bezalel and I spent the next several hours consoling friends and families within our tribe. Some homes had been visited by the death angel and some had not. For those that hadn't, they knew that their escape was only temporary. They knew that over the next several years, every adult male amongst them would die. Husbands, fathers, brothers, sons, fiancés, nephews, cousins – every adult male amongst them twenty years of age and older would indeed die. And there was nothing they could do to stop it. All they could do was brace themselves and prepare for it.

One of the people I visited would not lose any of her beloved family members in the wilderness. The death angel had, however, recently visited her in Egypt so she, too, was familiar with this depth of suffering. While there, I was a slave in the household of what was left of this Egyptian family. The husband, Husani, was a general in Egypt's army before being killed in battle. His wife Ayana was one of Pharaoh's officials. Wealthy and influential, they had many slaves. So my only task was to take care of their first and only child, a one-year-old boy. When the death angel came through Egypt during the night of the Passover, the child was killed. Ayana, inconsolably distraught, left Egypt with the Hebrew slaves. With her son dead and her country ruined, she was firmly convinced that the gods of Egypt had been killed that night along with all of the Egyptian's firstborn offspring. That was the only plausible explanation since they were unable to prevent the slaughter of her son and her people. She decided to follow not only the God who proved He is the only living God, but also the people He had delivered.

In spite of our official master-slave relationship in Egypt, Ayana and I were friends. We were close in age, both thirty-something, and had the same love of life and family. We laughed easily together and counseled each other when the need arose. In fact, right before the Israelites were to leave Egypt, I implored Ayana to come with us. Ayana consented because the nine devastating plagues that Egypt had encountered left nothing there for her. Her deceased husband's livestock business was ruined. And even though she had the financial wherewithal to rebuild it, they had no customers because their fellow Egyptians had lost all of their resources. Little did she know that within days her only son would be dead. When that happened, Ayana needed my friendship more than ever. For a part of the last two years, while we walked and followed God's miraculous cloud that led us through the wilderness, I helped Ayana carry the burden of her loss.

But tonight it was me who went to Ayana for comfort. When I arrived at her tent, I saw Ayana sitting at the table with her hands clasped, her eyes closed, and a look of anguish on her face. I was not sure if she was grieving because of the death of her son, or because the death of the Israelites reminded her of the deaths of the Egyptians. Maybe it was both. I stood there for a second waiting, not wanting to intrude if it was the wrong time. Detecting a presence, Ayana opened her eyes. Seeing her friend made her smile and took her mind off whatever had been bothering her. She silently motioned me over by waving her hand. I came and sat across from her at the table. I still couldn't make that pill go down, that terrible thought that my husband and son could die at any time. As if a dam had just broken, I began to cry.

"That's ok. Just take your time," Ayana said as she gently patted my hand and waited patiently for me to tell her what was wrong. "Crying is good for the soul. It's cleansing."

After a long while, I finally spoke. "I don't know how to live without him," I said, referring to Bezalel. "He's been my whole life for so long I'm afraid I won't know how to go on."

Listening to me speak, Ayana knew that this unsettledness was atypical of me who she knew as strong, resilient and capable of bouncing back from any adversity. So she offered her own story, hoping that it would help me.

"I know just how you feel," Ayana said convincingly. "I went through the same thing when Husani died. You'll learn to live without Bezalel. You will hurt badly at first. Then you will get up every day and keep putting one foot in front of the other. You will take life one step at a time. Not one day, not one hour, but one step at a time. And after a while you'll notice that, even though you miss him, it doesn't hurt as badly as it used to. In the meantime, you will pour your energy into getting to know your God, raising your children and doing whatever else He calls you to do. He will take His rightful place as your husband and will become your life."

I wiped my eyes and looked at Ayana, knowing that everything she had just told me was true. The only part that surprised me a bit was the part about getting to know the Lord and having Him become my husband. Being a Hebrew from the tribe of Judah and a direct descendant of Abraham, I was an Israelite in the truest sense of the word. I knew right from wrong because it had been passed down to me from my ancestors. I made every effort to do what was right. *When in need, I knew to call on the Lord, who cared about everything that concerned me.*[11] He was caring enough to deliver my people from slavery. But I never thought it was possible to really know and love Him the way I knew and loved Bezalel. So I wondered what Ayana, an Egyptian, could possibly know about it.

"Do you really know Him?" I asked her, genuinely curious.

"Well," Ayana pondered, "I grow closer to Him every day. When the baby died, I thought I would die too. The pain was so intense I didn't know what to do with it. A thought kept coming to me to take it to this "I Am" that I heard Moses telling the Israelites about. I now know that it was Him drawing me. I was desperate, so I came to Him because I had nowhere else to go. At first I questioned whether He would hear me because I have worshiped other gods all my life. But He had mercy on me because I had a change of heart and gave up those other gods, especially after I saw what He did to them. He healed my broken heart and comforted me. I get up early every morning, without fail, to worship Him. And He meets me there. He has become the love of my life."

Ayana chuckled and continued, "Right after He killed my child and my people, I thought He was a mean, vengeful God, and I hated Him. At that time, the only reason I followed through on my plan to leave Egypt is that I had no reason to stay. But when I started to seek Him, He softened my heart. He

---

[11] 1 Peter 5:7 (AMP)

showed me that He is a holy God who hates idolatry, one who will not share His glory with man-made gods. He destroyed Egypt to make it clear to the Egyptians, the Israelites and all of the surrounding nations that He is the only God and there is no other. I never thought I would ever say this but, as I look back, *I'm convinced that losing my only son and my country was worth it. One of the reasons I was put on this earth is to know the Lord intimately, and if those things had not happened I would never have found Him.*[12] *He took that terrible loss in my life and worked it out for my good."*[13]

I was stunned at Ayana's confession and testimony. I didn't think that God wanted to or could be known like that. Nor would He make Himself known to anyone who was not a leader and a descendant of Abraham, such as me. When that thought occurred to me, I realized that I was guilty of the sin of religious prejudice. Even though I loved Ayana, I thought that the Lord favored the Hebrews and reserved His best for us. I knew then that *God does not show favoritism but accepts people from every nation who fear Him and do what is right.*[14] Ayana's words were enlightening. If the God who calls Himself "I Am" could truly be known, then I would make getting to know Him my first priority.

"You've given me something to think about," I said as I reflected on Ayana's words. "I knew I could count on you for some wise counsel."

"Anytime," Ayana said sincerely. "Whenever you need anything, you can come to me day or night. I will always be here for you."

---

[12] Philippians 3:8 (AMP)
[13] Romans 8:28 (NLT)
[14] Acts 10: 34–35 (NIV)

I felt hopeful. I knew that if I could get to know the Lord, I would have a future even if most of my family died. Grateful for Ayana's friendship and encouragement, I embraced her tightly and stepped into the night.

When I returned home, my earlier conversation with Ayana was still on my mind. I knew that I, like Ayana, would one day lose both my husband and my son. It was too harsh a reality to come to accept. And to make it worse, I would have to raise my daughter by myself.

I loved and cherished my family. But after talking to Ayana I realized there was a longing deep inside of me – a craving for something they could not give me, even if they lived as long as I did. I wondered if this God of my ancestors, this God who called Himself "I Am" could meet that need. I knew that nothing on this earth could address it – not family or money or material things or fame or prestige – nothing at all. He had undoubtedly helped my friend Ayana. In spite of the death of her beloved husband and son, Ayana was totally at peace. She even glowed when she spoke of her new love, I Am. With my home quiet and my heart full of longing, I got down on my knees in search of this God.

Later that evening the desert air outside was cool and still thick with mourning. The loud wailing had evolved to quiet sobbing. I left my home and moved quickly to the tent of Bezalel's best friend, expecting to find my husband there. His wife, with a blank look on her face, came to the entrance and silently motioned me to come in. I nodded to acknowledge her presence, but she did not respond. As I entered, I saw Bezalel kneeling over his friend who was dead with his eyes still open, as though death caught him by surprise. They were all silent, so I, too, remained quiet.

Moments later, several men arrived at the tent. They stuck their heads into the entrance and inquired if there were any dead. The wife nodded slowly.

"We are burying now," one of the men said. "Some men are digging graves and the rest of us are picking up the bodies. It might take days, so we are starting tonight. We can take him now if you want. You don't want to wait too long because he's going to start smelling soon. You can have a few minutes to say goodbye if you need to."

The wife came out of her trance and started wailing again. Her two young children followed suit. The sudden reality of his death was too much for them to bear.

Bezalel and I quickly went outside to give them time to kiss him one last time and bid him farewell. The men who had come to pick up the body were waiting out there and told us that there were so many dead they had given up trying to count them. They had even resorted to using mass graves instead of individual ones.

"This is exactly what happened that last night we were in Egypt," one of them began. "We were in such a hurry to get out of there that we weren't paying attention. This is terrible. As much as I hated those Egyptians for how they treated us, I wouldn't wish this on anyone," he finished as he hung his head in dismay.

After what seemed like a long time, the wife came outside. "You can take him now," she said solemnly to the men waiting to bury him. When they went inside to get him, one of them closed his eyes with his hand, feeling it strange to look into the eyes of a dead person. They lifted him gently by the shoulders and the feet then took him out and laid him on top of the many other bodies piled on the cart.

"We need all the help we can get," one of the men said to Bezalel as the driver of the cart signaled the oxen to start pulling. While waiting for Bezalel to give him the answer he was hoping for, the man gave an order to the driver. "Come right back after you dump these bodies, and we'll be ready with some more," he said with no emotion in his voice. Without hesitation, Bezalel and I looked at each other, appalled at his insensitivity.

He saw the look on our faces and felt compelled to explain himself. "My father is lying on the bottom of that cart. And so is my oldest son. I'm doing everything I can to keep from falling apart. I can't let myself feel anything right now," he told us, hoping that we would understand, but not really caring if we didn't.

"Of course I can help," Bezalel said, eager to do whatever he could. "Just tell me where to find you and I'll meet up with you after I walk my wife back to our tent."

"Meet us just around the corner on the next row of tents. Our next pick up is at the third tent on the right," the driver said as he walked off.

Bezalel walked me home and saw me safely inside. Needing comfort, he held out his arms. I snuggled up close to him, as I needed his presence too. He kissed me gently without having to say a word. With his eyes, he told me that he loved me deeply before he slipped into the night.

Minutes later Bezalel found the other men at the exact location he had been given. Several more men had joined the body collection and disposal crew. They were already bringing three bodies out. The women were wailing, trying to get one last look, one last touch before their loved ones were forever gone. One of the men, visibly feeling their pain and grieving for their loss, gently held them back while the bodies were being carried off.

They worked tirelessly until after sunrise, encountering the same depressing scene at every stop. But the worst scenes were the mass graves. Several enormous holes had been dug, very deep and very wide. And they were piled high with motionless, expressionless bodies.

Bezalel knew that he needed to be a part of this effort, in spite of how dejected it made him feel, because this would soon be his reality and that of our son. One day, any day now, it would be them on those carts and in those mass graves. Being this close to death reminded him that he urgently needed to prepare for his demise and help our son do the same. And, above all else, he needed to prepare me, his wife, whom he loved with every fiber of his being, for the inevitability of his departure.

I had just returned from gathering the manna for the day when Bezalel arrived home. Exhausted from being up all night and desperately needing to enjoy whatever time we had left, we climbed into bed, held each other close, and reveled in our own thoughts.

Bezalel fondly reminisced about how we fell in love twenty-two years ago in Egypt. We would sit in the cool grass along the east bank of the Nile River and watch the sun go down. Palm trees swayed in the breeze and left their reflections on the still water. It was the season just between summer and autumn when the evening air was warm, and the pleasant sounds of crickets and birds signaled the end of a long day. The majestic setting was the perfect atmosphere for new love to take root in young hearts.

We met each other by happenstance. One evening after putting the child I took care of to sleep for the night, I decided to unwind a bit. The Nile River was the place where I always found solace. As I walked along the banks and allowed the environment to sooth away my tension, I saw a young man coming towards me whom I had occasionally seen from a distance.

"I've seen you before," he said, extending his hand. "I am Bezalel, son of Uri, the son of Hur, of the tribe of Judah.

I shook his hand. There was strength yet gentleness in his grip, and he exuded a confidence that was atypical of a young man of only seventeen years. I liked him immediately.

"My name is Chaya," I said, introducing myself. "I come from the tribe of Judah, too," I told him, pleased that we had this in common.

He seemed to like me also as he smiled from ear to ear, in no hurry to let go of my hand. Our eyes met, and we both knew that there was something substantive between us.

"I come here every evening to relax before going home," he said. "If you are not in a hurry you could join me." Even though his statement was more of a question, without answering, I sat down near him on the grass and we began to talk. We talked about everything – our families, tribal relationships, living in Egypt, responsibilities as slaves, likes and dislikes, and most of all, our dreams and hopes for the future. "I like listening to you. You are easy-going, and we think alike," he told me sincerely. "But the way you carry yourself says more about you than your words. Just being with you puts me at ease because you are at peace with who you are." It felt good to hear him say such nice things about me.

The time flew that evening, and we found ourselves still deep in conversation at sun up. A polite and respectful gentleman, Bezalel walked me to the home where I lived and worked.

"I hope the child you take care of didn't wake up last night," he said awkwardly, wanting to see me again but not knowing how to ask.

"I'm sure he didn't," I said, sensing his nervousness. "He's a quiet, predictable little thing. If I had thought that he would have awakened, I would have gone home sooner." Then I added, "We could meet again tonight if you want to?"

He was delighted with my invitation, and the sheer glee showed on his face. A woman who could read him and make up for what he lacked impressed him. "Yes, I want to," he said without even the slightest hesitation.

Our evening trysts were the highlight of both of our days. We would slip away after work, sit and talk until the wee hours of the morning, and then return to our respective homes to sleep for a few hours before going to our jobs. The indescribable magic between us made the fatigue we felt the next day worth the discomfort.

"Can I touch your hand?" Bezalel asked gently one evening, wanting only to express his feelings for me respectfully. He wasn't sure what to call this emotion, but it felt nice. I answered by slipping my hand into his. We both smiled and looked straight ahead, gazing at the calm water, pleased just to be in each other's company.

And so we met every evening in the same location along the Nile River for the next six months. When we were apart, we thought about each other every waking moment. We were barely able to wait until the next night, which seemed like an eternity, to be together again. Instead of a dull, dreary gray, we saw life in vivid color.

With his deepest, heartfelt declaration, Bezalel expressed that he was convinced beyond a shadow of a doubt that he wanted to spend the rest of his life with me. He asked me to marry him only six months after we met. And our life together had been magnificent. We loved each other with a deep, rich, pure love. Compatible in every way, it seemed as though God had made us exclusively for each other. After twenty-two wonderful years of wedded bliss, the mere thought of leaving me grieved him deeply.

While we lay there, I was also deep in thought. A realist, years as an Egyptian slave taught me that *life is what it is, and the sooner you emotionally come to terms with it, the sooner you position yourself to reap something good from it.* So I accepted the irrevocable fact that this desert would be my home until the day I died; that me, my husband, and my twenty-one-year-old son would meet our end here. I knew that I would probably outlive them for the sole purpose of raising my fifteen-year-old daughter, who would later enter the land.

With one awful decision to disobey God by not believing that He would bring us into the land and give it to us as He promised, we banished ourselves to the desert for the rest of our lives. Oh, the irrevocable consequences of one wrong decision![15]

Determined to make the best of it, I performed a post-mortem of sorts. *I asked myself what lessons I should glean from the mistakes that were made. Once I determined what they were, I engrained them in my mind so as not to ever repeat them.*

First, I believed that God sent the twelve men to explore the land in order to give them, and the rest of the congregation, an opportunity to trust Him. He knew that they would see the giants and fortified cities there. But He wanted to test us to see whether we would believe what He said or what they saw. They made

---

[15] Numbers 14:22–35 (TLB, NIV)

the fatal mistake of believing what they saw (with the natural eye) instead of what God promised (with the spiritual eye), and forfeited their future, and ours. We would never receive what He had planned for us. I learned from this experience that I should never again doubt God, no matter how things appear; that to receive what He promised, I had to believe Him first in order to see it come to pass later.[16] I was also convinced that seeing myself through God's eyes, as God saw me was crucial. There was to be no room for seeing myself as a powerless, insignificant victim who was hopelessly awaiting defeat by the enemy. Instead, I needed to remind myself continuously that the Lord has success planned for those who obey and trust Him.[17]

Second, when the twelve returned from exploring the land, ten of them brought back a negative report and spread it amongst the people. At first, I hesitated to believe them but later gave in to their persuasion. I allowed unbelieving naysayers to plant destructive thoughts and mental pictures of dead men, women and children into my mind. I learned from that experience to never listen to any person or voice, including my own, which contradicts the word that God has spoken. I understood that I needed to choose which voice to believe because listening to positive voices that encourage me to trust and obey God leads to victory. However, listening to negative voices such as doubt, discouragement, and the temptation to sin, leads to defeat.[18] Never was I to let an image of defeat stay in my mind. Negative mental images and thoughts must be replaced with positive ones. We are what we think. Therefore, our thoughts determine

---

[16] John 20:29(b) (NIV)

[17] Proverbs 2:7(a) (NIV)

[18] Psalm 1:1–3 (TLB); James 1:14–16 (AMP, NIV)

our future and our lives become what we envision.[19] *From now on, I would choose to view the wilderness as a valuable place, a place where I would flourish, somehow, someway. I would get an image of victory in my head for every area of my life and hold on to it tightly.*

Third, I learned how important it is to remember past victories. The Egyptians were the strongest, most powerful nation on earth during the time that they enslaved the Israelites. But, the Lord miraculously delivered us. He walked us out of Egypt in plain view with our enemy's gold, silver, and other possessions. He destroyed their country and killed its entire army to convince the Egyptians, Israelites, and the surrounding nations that He is the only God. Remembering this past victory would give me the faith to trust Him in the future.[20] *I would need this hope to successfully navigate the long stint in the wilderness, to persevere when my husband and son died, and to raise my daughter as a single parent.*

Fourth, and most of all, I understood the principle of God's timing. The Israelites had a window of opportunity. We needed to be spiritually ready, in faith mode, at the right time in order to receive what God had prepared for us. Instead of trusting God when faced with the choice, we responded with unbelief and rebellion and the window closed for our generation. If presented with an opportunity to trust God ever again, I would be ready.[21]

---

[19] 2 Corinthians 10:5(b) (NIV)
[20] Exodus chapters 1–14 (NIV)
[21] Galatians 6:9 (AMP)

How It All Began

Our story began with Moses who, after forty long years in the desert of Midian, learned how to survive the wilderness. His closest companions were emptiness, loneliness, nothingness, and discomfort. The days were hot, the nights were cold and tending a flock of mindless sheep only added to the monotony. The wilderness was not only physical for him, but a barrenness of soul as well.

Then one ordinary day while he was out at the edge of the desert watching the sheep graze, an unusual sight caught his eye. He saw a bush blazing with fire. Wondering how it began to burn and why it wouldn't burn up, he approached it slowly, with caution.

Suddenly a voice spoke to him from within the bush saying, "Moses! Moses!"

"Who are you?" Moses asked.

"Don't come any closer," the Lord told him. "Take off your sandals because you are standing on holy ground. I am the God of your fathers – the God of Abraham, Isaac and Jacob."

Moses covered his face with his hands because he was afraid to look at God.

"I have seen the way my people are being oppressed in Egypt, and I have heard their cries of distress because of their harsh slave drivers. I am aware of their suffering," the Lord continued. "So I have come down to rescue them from the Egyptians and lead them out of Egypt into their own fertile and spacious land. It is a land that flows with milk and honey – the land where the Canaanites and others now live. I am sending you to Pharaoh to demand that he let you lead my people, the Israelites, out of Egypt."

Moses was speechless. He just stood there for a few moments trying to let his mind digest what he had just experienced and heard. It wasn't every day that the living God came down from heaven and told him what he was put on earth to do. Suddenly, the events of Moses life made sense and finally fell into place.

Eighty years earlier, he was born in Egypt as a Hebrew slave. He and every other baby boy were supposed to be killed at birth according to the edict of the Pharaoh at that time. This order was given because the Israelites were multiplying rapidly and posed a threat to the nation of Egypt. Pharaoh knew that *the best way to destroy a people is through its male offspring.*[22]

Moses' mother understood from the day of his birth that he would one day be used by the Lord to do something great. So instead of doing away with him, she had his sister Miriam place him on the Nile River in a basket covered with tar, near where Pharaoh's daughter regularly went to bathe. The

---

[22] Exodus 1:1–22 (NLT)

princess saw him, took him to the palace, and raised him as her child. God's favor caused Pharaoh to disregard his own edict and adopt Moses as his grandson.

Growing up in Pharaoh's palace, his life was one of privilege, affluence, and position, even though his people, the Israelites, were slaves to the Egyptians. He was well-educated and afforded every creature comfort. In line to take the throne should anything happen to Pharaoh's son, Rameses, he was prepared to rule the country from the time of his birth.

But Moses felt another calling. Somehow, he always knew that his God, the God of his ancestors Abraham, Isaac, and Jacob, had chosen him to bring His people out of Egypt. So when he grew up, he refused to be called the son of Pharaoh's daughter. Instead, *he chose to fulfill his purpose rather than enjoy the temporary pleasures of sin* that were so prevalent in Egypt, even if it meant being mistreated along with the people of God. *He thought it was better to suffer for the sake of the Lord, who is The Christ, than to own* the *treasures* of Egypt *because he knew that he would be rewarded in due time.*[23]

One day he went out and watched his fellow Hebrews at their hard labor. Thinking that it was time for him to liberate them, he killed an Egyptian that he saw beating one of his own and hid him in the sand. The murder became known, and the same Pharaoh that once loved and raised him, now sought to kill him. He ran for his life and settled in the desert of Midian.

It had been almost forty years since he even thought about having been commissioned by God to deliver the Israelites, so long that he barely remembered it. The Lord was now confirming to Moses that he indeed had been called. He now knew that *he*

---

[23] Hebrews 11:24–26 (NIV)

failed forty years *earlier because he had impetuously acted on his own, with no regard for God's timing and method.*

Also, he had been in the wilderness for so long, doing nothing but tending sheep, that he didn't feel qualified to do much else. And he definitely wasn't equipped for such an awesome task as leading millions of people out of Egypt. Hoping that the Lord would understand his position and grant him an exemption, he said to Him, "Why me? I am not the one for a job like this. Who am I to appear before Pharaoh? Who am I to lead the people of Israel out of Egypt when I failed so badly the first time?"

God laughed and then spoke kindly to Moses. *"I let you fail to teach you many lessons that you could not have learned any other way. After you failed, your pride was gone, and you became humble and teachable. You learned not to assume that you know what I want you to do, or how, or when I want you to do it. You learned that it can be fatal for you and others when you get ahead of me. You learned the value of spending time with me, and how to listen to and hear my voice. And you learned how to obey me, trust me, and persevere no matter what happens."*

The Lord continued, "You are the person I have chosen for this assignment. I have spent the last forty years preparing you for it, so I know that you are ready. *I will be with you every step of the way to tell you exactly what to say and do.*[24] And this is your sign that I am the one who has sent you: When you have brought the people out of Egypt, all of you will worship me at this very mountain, Mount Sinai."

Having received the Lord's assurance that He would be right there with him, Moses began to warm up to the idea of

---

[24] Isaiah 30:21 (NIV)

doing what he had been commissioned to do. But his mind was still racing, thinking of every question he had that needed an answer. "If I go to the people of Israel and tell them, 'The God of your ancestors has sent me to you,' they will ask me what your name is. Then what should I tell them?" he asked the Lord.

God replied to Moses, "Say this to the people of Israel: 'I Am, the God of your ancestors – the God of Abraham, Isaac, and Jacob – has sent me to you.' I Am is my eternal name, the name by which I am to be known for all generations."

As his final set of instructions, the Lord told Moses to meet first with his brother Aaron and the other leaders of Israel. He was to tell them that He had appeared to Moses and sent him to liberate them from the cruel bondage of the Egyptians and lead them to a land flowing with milk and honey.

"I have prepared the hearts of the leaders of Israel so that they will accept your message," the Lord promised Moses. "Then you and the elders, in unity, must go to the king of Egypt and tell him, 'The Lord, the God of the Hebrews, has met with us. So please let us take a journey into the wilderness to worship the Lord, our God.'"

With his marching orders in his head and a special staff in his hand that God gave him to perform miracles, Moses left Midian and set out to return to the land of his birth. Forty years later, at the age of eighty, he was going back to Egypt on a mission to do the very thing he thought he was to do forty years earlier – to liberate his people. Only *this time he was acting at the right time, which was God's time, using God's method. And, above all else, God Himself was going with him.*

As Moses arrived back in Egypt and surveyed the country, old memories swept over him. It had retained all of its former beauty and splendor. Lush palm trees and exotic green foliage were everywhere. The crystal clear Nile still teemed with fish. It carried nutrients that enriched the soil, causing it to produce bountiful crops of all kinds.

The clothing styles had changed quite a bit in the forty years since he had been gone, but the Egyptians were still very well put together. They dressed in fine linen and wore soft leather sandals, expensive gold jewelry, and fragrant perfumes. Attention was paid to every detail including the make-up they applied to their eyes with precision. The Egyptians were and always had been healthy-looking, attractive people.

Their prosperity was evident. Many of them lived in beautiful homes and ran successful businesses. The people were literate and well-educated, which was one of the hallmarks of an advanced society. Their medical knowledge was far superior to that of any other country on earth. Other nations sent their doctors to Egypt to learn the latest medical procedures, treatments, and surgical techniques.

The pyramids that served as tombs for previous Pharaohs were still impressive, as were the colorful temples constructed to house some of Egypt's many gods.

Most evident of all were the massive structures built to honor the new Pharaoh, Rameses. There were colossal statues of him all over the country and a breath-taking monument in Abu Simbel that was intricately carved out of the side of a mountain.

As soon as Moses arrived in Rameses, the city where Pharaoh and the Israelites lived, he sought out his brother, Aaron, who was the leader of one of their twelve tribes. After a brief but happy reunion, Aaron notified the leaders and elders of the other eleven tribes of an important meeting that would take place early the next morning in a designated field.

They all arrived while it was still dark, long before the sun came up, to have ample time to discuss the business at hand and be at their respective jobs by daybreak. When Moses told them that the Lord was aware of their misery and was concerned about them, they bowed down and worshiped Him. They were convinced that I Am, the God of their ancestors, had indeed sent Moses to set them free, just as the Lord had said would happen. Eager to be liberated, they chose Aaron as their representative to accompany Moses when he went to Pharaoh.

Bezalel, one of the leaders of the twelve tribes who had attended the meeting, was so overwhelmed with the prospect of being free that he could hardly contain himself when he got to work later that morning. As an apprentice to an Egyptian craftsman and shop owner who worked for Pharaoh, his life as a slave wasn't as harsh as that of some of the others. But he was a slave, nonetheless, beholden to another person and unable to be his own man.

An apprenticeship was an unlikely trade for a slave, as those positions were traditionally passed down from Egyptian fathers to their sons. Many years ago Bezalel had begun by cleaning the craftsman's shop and doing whatever odd jobs he was given to do. But because he was observant and naturally gifted in workmanship, he was gradually given more and more responsibility. He was even allowed to make an occasional gold or wooden item that Pharaoh commissioned. His work was so superbly done that Pharaoh came to the shop in person to commend the shop owner. However, the owner didn't bother to mention that the work he was so impressed with had been done by his slave. Knowing that the one item yet to be completed in preparation for his death required impeccable skill, Pharaoh requested that the owner begin the highly coveted task of designing and building his sarcophagi. The owner in turn, with complete confidence in Bezalel's skill, gave the job to him. The day Bezalel heard the news that our people would soon be leaving Egypt, it took every ounce of mental discipline he had to complete the design of Pharaoh's coffin. As a master craftsman, his brain and hands painstakingly selected and penned every intricate, colorful detail of it on papyrus. But in his heart, he didn't much care what they buried Pharaoh in since he hoped to be long gone before that day came.

Bezalel wasn't the only leader who was brimming over with enthusiasm at the very thought of freedom. Within a few hours, all of the other leaders who attended the meeting had told someone, who told someone else. Before noon, almost every slave nearby had heard the news, including me as I worked in the home of Ayana, an Egyptian official. When one of the slaves who tended to the animals came inside hurriedly and told me that a man had come to town who was sent by God to liberate us, I was naturally skeptical. I had heard similar stories more than a few times. Throughout the course of my life, several different men had stepped forward with plans to set the Israelites free. Unfortunately, each and every attempt to overthrow Pharaoh ended in the torture and death of the leaders of the insurrections and their followers. Wanting to believe the news if it was true, but not knowing what to think, I decided to wait and discuss the matter with Bezalel later. I reasoned that the emergency meeting he attended early that morning with the other leaders had something to do with this issue.

Bezalel left work a few minutes early that evening, eager to get home and talk to me. "Chaya," he called to me excitedly as he opened the door and stepped into our humble home in the slave quarters. I looked up from the pot I was stirring over the fire and said with a little laugh, "You're out of breath. You sound like you ran all the way home."

"I did," he said, still winded, yet with a sense of urgency. "Please come and sit down so I can tell you what happened today." I followed him to the table and sat down, having decided not to mention what I heard earlier and ruin his surprise.

"Remember that meeting I went to early this morning with the other tribal leaders?" he began, after calming down a bit. "Well, Aaron from the tribe of Levi introduced us to his brother, Moses, who has been away in the desert of Midian for the last forty years. God sent him here to get us and take us to our own land."

Hearing the same thing from Bezalel that I heard from the slave earlier did make the story more credible. But I still had some questions. "If this Moses is Aaron's brother, which makes him a Hebrew like us, he was probably born as a slave here in Egypt, too," I presumed out loud. Then with my mind reeling with what seemed like inconsistencies, I asked, "So why was he in Midian for the last forty years?"

"I don't know," he responded, thinking that was an excellent question and wondering why he hadn't thought of it himself.

"If you know so little about him, what makes you think the Lord sent him here?" I inquired further, not doubting him but merely asking a logical question.

"He performed a miracle right before our eyes, and we were convinced," he told me simply as he shrugged his shoulders. "He put his hand in his cloak and when he pulled it out it was leprous. Then he put it back and when he pulled it out again it was completely normal. We all know what leprosy looks like. Only God could have done that."

"That makes sense," I said, finally persuaded. "So what happens next?"

"Moses and Aaron are going to meet with Pharaoh and tell him that the Lord wants him to let us go," he said as a matter of fact, hoping that it would be that uncomplicated.

"I don't know," I said, quickly thinking back over the years. "We've known Pharaoh all our lives. He's used to having everything his way. So it might take something significant to get us out of here."

"You might just be right," he told me. "We'll see."

Then we moved from the serious topic of freedom to a lighter agenda. Bezalel called the children to come inside from tending the animals while I put dinner on the table. Talking, laughing, and enjoying each other's company, we couldn't have been freer at that moment in time.

The next day Moses walked through Pharaoh's palace and into his court. In spite of the fact that he had been raised in the midst of the former Pharaoh's opulence, he was in awe. The splendor he had seen earlier as he surveyed the country paled in comparison to Pharaoh's personal surroundings.

However, what caught his eye more than anything else was the woman who sat next to Pharaoh. She was stunningly beautiful, one of the most captivating women he had ever seen. Regal in appearance, she exuded royalty. At first he thought she may have been one of Pharaoh's wives. But somehow Pharaoh's interaction with her told Moses that she knew him on a less personal level, perhaps as a member of his council. This was conceivable since Egypt had had female Pharaohs in the past and was wise enough as a nation to appreciate a woman's wisdom. When Pharaoh motioned Moses to come forth, he walked forward, immediately forcing himself to focus on his purpose for being there, and not the woman.

Moses approached Pharaoh with confidence. Before he even spoke, Pharaoh's demeanor reeked of arrogance and self-appointed superiority. This was the same man who had filled the land with statues of himself not just to make the subjects of his kingdom believe that he was god, but because he believed it himself. But Moses was not concerned. *He knew that his God was the only true God and that His purpose would prevail. Therefore, he feared no man.*[25]

"Who are you and what do you want?" Pharaoh asked Moses, looking at him as though he were an insignificant bug and letting him know that he needed to make his point quickly. If he recognized Moses as a relative from his past, he didn't bother to mention it. And Moses saw no point in bringing it to his attention, as it would not have any bearing on the outcome of his mission. Relative or not, Pharaoh would ultimately let the people go.

"My name is Moses and I have been sent here by I Am, the Lord, and the God of the Israelites who are enslaved here in Egypt. He has told me to tell you to let His people go so they can worship Him," Moses said, clearly and succinctly stating his purpose. "*They are very important to Him and He wants to establish a closer relationship with them.*"[26]

"I'm sorry. I must not have heard you correctly. What did you just say to me?" Pharaoh said mockingly, feigning disbelief.

Without flinching, Moses repeated himself. "My name is Moses and I have been sent here by I Am, the God of the

---

[25] Hebrews 13:6 (TLB, NLT)
[26] Psalm 100:4(a) (NLT); Romans 12:1 (NLT, AMP)

Israelites whom you have enslaved, to tell you to let His people go."

"You are looking at the only god on this earth," Pharaoh stood and exclaimed, lifting his hands to the sky in glorification of himself. "Egypt is the most powerful nation on earth and the most advanced in every way. And I am its leader. I am god. Anyway, who is this I Am that I should obey Him and let the Hebrews go?"

Moses continued, without fear of reprisal. "Pharaoh, you are a great man, the leader of the greatest nation on earth. But with all due respect, you are not God. There is only one living God, and his name is I Am. He sent me to tell you to let His people go. And I promise you, when He is finished with you and your country, you will gladly let them go."

Pharaoh threw his head back and laughed a long, deep, guttural laugh from the bottom of his stomach. He laughed so hard that he cried. His officials also laughed, not because they thought what Moses had said was funny. They laughed instead because they were "yes" people who were afraid not to laugh when Pharaoh laughed, for fear that they might seem to not be in agreement with him.

When he could laugh no more, Pharaoh, ready to be done with the issue said very seriously, "I do not know the Lord, and I will not let the Hebrews go. But I'll tell you what. If this God of yours is real, He should have some power. Let him prove Himself and maybe I'll reconsider."

Moses was certain that Pharaoh would not reconsider no matter what he saw, but he went ahead and performed the first miracle anyway. In the presence of the king, his court, and the leaders of the Israelites, Aaron took the staff the Lord had given Moses and threw it on the ground. It immediately turned into a massive, hissing, deadly snake. Everyone gasped, astounded by the Lord's display of power. But Pharaoh sat there stone-faced and unimpressed. He beckoned to his magicians who were standing nearby, and they stepped forward. Each of them did as Aaron had done and threw their staffs on the ground, and they too became snakes. But to everyone's dismay, Aaron's snake quickly devoured all of the other snakes. Pharaoh, still stubborn and unyielding, hardened his heart and would not change his position.

"As I said before," he began. "I will not let the Hebrews go. Furthermore, you are planting foolish ideas of freedom in their heads and keeping them from their work. They are my slaves for life, and because you had the audacity to come to me with this nonsense, I am going to make their lives even more miserable. This conversation is over. Now leave my presence."

Before Moses turned to leave, he stole a quick glance at the beautiful woman. For a split second, he thought he saw her smile at him but he couldn't be sure. He wondered if he only saw what he wanted to see and was merely engaging himself in wishful thinking.

As Moses and Aaron were being shown the door, Pharaoh summoned the Egyptian leader of the Israelite slave workforce. He told him to make the work harder for the slaves so they would not have time to fantasize about ever leaving Egypt. Instead of giving them the straw needed to make bricks, the slaves were told they would have to scour the land to find their own straw. Then they had to make their daily quota of bricks within the same period as before.

Once the Israelite foremen informed the slaves of their new responsibilities, they mourned deeply. They got up earlier to look for straw and worked late into the night to make the bricks. But no matter how hard they tried, they couldn't make their quota. So they were whipped until they were raw and bleeding. And the same Israelites, who only days before were hoping and praying they would soon be free, were now hating Moses for ever having mentioned the elusive idea of freedom to them. He was a stench in their nostrils and no longer credible.

The Israelite foremen who had been given the task of whipping the slaves went to their elders, who in turn went to Moses and told him that his plan had not worked. Moses was dumbfounded but did the only thing he knew to do. He went to the Lord for an answer.

He bowed before I Am in reverence and with the utmost humility spoke from his heart. "Lord, I do not understand. I did what you told me to, but it did not work. Pharaoh has put more work on the Israelites and whips on their backs when they can't get it done, all because I told him that you said to let your people go. They are angry with you and me, and are even more miserable than they were before. Now, what do I do?" Moses said, desperate for an answer.

"You need to trust me even when things don't happen like you think they should," I Am told him gently. *"Victory is a process that is not measured by one outcome. So don't expect to understand everything that happens along the way. Just keep doing what I tell you to do and leave the results to me.*[27] Now go back to Pharaoh. He is not yet convinced that I am the only living God. So you will need to show him another miracle to get his attention. Take your staff with you, and I will tell you what to do when you get there. Don't worry. I will be with you."

---

[27] Proverbs 3:5–6 (NLT, NIV)

The Lord always said exactly what He knew Moses needed to hear. Moses had been concerned. Pharaoh threw him out of his palace the last time he saw him and didn't leave him with the impression that he could come back.

So Moses went back to Pharaoh a second time. He was ready to convince him that I Am is the only living God and very serious when He told him to let His people go. This time Moses was waiting for Pharaoh very early in the morning when he came out of the palace to take a walk along the Nile River. The beautiful woman was part of his entourage. "So you're back again," Pharaoh said with his usual pompous arrogance. "I would have had you killed for even thinking of coming into my presence again but you make me laugh, which is something I don't get to do very often. So humor me. What do you want this time?"

"You humor me too," Moses replied. "And I don't get to laugh often either." The two men joked a bit, appreciating each other's sense of humor.

Moses quickly reminded himself that he was there on official business with no time to exchange pleasantries. So he went straight to the point.

"I Am, the God of the Hebrews, has sent me to tell you, 'Let my people go so they can worship me in the desert. Until now you have not listened, so I will strike the water of the Nile, and it will be changed into blood. The fish will die, the river will stink, and the Egyptians will not be able to drink its water.'"

Moses then told Aaron to stretch out the staff over all the waters of Egypt – over the Nile, the streams, the canals, the ponds and even all the reservoirs. They immediately all turned to blood. Blood was everywhere in Egypt, even in wooden buckets and stone jars.

Pharaoh's entourage was noticeably alarmed, including the beautiful woman. But Pharaoh himself wasn't fazed. His magicians were able to do the same thing with their secret arts. So he hardened his heart a second time, turned and went into his palace with his officials, and did not give it a second thought. But the beautiful woman turned and looked at Moses with a look that said there was something she wanted to say. Moses looked at her too, eager to hear whatever was on her mind. But instead of speaking, she followed Pharaoh into the palace.

Shortly after that, just after sun up, I left my home and quickly walked the short distance to the luxurious mansion where I worked, enjoying the cool, fresh air. My master was Ayana, a member of Pharaoh's court. She was also my friend. Her chariot driver had picked her up even earlier than usual for an important meeting at Pharaoh's request, leaving the slaves to tend to the estate.

I let myself in through the back door and immediately went to the room where the woman's son slept since I assumed responsibility for him during the day shift. He was just beginning to stir, so I lifted him from his crib and cooed and played with him for a few minutes before taking him to the kitchen to feed him breakfast. I strapped him into his high chair, and he began to whimper and reach for his cup, letting me know that he was thirsty. With his cup in one hand and the water pitcher in the other, I began to pour before I realized that it was not water streaming from the pitcher, but rich, red blood.

Terribly startled, I dropped the clay pitcher and the cup. They both shattered causing the baby to scream and leaving the floor covered with blood. I unstrapped and picked the baby up right away, wondering if this strange phenomenon could have anything to do with the mission to free us. As a mother, it horrified me to think that I almost gave a baby, any baby, blood to drink.

Within seconds, two other slaves ran into the room. When they saw the blood and broken clay pieces on the floor, they promptly began to clean them up.

"What's going on?" I asked them, still shaken. "How did blood get into that pitcher?"

"Someone just came and told us that to get Pharaoh's attention, the Lord has turned all the water in Egypt into blood except the water below the ground," one of them explained to me. "Don't worry. The other slaves are out digging. We will have some fresh water for the baby soon." Oddly, the baby stopped crying as though he understood what he had just heard. When I saw that he had settled down, I strapped him back in his chair.

Then I got down on my hands and knees and helped the other two slaves clean up the mess. Not that I had to, since I was only responsible for the baby, but because it was the right thing to do.

Later that day Ayana returned home and told me about the unusual events that had recently occurred. "An interesting man named Moses came to see Pharaoh a few days ago," she began. Ayana knew that the slaves always knew as much or more about what was going on in the country as the Egyptians did, and I might have some information. "He says that his God told him to tell Pharaoh to let your people go so you can worship Him."

"I know," I said to her. "Everyone's been talking about it. He came to see Bezalel and our other leaders when he first got here, and he convinced them that he is legitimate. In fact, I met him a day later when Bezalel brought him to the house. So what did Pharaoh say?"

"He said the same thing anyone in his position would say," Ayana explained. "What leader would let their entire labor force walk away?"

"Is that why all of our water has been turned to blood – because Pharaoh won't do what our God is telling him to do?" I asked, even though I already knew the answer.

"That's it," Ayana said. "But Pharaoh doesn't care. His slaves have been bringing water into the palace from wells that tap into underground water sources. As long as he has what he needs, he won't budge."

"Well, our people are still hopeful that our God can change his mind," I said, thinking it would be a dream come true.

"If I were in your shoes, I would feel the same way," Ayana told me empathetically. "When I get more information, I will tell you as much as I can."

I understood without Ayana having to say so that whatever information she gave me was confidential unless she told me otherwise. And even though I was a slave, Ayana knew not to divulge what she learned from me, either. In spite of our opposite economic, social and political positions, *our close friendship thrived because of respect and high regard for each other. It was an excellent example of true sisterhood.*

CHAPTER

FORBIDDEN FRUIT

Later that evening when Moses was praying in the small garden at Aaron's house where he was staying, Aaron came to see him. "You have a visitor," his brother said with a sparkle in his eye.

Moses knew that Pharaoh would never break protocol and come to see him. But he hoped that he had sent one of his officials to say that he was ready to release the Hebrews.

"Is it one of Pharaoh's officials?" Moses asked, seeing Aaron's enthusiasm and thinking of the concern that the officials showed earlier when the Lord turned their water into blood. "Maybe they talked some sense into Pharaoh. I'm ready to get this thing over with and get out of this God-forsaken country."

"It's that woman you've been making eyes at since you got here," Aaron said, letting him know that he was watching him carefully. "You thought I didn't see you, but I did. Anyway, I hope she came to bring us some good news."

Moses was even more elated now that he knew who the visitor was. "Did she say why she wants to see me?" Moses asked Aaron, not doing a good job of hiding his enthusiasm. He felt more like a teenager that an eighty-year-old.

"I tried to find out but she said that she had a word from Pharaoh that she could only tell you. Listen. Don't lose your head over this woman and get us all killed. She's beautiful, but you need to keep your focus and remember what we're here for," Aaron said.

"Thank you for your concern, brother," Moses said, not really hearing what Aaron was saying. "Just show her in."

The woman entered the garden gracefully. She was even more beautiful and exotic up close than she was from a distance. The Egyptians were a good-looking people, but she stood out in a crowd.

"Won't you have a seat?" Moses asked her as he smiled and pulled a chair out from the table for her.

"Yes, yes I will," she said, maintaining eye contact with him as she sat down.

Moses took a seat at the table across from her, eager to hear what she had to say. Fortunately for him, she broke the ice and spoke first because he was too awe-stricken to begin.

"I lied to your brother," she said candidly. "Pharaoh did not send me to see you. I came on my own."

Moses' face lit up. He felt encouraged, hoping that this was a personal visit. "Please speak freely," he told her.

"My name is Ayana, and I am one of Pharaoh's personal advisors," she said with dignity, carefully enunciating each word as a queen would do. "Pharaoh is a proud man who does not always listen to reason. It may not seem like it, but this God of yours has gotten his attention. My concern is that our country will be destroyed while we are waiting for him to realize that there is a power greater than him. I am here because I want to get a better understanding of your God and His plan. Pharaoh respects my opinion. If your God is willing to negotiate, perhaps I can get Pharaoh to do the same."

Moses found her proposition amusing. He chuckled inside at the idea of I Am negotiating with Pharaoh. I Am is jealous for his glory and not at all pleased with seeing those He created worshipping anything or anyone besides Himself. Pharaoh presented himself as God and, therefore, one to be worshiped. This ridiculous notion of Pharaoh's deity would have to be abolished before the Lord would even consider listening to anything he had to say.

"Let me tell you about the God that I serve," Moses began. "His name is I Am and He is the only living God and the Creator of everything that lives and exists." For the next several minutes, she listened with fascination as he went back to the beginning and told her the whole story. He recounted it so vividly that she could envision every detail as he spoke.

"When He created the earth, He placed a magnificent garden in it. It was the perfect environment with a warm, pleasant climate, lush green vegetation, fruit trees of every kind, aromatic flowers, flowing rivers, and animals living in perfect harmony with each other. But His greatest creation was man and woman, whom He made and placed in the garden just for friendship with Himself. The only thing He asked of them was that they obey Him so that their lives would continue to be delightful. He told them not to eat from the tree in the middle of the garden. One day, the devil, the source of all evil, lied to them and tricked them into eating the fruit of the tree. God punished them for their disobedience by putting them out of the garden, forcing them to work and make a living by the sweat of their brow. Worst of all, they destroyed the intimate relationship they once had with the Lord. But, the Lord still loved mankind. So He put together a plan to draw them and their descendants back to Him. Years later, He appeared to a man named Abram who lived in the city of Ur along the Euphrates River. He told him to leave his home and his family and go to a place that He would show him. He chose Abram because he was looking for someone with whom He could have a loving, intimate relationship. He wanted someone He could count on to worship, trust, and obey Him, and to teach his children to do the same for generations to come. Abram obeyed, left Ur, and settled in the land of Canaan where God told him. After he arrived there, the Lord appeared to him again, changed his name to Abraham which means "father of many," and told him that He would one day give that entire land to his descendants. At that time, Abraham did not have any children because his wife Sarah was barren. Therefore, having a child did not seem possible, but Abraham believed what God promised him. Twenty-five years later, when he was one hundred and his wife was ninety, she gave birth to a son whom they named Isaac. Isaac grew up and had a son named Jacob. Jacob had twelve sons, one of whom was named Joseph. Joseph came to Egypt over four hundred years ago when his jealous brothers sold him into slavery. He obeyed God, and God gave him favor with the Pharaoh at that time who made him Governor of Egypt. There was a terrible famine in the land, and the Lord used Joseph to save Egypt, and all of the surrounding nations, including Canaan, from starving to death. Joseph sent for his father Jacob, who was also known as Israel, and he and his entire family came from Canaan and settled in Egypt. They multiplied rapidly over the next four hundred years. The new Pharaoh, who knew nothing about Joseph, thought the Israelites might be a threat to Egypt and he enslaved them. During their centuries of bondage, they have cried out to the Lord, asking Him to deliver them. He heard them and sent me to tell Pharaoh to let them go."

"So the answer to your question is no," he candidly told her. "I Am will not negotiate with Pharaoh because He alone is God, and He does not need to. *He has a very specific purpose in mind. He will bring His people out of Egypt, through the wilderness, where they will learn to worship, trust, and obey Him, and into Canaan, a land flowing with milk and honey.*[28] In the process, *He will convince* Egypt and *all of the* surrounding *idol-worshipping nations that He is the only living God. And the wise people who are living in those nations will come to Him, forsake their worthless, hand-made gods, and worship Him only.*"[29]

"That story is so unbelievable that it must be true," Ayana said, looking off reflectively and then back at Moses. "Your God has put a lot of thought and effort into this plan of His. And He has chosen a strong, wise, God-fearing man like you to help him bring it to pass," she said with admiration and respect. Moses was inwardly flattered by her verbal and visual compliments. Then she continued. "I need some time to think about how to bring this before Pharaoh. If what you are telling me is true, this has serious implications for Egypt's future and mine."

"You are right," Moses told her frankly. "If Pharaoh continues to be stubborn, I Am will destroy this country. You

---

[28] Deuteronomy 6:23 (NLT)
[29] Isaiah 56:6–7 (NLT)

might want to consider leaving Egypt with us when we leave. You can bring your family and make a new life in the land of Canaan." Moses mentioned her family not only because he cared about her well-being, but mainly with the hope that she would divulge her marital status to him.

"I have no family except a small son," she told him, quickly picking up on his motive for asking, and hoping that he didn't have a spouse either. "My husband was the highest ranking general in Pharaoh's army. He was killed in Egypt's last military campaign. We won the war and acquired more land, but I lost my beloved. I have had many proposals, but I never remarried because I haven't met a man that appeals to me yet."

Moses felt sorry for her loss but could not hide his jubilation that she was unattached. This woman appealed to him, immensely. It was not just her beauty. It was also her spirit. Even though she was an Egyptian living in a country that worshiped many gods, she seemed drawn to his God, not out of fear, but out of a genuine interest in and reverence for Him. And Moses liked that.

Moses appealed to her too. She liked men who had a vision and a purpose – men who knew who they were, what they wanted, where they were going, and the wisdom and power to make it happen. In fact, that was partially why she had come to see him that evening. She was concerned about the future of Egypt and wanted to intercede in any way she could to save it. But she also saw a man that she wanted to get to know better and didn't have an issue with making her intentions known to him.

There was only one problem. Moses was already married. When he left Egypt 40 years ago after murdering an Egyptian, he fled to Midian where he married a woman named Zipporah.

Her father Jethro had moved the family to Midian from Cush when she was a child. Moses loved Zipporah dearly and knew that she was waiting for him back in Midian. But he was intrigued by this woman also. So he conveniently chose not to mention that he was married. As he always did, he decided to talk to God about the matter first.

"It's getting late," Moses said, motioning with his head to the setting sun. She turned and looked, puzzled that he had abruptly moved on from their conversation about her not having a husband. She was sure that there was a connection between them and wondered why he so quickly turned back to business.

"I understand your reason for coming here, but I can assure you that the Lord will not negotiate with Pharaoh," Moses told her. "Hopefully, when you go back you can convince him to let the Hebrews go right away so that he can save his country. You need to tell him that we will leave one way or another. He did not become Egypt's greatest Pharaoh by being a foolish man. Perhaps he will listen to your voice of reason and make a wise decision."

He stood to see her out and made the mistake of taking her hand in his to say goodbye. He felt an attraction to her that he liked very much, but also found disturbing since he was a married man who loved God. She looked into his eyes, the window to his soul, to see what was there, and she knew beyond a shadow of a doubt that there was something real between them. She squeezed his hand gently to let him know that she knew. Seeing that this encounter was awkward for him, she simply told him goodbye and left.

As soon as she was gone, Aaron came to Moses. He had been listening to the entire conversation between him and

Ayana from inside. For a moment, he just stood there glaring at his brother without saying a word.

"What are you doing?" Aaron asked Moses, finally breaking the silence.

"I don't know what you're talking about," Moses answered, not wanting to have that conversation.

"You know exactly what I'm talking about," Aaron retorted. "You're interested in that woman."

When Moses just stood there and looked at Aaron without saying a word, Aaron knew that he was right. And he was gravely concerned. Moses was a married man on a very important mission for God. The last thing they needed was for Moses to lose his focus and make a costly mistake that might affect all of them.

"Moses," Aaron began, trying carefully to choose his words. "God hand-picked you and spent forty years preparing you to lead us out of Egypt. Don't blow this. I know that you need Zipporah here with you now, that it is hard for you to be here alone. That is the way God created us – to need the companionship and comfort of someone we love. But He has decided that the best thing for now is that you focus on what He sent you here to do. When we get out of here, you can be with your wife again. Until then you need to keep your thoughts from wandering into dangerous territory. You need to tell that woman that you are a married man who loves the only wife he will ever have. That way she can get any thoughts of you two living happily ever after out of her head," Aaron finally said as he wagged his finger at Moses and walked off.

Moses knew that everything Aaron had just said was true and came straight from the Lord's mouth. His mind had momentarily wandered off into dangerous territory, and he needed to bring it back. Even though he desperately needed to be with Zipporah but couldn't, he was grateful that God had placed his brother there to hold him accountable. He knew that *no matter how long a person has walked with God, if they entertain the wrong thought, even for an instant, they are susceptible to sin.*[30]

So Moses did what he had done for the last forty years *when he had a problem or was in any way tempted or uncomfortable. He talked to the Lord about it.*[31]

Needing privacy, Moses left the house and walked down to the Nile. It was majestic at sunset, like the Garden of Eden. There was nothing like seeing the awesome beauty of God's creation to put one immediately in touch with Him. Apparently, God was just as eager to talk to Moses because He spoke first.

"Moses," God began, calling him by name. "I am pleased with you. Your heart is pleasing to me."

"You are?" Moses said quizzically. "But I was thinking some thoughts that I should not have been thinking. I was tempted to become involved with a woman who is not my wife."

"Yes, but you recognized the temptation and did not act on those thoughts. You changed the subject and sent Ayana away instead of letting that conversation take its course, which would have ultimately led you into a sexual relationship with her. *Sin is a process that can begin simply with the wrong conversation. But remember that being tempted is not a sin. It only becomes a sin when you choose to dwell on the thought or carry out the act. Also, remember that your enemy, the devil, is very cunning, and he uses different strategies for different people.*

---

[30] 2 Corinthians 10:5(b) (NIV)
[31] 1 Peter 5:7 (AMP)

Knowing that you are a man who has a close relationship with me, he knows that the best way to lure you into sexual sin is with a woman who appears to be spiritual. So he will present a woman to you that you think is, or may become, drawn to me. *And he is not in a hurry. He will slow-walk you. He doesn't care if you sin now or later, just as long as he can get you to ultimately ruin your life and my purpose for it.*[32] *So be on your guard because he won't give up. He will just come back at a more opportune time.*[33] You also need to know that Ayana is not the problem. She is not maliciously trying to ruin you. In fact, she means you no harm at all. She is merely an unwitting tool of the devil to get you to sin, lose credibility with the Israelites, Egyptians, and Pharaoh, and ruin my plan. *Always remember that the devil is your real enemy, not people.*[34] So continue to come to me and pray whenever you feel tempted so that I can help you. *You are human, and you can want with all your heart not to sin, but the flesh is weak.*[35] *I will not let you experience any more temptation than you can endure. When you do your part and resist the temptation, I will give you the ability to overcome it so that you do not give in to it.*"[36]

God paused for a while to give Moses time to absorb the depth of what He had just said. When He saw that Moses was ready, He continued. "I know that it is hard for you to be alone right now. But this is my will for you at the moment. I need you to remain sober-minded and completely focused on the task I have called you to do – to lead my people out of Egypt.

---

[32] John 10:10(a) (NIV)
[33] Luke 4:1–13, especially verse 13 (TLB, NLT)
[34] Ephesians 6:11–12 (TLB)
[35] Matthew 26:41 (NLT, AMP)
[36] 1 Corinthians 10:13 (NLT, TLB)

I have spent forty years preparing you for this mission. Only someone who has spent decades in the wilderness with me can successfully lead millions of others through it. So for the sake of my name and my purpose, I will be right here with you to help you every step of the way. And when the time is right, I will bring Zipporah back to you. She is the woman I have chosen for you, the wife of your youth, and the only wife and woman you are ever to have. She knows me and hears from me. She is my gift to you, a woman after my own heart, your helper, and the mother of your children."

As he always did, Moses felt encouraged after his conversation with the Lord. Spending time in His presence, talking and listening to Him, refreshed and energized Moses and gave him the strength to continue with the task before him. With nothing more to be said, Moses bowed his head. He was overwhelmed with gratitude for the Lord's loving care and honored to have been chosen to serve Him.

Later that day, Ayana couldn't wait to get home and tell me what happened during her meeting with Moses. Her head slave and personal assistant greeted her at the door with her slippers and asked her how else he might be of assistance to her.

"Please bring two cool cups of beer out onto the patio and tell Chaya to join me," she told him as she changed her shoes and handed him the dressier, less comfortable pair. He scurried off and gave her instructions to two other slaves. One of them relieved me while the other one saw to the refreshments. I was more than happy to take a break and eager to get an update on the status of our deliverance. Minutes later, both of us were seated on a bench outside, enjoying the beautiful garden.

"How was your day?" I asked, noticing Ayana's cheerful demeanor right away. I was sure that something special must have happened.

"I went to see Moses at his brother's house today," Ayana said, as I gave her a surprised look. "And we had a very interesting conversation."

"Don't you leave out one word," I told her as I took a sip of my beer and leaned forward with my interest piqued, not wanting to miss a thing.

Ayana explained how she went there hoping to understand the Lord's plan better so she could intercede with Pharaoh to prevent any further damage to the country. She went on to share everything Moses told her, expounding on God's plan to deliver the Israelites from bondage so we could worship Him, and to ultimately use us to draw all mankind to Himself.

"I know the plan well," I said, grateful to have such a conscientious God on our side. "Moses told my husband and the other leaders the same thing when he met with them. And he told it again when he came and had dinner my family. *The Lord has our entire future mapped out for us.*[37] No other god does that for his people. You know, I wish you would give some more thought to coming with us when we leave."

"Moses and I talked about that very idea today," Ayana told me with a sly smile as if she thought he might have had a motive for the suggestion.

"So what did you tell him?" I asked, detecting more than just a political reason for Ayana's visit."

"I didn't tell him anything," Ayana began. "But I have been considering it."

---

[37] Jeremiah 29:11 (NIV); Ephesians 2:10 (AMP, TLB)

"Why now, and not before?" I inquired. "When you and I talked about it a while ago you weren't interested."

"Because I find Moses appealing," Ayana finally admitted.

"So what do you like about him?" I asked.

"Well, from what I can tell from his interaction with Pharaoh and my conversation with him, he's a very impressive man. He's well-spoken, wise, and very focused on his purpose for being here. He seems like a man of character, a deliberate man who does what he says he's going to do. And he's funny too. He could be good husband material."

"Husband material?" I asked, sincerely interested in hearing more about him. My friend Ayana was top-shelf and would never settle for anything less. "So does he meet all of your criteria? I know how particular you can be."

"Yes, he does." Ayana began, then hesitated. "Except for a couple of things. He's wise, but I'm not sure that he's educated. And he's a little rough around the edges."

I threw my head back and laughed long and hard. When I finally collected myself, I said, "I don't like being a slave, but it makes life so much easier. When we are choosing a mate for life, we don't have to consider whether he's educated, polished, or has money, or position. We look at who he is as a person. From everything you've just told me about Moses, he passes that test. So why does it matter if he is educated? You said he's wise, and *wisdom is better than education*. And the right woman can polish the rough edges off of a man. Am I right?"

Ayana thought about it for a moment then said, "Yes, you're right as usual. I need to stop thinking like Egyptian royalty and start thinking like a woman who's looking for a real love that can stand the test of time."

"Good," I said, smiling. "Now one more question. Is he available?"

"I'm not sure," Ayana replied. "But I do know that he is as interested in me as I am in him. So we'll see what happens."

Then the two of us went on to laugh and talk about other things. I was pleased to see my friend happy and full of life. I hadn't seen her like that since before her husband, Husani, died. And Ayana gave me the highest compliment. She told me that she was grateful to have *a friend* like me, *a trustworthy confidant who listened, gave wise counsel, never repeated anything she shared with me and always meant her well.*

CHAPTER 6

THE DEVASTATION OF EGYPT

One week after the Lord turned the water into blood, it was completely clear again. Fresh water from the place where the Nile originates deep in Africa had flowed from there through Egypt, washed the tainted water away, and restored life back to normal. Everyone, whether Egyptian or Hebrew slave, couldn't have been more relieved because the blood in the river had brought with it a thick, nauseating stench that made our stomachs sick and our heads hurt. And digging for water underground made the already burdensome lives of the slaves even worse. Pharaoh, however, had not yet come to the realization that he and his country would be better off without us. He hardened his heart, and his decision not to let us go remained unchanged.

So Moses went back to Pharaoh and told him the Lord said, "Let my people go so they can worship me. If you refuse to let them go, I will send a plague of frogs across your entire land. The Nile River will swarm with frogs. They will come up out of every river, canal, and pond in Egypt and into your palace, even into your bedroom and onto your bed! They will even jump into your ovens and your kneading bowls. They will enter not just your palace but the houses of all your people."

Again, Pharaoh foolishly refused to heed the warning. So the Lord brought large frogs up out of every body of water in Egypt, and they infiltrated the entire country within hours.

I was attending to my regular duties at Ayana's house on the day of the invasion. Though usually calm and agreeable, the baby was irritable and restless for no apparent reason. I tried to feed him everything I knew he liked, including his favorite mashed barley drizzled with honey. But he wouldn't eat a drop. I changed him to be sure that he was dry, but that didn't help. He whimpered when I sat down and rocked him. He squealed when I stood up and walked with him. But nothing made him happy. Finally, I decided to take him into the garden to see if the sunlight, fresh air, and fragrant flowers that ordinarily pleased him, might settle him down.

As soon as we stepped outside he looked to his left, and his little round face lit up, distracted by something he saw. Thinking it must have been a bird or a butterfly, I looked in the direction he was looking. At first I didn't believe my eyes. Jumping over the tall privacy fence like soldiers on a mission were what must have been hundreds of huge, croaking bullfrogs. The baby began to laugh as he watched them land on the ground and come toward us, but I panicked. I had lived in Egypt all my life and had never seen such a thing. So I knew immediately that, like all the water turning to blood, this was the Lord's hand pressuring Pharaoh to let us go.

I ran back into the house thinking we would be safe there from the bizarre reptilian invasion. But no sooner than I closed the door and turned around, I saw dozens more of them fast approaching. As concern for the baby's welfare superseded my own fear, I quickly stepped over them, desperately seeking a place of safety. But they brazenly climbed on my feet as though they would have given anything to be big enough to reach my head. I lifted my feet, first one then the other and shook them off, making every effort to maintain my balance. They were hideous, slimy and covered with warts, and I was sure that if I fell to the floor and they crawled all over me, I would go insane.

"Help me!" I cried loudly in desperation. "Somebody help me!"

One of the other slaves came around the corner with a shovel in one hand and a sack in the other. He quickly scooped the frogs up two at a time and dumped them in the bag. The other slaves were running around feverishly closing all of the doors and shutters to keep any more frogs from entering the house. All I could do was stay out of their way and hold the baby, who by this time was laughing and pointing at them. About an hour later they had filled a countless number of sacks with the jumping, croaking creatures. Then they double-knotted the bags to keep the frogs from escaping and left them in an empty room to die a slow death.

With the problem of getting the frogs out of the way resolved, a problem that was equally as intolerable emerged. The outside temperature was one hundred and forty degrees. Once the house was completely closed up with no air circulating, the indoor temperature quickly rose until it was just as hot inside. The heat was smoldering and virtually unbearable. In spite of their discomfort, the other slaves went back to their individual household tasks. I made my way into the baby's room and sat in the rocker, drenched in sweat and weak from the heat. With barely enough strength to make the chair move, I rocked him. Seeming to prefer the comfort of rest to the miserable heat, he quickly went to sleep.

I was glad that he was asleep because it gave me time to think, to reason this thing out. Ayana had warned me that more bizarre occurrences could be coming, but I never expected anything like this. It was nightmarishly surreal. I was stranded in a sweltering house unable to reach my husband and children. A frog invasion had brought the entire country to a standstill. If it were not so uncomfortable, it would have been funny. I wondered what kind of God would choose such a plague. Then looking up towards heaven, I had to shake my head and smile as I realized that only a God with a sense of humor would do such a thing. This plague was not life-threatening or harmful in any way, just attention-getting because it was incredibly unreal. In fact, at that very moment I could hear the frogs outside the house, croaking loudly and bouncing against the walls, looking for a way to get in. I reasoned that the Lord had to be a loving God to send a warning as merciful as this. And I hoped that Pharaoh was as miserable as everyone else in the country so he would come to the same realization soon in order to spare us all any more discomfort.

The following day, Pharaoh, desperate for relief, summoned Moses and asked him to beg the Lord to get rid of the frogs in exchange for the release of the Israelites. The word that leaked from the palace was that Pharaoh was given a double dose of the slimy reptiles. We heard that his highness, the proud king, sat up in a chair all night because he was afraid to sleep in his bed. And the Lord did just what Moses asked. The frogs in the houses, the courtyards, and the fields all died. The Egyptians and the slaves piled them into large heaps, and a terrible stench filled the entire land. But when Pharaoh saw that there was relief, he became stubborn and hardened his heart again. He refused to listen to I Am and let us go.

Over the next few weeks, the Lord bombarded the country with plague after devastating plague, in unending succession. Next, dense swarms of gnats then flies infested the land and covered everything that breathed, both people and animals alike. In frustration, we covered our entire heads with sacks to keep the aggravating insects out of our mouths, noses, and ears. The whole land of Egypt was thrown into chaos by them. After that plague, all of the livestock of the Egyptians, including Pharaoh's, were stricken and died. Not one cattle, horse, donkey, camel, sheep, goat, or ox remained alive.

Ayana's husband had been in the business of buying and selling thoroughbred cattle and horses for decades. After his death she continued the trade, and it prospered greatly. Before she arrived home that day, she knew what had happened because she was with Pharaoh when Moses told him what would happen. And she also saw the carnage with her own eyes, as every field that her chariot driver passed by on the way to her house was full of dead livestock. Instead of immediately going into the house, she went straight to the stables. She stood inside the door in disbelief, looking at the death not only of her animals, but of her wealth and financial future as well. Though she owned her land, her home, and all of its contents, the thriving business she relied on as a source of income and as her son's inheritance no longer existed.

I watched her from the house, not sure if I should go to her or not, because I didn't know what to say. I did not want to say I understood because I didn't. As a slave, I didn't have any idea what it felt like to have wealth and lose it because I never had it to lose. So I waited for her. A little while later she came into the house, and I made myself available in case she wanted to talk.

"Can I get you something?" I asked her as she sat down in her favorite chair in the main room, her face expressionless. She shook her head to say "no" and motioned for me to take a seat across from her.

"I understand that none of the livestock of your people died today?" she said, more as a question than a statement.

"The Lord spared ours," I said softly, not wanting to make her feel any worse than she already did.

She thought about it for a moment then said, more to herself than to me, "It seems like your God is trying to send a message to us Egyptians. *Maybe there is more to life than money, power, and comfort. Maybe there is much, much more.*"[38]

Knowing that she was in the process of making a life changing realization and needed to draw the right conclusions on her own, I remained quiet and just listened.

"Something very serious is getting ready to happen, and I can't afford to come out on the losing end of this equation," she said with conviction. "I have a son to raise and I have to take care of his future and mine."

I sat there and continued to listen until finally she said, "I have a lot to think about. You are free to leave. I'll see you tomorrow morning."

On the way home I thought about what she was discovering that I already knew. I was a slave working for a woman from the highest level of Egyptian society, a woman of wealth who was also a member of Pharaoh's inner circle. I had seen *riches, influence and privilege* up close in her life and in the lives of her

---

[38] Luke 12:15 (NLT)

peers. *While they are not detrimental in and of themselves, they do not bring real happiness, peace of mind or purpose.* I was merely a slave, but I knew this to be a fact. And if it took a great loss for my beloved friend to learn this, I knew she would be all the better for it because *the greatest gains can come from the greatest losses.*[39]

Just a few days later, while the Egyptians were still burning the carcasses of their dead animals, another plague fell on the country. They were becoming progressively more severe, and this was the worst one yet. Because Pharaoh continued to disobey the Lord's command to "Let my people go so they can worship me," the Lord caused ugly, festering boils to break out on all the Egyptians. They were in such excruciating pain that it hurt to sit, hurt to stand, and hurt to even breathe. It was hard to see my dear friend Ayana in that state, but there was nothing I could do to relieve her suffering. No one was exempt from the misery, not even Pharaoh. Because he had stubbornly refused to listen to the Lord several times before, but hardened his own heart instead, this time the Lord Himself hardened Pharaoh's heart. The king would soon learn that *I Am is a gracious God, who warns before He executes judgment. The wise person heeds His voice the very day they hear it. If they wait too long, it may be too late, and He will no longer give them the option to change their mind and obey Him.*[40] So in spite of his own dreadful suffering, he again refused to let us go.

Three weeks later, as soon as the Egyptian's oozing boils healed and Pharaoh thought he had gotten some relief, the Lord again sent Moses to warn him. "Let my people go so they can worship me," Moses told him on God's behalf. "If you don't,

---

[39] Philippians 3:8 (AMP)
[40] Hebrews 3:7–11 (NLT)

I will send a hailstorm more devastating than any that Egypt has ever seen. By now I could have lifted my hand, struck you and your people with a plague, and wiped you off the face of the earth. But I have spared you for a specific purpose. I want to show you, the king of the most prosperous nation that has ever existed, that I am the only living God. And I want to use you to make myself known throughout the world." But Pharaoh refused to heed the warning, so the Lord sent a tremendous hailstorm against the land of Egypt. Sheets of rain poured down, brilliant lightning illuminated the sky, and roaring thunder crackled loudly as hailstones the size of pomegranates bombarded the country. The hail struck down everything in the open field – people and plants alike. Even the large, majestic palm trees were destroyed. I had been outside cutting fresh flowers from the garden and made it inside just in time. Many of Ayana's slaves who worked in the fields were less fortunate. The massive hailstones killed them. The storm left all of Egypt utterly ruined. The only place without hail damage was the region of Goshen, where I and the other Hebrew slaves lived.

Seemingly convinced that the Lord meant business, Pharaoh quickly summoned Moses. He asked him to plead with the Lord to end the terrifying thunder and hail, promising to let the people go in exchange. But as soon as the Lord did as Moses requested and the storm ceased, Pharaoh again refused to let us leave.

So the Lord sent a strong east wind that brought locusts that swarmed over the entire country and settled like a thick, dark blanket from one end to the other. They devoured every crop and plant in the fields as well as all the fruit on the trees that had sprouted right after the hailstorm. Not a single green leaf remained on the trees and plants. The entire country, once lush with greenery, was now brown, barren, and eerily lifeless. Everyone was left with only what they had in reserve to eat. Again, Pharaoh promised to let us go, and the Lord took the locusts away with a strong west wind. Then Pharaoh changed his mind, just as he had done every time before.

Finally, the Lord sent a deep darkness over the whole country for three days, a darkness so thick it could be felt. Blackness fell unexpectedly, all of a sudden, during the middle of the day, leaving no one time to find or light a lamp. During that entire time, the Egyptians could not even see each other, let alone anything else. So no one moved. Wherever they were when the darkness descended is where they stayed, sitting in total blackness, fearful for their lives and their future, not knowing what to think or expect. When the darkness ultimately lifted, Pharaoh again refused to let us go.

Ayana was with Pharaoh every time Moses informed him that the Lord told him to let His people go so they could worship Him. And every time he refused and brought God's wrath on Egypt, I watched her suffer along with all of the other Egyptians. Observing her allowed me to understand the massive extent of their loss and the depth of their misery. I understood why after this ninth plague she knew she had to do something. The plagues had strategically progressed from being irritating to physically, financially, and emotionally crippling. She was afraid the Lord's patience was wearing thin. She finally understood that I Am merely wanted us free so He could draw us into a close, intimate relationship with Himself. Our loving God was ready to take some very drastic measures to deliver us so we could worship Him. Therefore, she determined that when the time was right, she would try to reason with Pharaoh, the once great king of Egypt.

CHAPTER 7

A PLEA TO PHARAOH

One evening when Pharaoh was alone, Ayana approached his throne. She had chosen this specific day and time to come to him because his demeanor over the last few days indicated that he knew his time was running out. She hoped that if she were right, once he honestly assessed the state of his country he would be logical and bid the Israelites farewell.

She could see that he was emotionally dejected, yet deep in thought, pondering how to repair the damage the plagues had done to his country and his reputation. The king who was once proud and boastful was worn down and no longer sure of himself. Ordinarily he would have put on a façade to keep anyone else from seeing him in that condition, but Ayana was one of the few people he trusted enough to be his true self.

"Rameses," she said softly as she sat down in front of him, choosing her words carefully as she prepared to make her appeal. He turned his head and looked at her, and she continued. "The Egyptian people are tired and hungry. We have lost our crops, and our animals, and our country has been destroyed. You are our king, and we love you. We want to continue to stand by you, but we are afraid that the God of the Hebrews will kill us and destroy our land if you do not let them go. He loves them, and He just wants them to be free so they can worship Him." She paused for a moment and looked away as she thought of what to say before continuing. Then she looked back at him and said with conviction, "We can survive without the Hebrews. We still have our lives, our crops will grow back, we can buy animals from other countries, and we can do our own work until we can find other slaves."

For a moment, he was silent and did not respond, leaving her to wonder if he understood the magnitude of what she had just said. She had been trying to tell him without explicitly saying so that she and many of his once-loyal people, including his officials, were ready to abandon him to save their lives. After seeing the miracles displayed in the plagues, they were convinced that I Am is the only true God, even though Pharaoh was not. With a newly found reverence and fear of the Lord, they no longer believed in any of the gods of Egypt. And they certainly no longer believed that Pharaoh was God. In fact, most of them not only questioned his deity, but his common sense as well. She knew he had understood what she was subtly trying to convey to him when he turned his entire body towards her. Then he gazed at her as though he could not believe that she had just said what she said to him.

"I don't care what any of you think," he said with fury in his eyes. "And no matter what, I will not give in to this God who calls Himself I Am. This is my country, and I will not be told what to do. Not by you, Moses, this I Am, or anyone else. And anyone who doesn't like it can leave."

"I am begging you to reconsider," she pleaded with Pharaoh, knowing that she was in danger of angering him even further, but needing to take the risk. "I went to see Moses some time ago, and from what he told me, the God of the Hebrews will do whatever it takes to get His people out of here. Their release is part of a much larger plan of His. You should know by now that He is more powerful than any of Egypt's gods. You are a wise man. Just look at what He is doing. He is making a mockery of them one by one. We worship the god of the Nile River, the source of our life, and He turned it to blood. We worship the gods of our animals, and He sent a plague and killed them all. We worship the gods of our bountiful crops, and He destroyed them with hail and locusts. We worship the sun, and He caused it not to shine and darkened our land. He is slowly proving that our gods are not real and that He is the only living God. You can end this destruction now so that we can survive as a nation."

"You went to see Moses behind my back?" he said, wondering what on earth made her think he thought that was permissible since she was one of his employees. Before she could answer, Pharaoh, still angry but obviously curious, asked, "Since you took it upon yourself to disregard my authority, what did he tell you is his God's great plan?"

Just as Moses had done for her, Ayana recounted to Pharaoh the entire story of how the Lord had created mankind for an intimate relationship with Himself. With enthusiasm, she told how God planned to deliver the Israelites from Egyptian bondage. He would then lead them through the wilderness, where they would learn to worship, trust, and obey Him, and into a land of abundance. She finished by telling him that through the miracles He performed on behalf of the Israelites and the goodness He showed them, He would prove that He is the only living God. As a result, He would draw people from every nation to Himself.

He listened silently, meditating on what she had said. The look on his face revealed his concern. He seemed to understand that if this were true, he could let the Israelites go and save what was left of his country and his reputation. Or, he could continue to rebel against this God, who had already proven that He is quite a force to be reckoned with, and bring about his own demise. *But even while he was thinking, the Lord was hardening his heart so that he could not do what his logical mind knew would be in his best interest.*[41] *Because he refused to repent and obey the Lord when he was initially told to do so, he waited too long and lost the opportunity to repent. Now he had no choice but to do what would ultimately lead to his own ruin.*

"I do not want to talk about this anymore. This conversation is over," Pharaoh said as he waved his hand to let her know that it was time for her to leave. As she was walking away, he snidely added, "I saw you and that man Moses eyeing each other. You know that I don't miss a thing. If he is who he thinks he is, he shouldn't need to send his woman to do his bidding."

She ignored his last comment and left quickly, sorry that she had not gotten the outcome she had sought and thinking how foolish Pharaoh was. Contrary to what he believed, he did miss something. He missed an opportunity to make the most important decision of his life. A truly wise man would know that he was beaten, but he was too stubborn and hard-hearted to recognize the truth. He so needed to be right and to have things his way that he couldn't see his own impending doom.

---

[41] Romans 1:28 (NIV)

Ayana knew even before she left the palace what she had to do. She had an obligation to save herself, and anyone else who did not want to incur the fate of those who would remain in what would be left of Egypt after its destruction. Since Moses had encouraged her to leave with the Hebrews, she intended to do just that and to encourage others to do the same.

As an official in Pharaoh's court, Ayana was an insider. She knew from her private conversations with Pharaoh's other officials how they felt about Moses, the plagues that had devastated the country, and the God of the Hebrews. They liked and respected Moses because he was not arrogant, spoke with authority, and backed his words up with action. What he said would happen, always happened. They hated the plagues because they were just as much a source of misery for them as the ordinary Egyptians. And, above all, they feared this unquestionably powerful God, I Am, who was previously unknown to them. Many of them were ready to abandon Pharaoh unless he relented and did what was best for the country, which was to let the Hebrews go.

Ayana sent trusted couriers throughout the city to call an urgent meeting with the officials, whom she believed were more interested in the well-being of Egypt than their allegiance to Pharaoh. She was very careful not to invite his die-hard loyalists, knowing that they would alert Pharaoh to their plan, and he in turn would have her and the other officials executed for inciting an insurrection. The next day they all attended, glad that one of them had taken the initiative to begin a conversation they all wanted to have anyway. Even though she was not the senior official in the group, she took the lead and presented her well-crafted plan to them.

"You all know why we are here, so let's get down to business," she said with authority as they listened intently. "Our country and our lives are in jeopardy. The God of the Hebrews wants His people out of here, and He has made it clear to us with the terrible plagues that He will do whatever it takes to achieve His objective. Up until now, I believe that He has held back His hand and not been as harsh with us as He could have been. That may be about to change. If Pharaoh does not let His people go, I suspect that some of our people are going to start dying soon." With worried looks on their faces, all of the officials nodded in agreement, indicating that some of the same thoughts had crossed their minds.

"I met with Pharaoh to try to reason with him, but he wouldn't listen," she continued. She noted that some of them were surprised that she had approached him and run the risk of being punished for disagreeing with him. They all knew that Pharaoh despised anything that even smelled like disloyalty. The only reason he did not have her killed was because he liked and respected her, and he was also partial to beautiful women.

"So we need to leave when the Israelites leave," she stated matter-of-factly. "I met with Moses, and he told me that we are welcome to come with them. They are headed for Canaan, and we can settle there and make new lives for ourselves." She could see wheels turning in their minds while she presented her solution. Naturally, they had many questions about how this would work.

The highest ranking official spoke out, asking, "First of all, how do we know that Pharaoh is just going to let us walk out of here?"

"We are going to walk out of here the same way the Hebrews do," she told him confidently. "Their God is powerful and *He will protect us just like He will protect them. He is fair. As long as we acknowledge that He is the only God and determine to follow Him, we become His people too, and we receive what they receive.*"[42]

"How do you know this about Him?" asked one of the others, liking the idea and genuinely wanting to know how she knew this.

"Because I have already started talking to Him myself, and He has impressed this upon my heart," she said with conviction. "The gods of Egypt are silent, but this God communicates."

They all looked stunned as though they had never heard of such a thing. But since they respected her and viewed her as credible, they believed it was possible. Furthermore, Egypt had hundreds of gods, and not one of them had ever been on record as having communicated anything to anyone. In fact, now that they thought about it, the gods of Egypt had been of no use during the plagues, but powerless and impotent instead.

"Well, one thing is clear," another official interjected. "If we stay here, we will be starting our lives over in a ruined country. It could take many years for Egypt to recover. Not to mention what it would be like to work for a stubborn and defeated tyrant king. And this is the best case scenario. The worst case is that we could be killed for getting in the way of this God. I say we quietly put the word out and let the Egyptians and foreigners living here know that whoever wants to can leave with us when the Hebrews leave."

---

[42] Acts 10:34–35 (NIV)

"So do we all agree that this is the best plan?" Ayana asked as she made eye contact with each of the officials, especially the two who had not previously shared their thoughts.

One of the two quickly spoke up. "You are forgetting something. Canaan is not uninhabited. There are people living there. How are millions of Hebrews and all of us going to just walk in and settle down there? Those Canaanites are a force to be reckoned with. They are the biggest and strongest people we know of. We made a treaty with them a few years ago so that we wouldn't ever have to go to war with them. Are we prepared to fight them now if we need to?"

"If we have to fight, we'll fight. But let's cross that bridge when we come to it. *I Am will tell us what to do, and when to do it. All we have to do is follow His instructions*,"[43] Ayana said, to the concern of the other two men.

She had a reputation for being wise and methodical, a logical thinker whose every decision was calculated for success. They all knew that Egypt had achieved its status as a premier world power partially due to the counsel she gave to Pharaoh. But this was the second time she had expressed such confidence in this new God, and they needed to be sure that she was right.

"Until five minutes ago, you believed in Egypt's gods just like we do," the other of the two, a fast speaking, shifty-eyed character said. "How can you be so sure that this God of the Hebrews can be trusted? If we are wrong about Him, we may all die. And we might as well die here in Egypt as somewhere in that desert, or fighting to get into Canaan."

---

[43] Isaiah 30:21 (NIV); Psalm 32:8 (NIV)

She tactfully addressed his concern. "You are right," she began. "I did believe in Egypt's gods – until recently. But I am a realist. I Am has proven Himself to be more powerful than Egypt's gods. I would be foolish to ignore this fact. And with all due respect, so would all of you. Plus, He is accessible. I know that He is telling me to leave this place, and I want to save the lives of as many of us as possible. So again, does everyone agree that leaving with the Hebrews is the best plan?"

Everyone nodded in agreement, relieved that they had a way out. They had all secretly worried that Pharaoh's stubbornness would cause the situation to end badly and that by mere association with him, they would incur an unfortunate fate.

As soon as their meeting was over, Ayana went to work. Not wanting to put the message in writing and run the risk of having Pharaoh discover it, she called in several trusted heralds. Egypt had a well-organized verbal network, so she knew it would not take long for the offer to spread throughout the country. The message instructed the people to start heading toward the city of Rameses so they would be ready to move out when the time came.

By the time Ayana arrived home that evening, I had already heard the news through the slave grapevine that some of the Egyptians would be leaving the country when we left. "So you'll be coming with us after all," I said cheerfully to Ayana as soon as she walked through the door.

"Yes, we will," Ayana told me enthusiastically, pleased to have finally made a decision. "Lots of Egyptians will be going and some foreigners who have settled here from other countries too. Pharaoh is as stubborn as an old mule. We all need to get out of here before this place totally falls apart."

"I understand we might be leaving any day now," I informed her, wanting with all my heart to believe that the news I had received was correct. "I can smell freedom already."

So in anticipation of our imminent departure, we spent the rest of the evening with our heads together deciding what to take with us.

CHAPTER 8

SOME UNFINISHED BUSINESS

Ayana's next step was to address some unfinished business that she had with Moses. As any emotionally mature woman would do, she carefully analyzed her true motive for wanting to leave Egypt. She admitted to herself that escaping Egypt's impending doom was only half of it. The other half was that she liked this man named Moses and hoped they might have a future together. She knew from their last encounter that he was attracted to her, and she needed to find out if he had the same long-term interest in her that she had in him.

She went to Aaron's humble abode down by the Nile, knocked on the door, and then called for Moses. He came to the entrance as soon as he heard her voice. The look on his face told her that either he had been thinking about her or talking about her since the last time they were together. He was the most transparent man she had ever met.

"Hello Ayana," he said politely, as though he were greeting a mere acquaintance.

"Hello Moses," she responded with a smile, deliberately hiding her disappointment.

To make matters worse, he did not invite her in. Instead, he called back into the house and told Aaron that he was going down to the Nile with Ayana and would be back soon. He was clearly sending a signal to her that their conversation would be short and strictly business.

"How can I help you?" Moses asked Ayana as they walked towards the Nile River.

"I talked to Pharaoh about letting the Hebrews leave," she began. "He would never let you see it, but these plagues are wearing him out. He knows that he has been beaten, but he is too proud to give up. So I met with some of the Egyptian officials, the ones I know I can trust. We decided that it's best if we leave Egypt when you all leave. We spread the word throughout Egypt, and our people are looking forward to making a life with your people in Canaan."

Moses seized this opportunity to tell her what he knew she did not want to hear. "Your people are welcome to join us," he said with sincerity. "You can bring your families and whomever else you wish. I am just as eager to see my wife and children again and settle down in Canaan with them."

His last sentence caught Ayana completely by surprise. Her countenance fell as she heard his unwelcome, disappointing words. Knowing that the look on her face exposed her emotions, she quickly collected herself.

"How nice," she said, curious to know more. "Tell me about your family. I can see that they mean a lot to you."

Moses beamed with pride. It wasn't every day that he had an opportunity to talk about the three people on earth who meant the most to him. "I have two wonderful teenage boys," he began. "They are soft-hearted and teachable. I tell them what God says, and they do it. Don't get me wrong. They are still boys who can be strong-willed at times. But they have grown to love God like I do, and they always come around to doing the right thing. It has been a joy to raise them."

Because Moses was taking too long to get to the part she wanted most to hear about, Ayana came right out and stated what she wanted to know. "Tell me about your wife. I'm sure she's an exceptional woman," she said, as pleasantly as she could, certain that this was true. It only made sense that a man like Moses had married well.

"Her name is Zipporah," he exclaimed with adoration in his eyes and voice. "She is the most beautiful woman I have ever laid eyes on. She is pretty, yes, but she is so much more than that. *I am important to her, and she lets me know it by everything she says and does. She listens to me and offers wise counsel.* Even though she is busy with the boys, the animals and the crops, *she always makes time for me.* When I am having a bad day, *she always knows what to say to make me feel better.* We are compatible in every way. *She encourages me and makes me want to be the best man I can be – an excellent husband, father, and a man who achieves great things.* Even though I don't have any money, *she makes me feel like a very rich man.*[44] There is no way I could have been wise enough to choose such a woman for myself. God chose her for me, and He taught me how to love her. Besides Himself, she and I are the greatest gift God has ever given to us."

As Ayana listened to Moses describe his relationship with Zipporah, she was both happy for him and a bit envious. He had found a love that most people would never find in a

---

[44] Proverbs 31:11–12 (AMP, TLB, NLT)

thousand years. She knew that her husband had loved her, but she wondered if he had cherished her the same way. Listening to Moses gave her a new respect for *I Am. Here was a God who cared enough about His children to choose the best mates for them and teach them how to love each other.* Egypt's lifeless gods paled in comparison to Him.

"I can see that what you have with her is very special," Ayana said with all sincerity. *"I admire a man who is wise enough to only drink water out of his own well.*[45] I know men well, and I perceived that you were attracted to me, as I am to you. Your wife is not here so you could very easily have not mentioned her and let yourself become involved with me. But you didn't. I can tell that your God truly has your heart because you're serious about obeying Him."

He mentally acknowledged that she was right. *He wanted to please God with all of his heart. And the very thought of grieving Him by being disobedient made him uncomfortable.*[46] Moses also admired her. *She was wise enough to respect his relationship with his wife and the sanctity of marriage, and not pursue him any further.*

Eager to move on now that they had addressed that uncomfortable issue, Moses returned to the subject of Pharaoh.

"Anyway, I'm not surprised that Pharaoh is still being stubborn," Moses said as he shook his head. "He does not understand that we will leave here, one way or another."

"So what is the next step?" Ayana asked.

"Another plague," he told her. "This one will be the worst one, the one that will break Pharaoh's will. So prepare yourself, because all of the Egyptians will feel it."

---

[45] Proverbs 5:15 (NLT)
[46] Ephesians 5:10–11 (NLT, NIV)

She looked at him with a puzzled expression on her face, wondering what he meant, but hoping it wasn't what she thought he meant. "Is someone going to die?" she asked, alarmed even though she had strongly suspected that it might come to this.

"Just be ready to leave when we leave," he told her candidly, letting her know that he was not in a position to answer any more questions at that time.

"We'll be ready," she promised. Then she slipped into the night.

As she walked to her house, she nursed her disappointment. She had such high hopes that a relationship might evolve between her and Moses. He seemed just right for her, and she was a woman with very lofty standards. She wondered what the odds were that she would ever meet a man like him again in her life.

By the time she arrived home, I could see it all over her face. "Something happened today, didn't it?" I inquired. "Did you see Moses?"

"Yes, I saw him," Ayana replied, not wanting to verbalize what she found out because saying it made it feel worse.

"And?" I asked, trying to get her to tell me what happened.

"And he's married to a wonderful woman," Ayana revealed emotionally. "They have two children and he'll be joining up with them soon so they can settle down in Canaan. But I wish him well. I really do."

I knew that no words could erase the disappointment my friend felt. So I simply gave her a hug, pleased that she was mature enough to want what was best for the man she could not have.

Traditional
Route of
the Exodus

CANAAN

Mediterranean Sea

City of Rameses

EGYPT

Desert of Zin

Desert of Shur

12 Spies

Desert of Paran

Sinai Peninsula

Desert of Sin

Marah

Elim

Rephidim

Manna

Mt. Sinai

Red Sea

CHAPTER 9

THE DEPARTURE

Moses went to Pharaoh one last time to give him a final word from the Lord. He stood before him in his throne room and told him, "The Lord says: 'About midnight I will pass through your entire country. Every firstborn son will die, including your firstborn son who is the heir to your throne. The loud wail of death will be heard throughout Egypt. But among the Israelites, not a person will die. Then you will know that I make a distinction between Israel and Egypt, between those who belong to me and those who don't.'" Then Moses walked out of Pharaoh's presence without waiting for him to respond. He knew that in spite of the terrifying warning Pharaoh had just received, nothing Pharaoh said or thought mattered at that point. *He couldn't relent even if he wanted to because the Lord had hardened his heart.*[47] After each horrific plague, the Lord had given him an opportunity to obey Him and let the people go, yet he had hardened his own heart every time.

---

[47] Romans 1:28 (AMP)

So now the Lord would use Pharaoh's refusal to repent to establish Himself as the only living God to Egypt and every other nation.

In preparation for our upcoming departure, Moses met with the leaders of the people later that day and gave them specific instructions that were to be followed to the letter.

Bezalel came home late that evening after a full day's work and two long meetings. One was with Moses and the other leaders, and the other with those in our tribe under his authority. Instead of being tired as he usually was at the end of the day, he was full of energy, fueled by just the thought that we would be leaving Egypt that very night.

"This is it!" he told me happily, grinning from ear to ear. "By this time tomorrow we will be free."

I knew freedom was coming, but it happened so quickly that I was still processing the reality of it. I needed more information so I asked him every question I could think of. "What time are we leaving tonight?" I inquired. "Can we take anything we want with us? How long will it take to get to Canaan?"

"One question at a time," he said laughingly before switching to a more serious tone. "Let's sit down and go over the plan. All of us need to know exactly what to do so our departure will go smoothly. I told the other people in our tribe earlier, and now I need to tell you." Then he called the children in from the other room, and they joined us at the table. They knew what was about to happen and were as eager as I was to know what to expect.

"Listen carefully," Bezalel began as we all gave him our undivided attention. "The Lord told Moses to have us follow these instructions thoroughly. We need to take our best lamb from the flock, one without a spot or a blemish and slaughter it at nightfall. Then we have to place its blood outside on the two side frames of the door and the panel above it."

We all looked at him with puzzled expressions, wondering what the purpose was for killing the lamb and applying its blood to the outside of the door. After reading our faces, Bezalel explained, "Tonight I Am will go throughout Egypt and kill every firstborn person, finally proving that He is the only living God. When He sees the blood on the outside of our doors, we will be saved from death by the blood of the lamb, and He will pass over us. The blood must be applied tonight because this day will become the first day of our new year, the day when our lives are beginning anew, just as if we are being born again."

I smiled, pleased with a thought that had never crossed my mind before. I realized that *we were not just starting new lives, but becoming new people because we were entering into a special, new relationship with I Am.*[48]

Then Bezalel continued. "Next, we have to roast the lamb and eat it quickly while we are dressed and ready to go. Once Pharaoh finds out that his firstborn son and all the other firstborn Egyptians are dead, he will want us gone so badly he will put us out. But we will not leave empty-handed. We are to ask the Egyptians for expensive articles of gold, silver, clothing and other valuables that they will gladly give us. The Lord has already touched all of their hearts and given us favor with them, so they will give us all the resources we will need later."

With freedom so close we could taste it, we all got up and eagerly set about preparing to leave. Bezalel selected,

---

[48] 2 Corinthians 3:18(b) (TLB)

slaughtered and prepared the lamb. I started the fire and packed our belongings, and the children watered and fed the animals since they too would be going with us. After applying the blood to the door, roasting the lamb, and eating our last meal in Egypt in haste, we waited patiently for the Lord to come through.

While standing there with my family I became filled with mixed emotions, feelings of hope for our future, yet a sinking sorrow as my thoughts turned to my dear friend Ayana. My heart went out to her because I knew she would lose her beloved son that very night. Only she did not know this because she was not there when Moses met with Pharaoh earlier that day. In spite of how close we were, I didn't tell her that her child would die because I knew it had to happen. The Lord had determined that every firstborn Egyptian would die, and there was nothing I could do to change that. And telling her about the blood remedy would have meant disobeying the Lord's command because the remedy was only for the Israelites. I knew that the Lord would have seen me tell her, her son would have died anyway, and I would have faced some undesirable consequences.

Suddenly I heard a strong wind outside our house that snapped me out of my reverie. Bezalel and I looked at each other and then at the children. We all knew what the sound meant. The Lord was doing exactly what He said He would do. It was midnight. And He was striking down all the firstborn sons in the land of Egypt, from Pharaoh's firstborn who was the heir to the throne, to the firstborn of the prisoner, who was in the dungeon.

Pharaoh, his officials, and all the people of Egypt woke up during the night and found their loved ones dead. Loud agonizing wailing was heard throughout the land. There was not a single house where someone had not died, including Ayana's. When she found her son dead, she screamed at the top of her lungs in agony and disbelief.

Pharaoh sent for Moses and Aaron during the night. "Get out!" he ordered. "Leave right now and take the rest of the Israelites with you! Go and worship your God, who calls Himself I Am. Take your flocks and herds and everything else that belongs to you and get out. And pray for me before you leave." All the other Egyptians also urged the people of Israel to leave as quickly as possible because they were afraid that they too would die. Then Pharaoh went to the bedside of his dead son and wept bitterly.

As soon as the wind died down the word spread quickly that Pharaoh had agreed to let us go. We set out to meet up with the other Israelites on the outskirts of the city. Amidst the terrible sounds of wailing which came from everywhere, Bezalel and I carried our things while the children herded the animals. We went first to Ayana's house to bring her along with us. When we arrived there, we found her in her son's room with her body covering her dead child as if she couldn't part with him.

"Ayana, we have to leave now," I told her as I gently tried to pull her away from the boy. But it was no use. She refused to let him go. So Bezalel stepped forward and took the child from her. She frantically grasped for him, but Bezalel kept him out of her reach.

"We cannot take him with us Ayana!" Bezalel exclaimed, understanding her dilemma but needing to make her understand that we had to move on. "I can bury him for you and then we have to go. The group is leaving now, and we need to stay with them." Through her grief, she nodded in agreement.

While Bezalel buried the child, I helped Ayana gather the possessions she had already decided to take with her. Amongst the things she was leaving behind I saw many valuables that I wanted, and she gave me everything I asked for. When Bezalel returned, we all left as a group and joined the mass exodus of people headed out of the city. I knew that there were many of us in Egypt, but I had never seen us all together at one time. It felt good to see them and to know that we, who had been slaves our entire lives, were now free.

We found Moses at the exact location where he told the leaders to meet up with him. He greeted each of us warmly, noticeably as excited as we were to finally be leaving. When Ayana did not respond when he spoke to her, I looked at Moses and shook my head to let him know not to press her any further and that she would be alright. He nodded in turn to let me know that he understood since there were many grieving people in the group who had just lost loved ones.

"Are you ready to do this?" Moses asked Bezalel enthusiastically, moving on to the task at hand.

"I couldn't be readier," Bezalel responded with much cheer. "Just let me know when you need my help. That's what I'm here for." Then Moses signaled to the group, and we set out.

That very night we boldly marched out of the city of Rameses, with our heads held high. There were approximately six hundred thousand men in our group, in addition to a multitude of women, children, and large droves of bellowing livestock. Many other people from Egypt and from the surrounding nations who had settled in Egypt were desperate for relief from the crippling plagues, and in search of new lives. With eyes full of promise, they walked out with us.

We had lived in Egypt for exactly four hundred thirty years. Our ancestor, Joseph, brought the Israelites there when there were only seventy of them, to save their lives during a famine. At the end of the four hundred thirty years, to the very day, the Lord kept the promise He had made to Joseph, his father Jacob, his grandfather Isaac, and his great-grandfather Abraham. Joseph was so sure that the Lord would keep His word that he said to the Israelites, "God will surely come and deliver you from slavery to take you to Canaan. And when He does, you must take my bones with you when you leave this place." So Moses took Joseph's bones with us. *The Lord brought us out of the land of Egypt exactly when He said He would, again proving that He can be trusted to do what He says He will do.*[49]

The Lord not only delivered us out of Egypt, but *He stayed with us and led us every step of the way.* Shortly after we left the city, He appeared in a massive, bright orange pillar of fire in the sky. We knew that I Am was leading us, not only because Moses told us, but because we had never before seen such a breathtaking sight. It was consistent with all of the other miraculous wonders we had recently witnessed in Egypt. By day the Lord would go ahead of us in a pillar of cloud to lead us, and by night in a pillar of fire to give us light. So we could travel by day or night. The cloud and fire were never out of our sight.

"Look," I said to Ayana as I pointed to the pillar of fire, hoping that the sight of it would perk her up a bit. She looked up from her daze and gazed at it for a few moments. Then she

---

[49] Genesis 15:12–14 (NIV) and Exodus 12:40–41 (NIV)

smiled as if the Lord had somehow communicated to her that He cared about her and was with her, in spite of the fact that He killed her son. I looked at it more carefully too, sure that He must have also cared about me.

We traveled for about twenty-five miles before stopping to rest at Succoth. Then we moved on and camped at Etham on the edge of the desert. There the Lord told Moses, "Tell the Israelites to turn back and camp by Pi-hahiroth between Migdol and the sea. Camp there along the shore, across from Baal-zephon. Then Pharaoh will think, 'The Israelites are wandering around confused. They are trapped in the wilderness!' Once again, I will harden Pharaoh's heart, and he will chase after you. I have planned this in order to gain great glory for myself at the expense of Pharaoh and his entire army. After this, the Egyptians and the people from all of the other idol-worshipping nations around them will know that I am the Lord!" So we followed the Lord's specific instructions and camped there as we were told.

From the time Pharaoh found out that his firstborn son and heir to his throne had died, he mourned by his bedside. He was still there when one of his officials came to him and told him that all of the Israelites were gone. When he understood the magnitude of what he had just been told, he changed his mind and said, "We have made a terrible mistake by letting our entire slave labor force walk out of here. We have to go and bring them back."

So Pharaoh gave orders to his general to prepare the army for battle. They harnessed his chariot and called up the troops. He led them out, taking with him Egypt's six hundred best chariots, along with every other chariot in the country, and all of his foot soldiers and commanders as well.

The Lord hardened Pharaoh's heart so that he would go after the Israelites. The Egyptians pursued us with all the forces in Pharaoh's army – all of his horses, chariots, charioteers, troops, and commanders. They caught up with us as we were camped exactly where the Lord told us, on the shore of the Red Sea.

We panicked when we looked up and saw Pharaoh and the entire Egyptian army coming towards us. Terrified and feeling trapped, we cried out to the Lord. But some in the group said to Moses, "Why did you bring us out here to die in the desert? What have you done to us by making us leave Egypt? We told you this would happen before we even left. We said, 'Leave us alone! Let us be slaves to the Egyptians. It's better to be a slave in Egypt than to die in the wilderness!'" Instead of trusting the Lord, who had miraculously delivered them from slavery and led them thus far, they began to doubt that He would protect them this time and safely lead them on.

In an effort to encourage them, Moses said, *"Don't be afraid. Just stand still and watch the Lord deliver you* again today just as He delivered you from Egypt. The Egyptians you see now will never be seen again. *The Lord Himself will fight for you. Just stay calm and trust Him."*[50]

Facing the deep waters of the Red Sea with an angry Pharaoh and his army at our backs, the Lord then instructed Moses, "Tell the people to start moving! Pick up your staff and raise your hand over the water. It will open up so the Israelites can walk through the middle of the sea on dry ground. I will harden the hearts of the Egyptians, and they will go in after the Israelites. And I will receive great glory

---

[50] Exodus 14:13–14 (TLB); 2 Chronicles 20:1– 30, (NLT) especially 15 and 17

at the expense of Pharaoh and his entire army – his troops, chariots, charioteers, and commanders. Then the Egyptians and the people from all the other nations will know that I am the Lord, the only living God."

Then the Lord, who was traveling in the cloud in front and leading us, moved the cloud around behind us, and it stood between us and the Egyptians. At nightfall, the cloud turned to fire, lighting up the sky so we could see. But the Egyptians were unable to move because of the darkness on their side. So they could not approach us that night.

Meanwhile, Moses raised his staff over the sea and with our very eyes we saw the Lord miraculously open up a path through the water with a strong east wind. The wind blew all that night, turning the floor of the sea into dry land. We walked through the middle of the sea on dry ground, with a wall of water on each side. Words could not explain the awesome experience. A light, refreshing spray fell on our faces as we marveled at how the water stood up, and the fish swam without falling out. We even stuck our fingers into it to convince ourselves that it was really wet.

When Pharaoh's army saw that we were walking through the middle of the sea, they all followed us into the water. Of all the Egyptians, only Pharaoh remained on the shore. From the cloud of fire, the Lord looked down on the Egyptian army during the last watch of the night and threw their forces into total confusion. To their dismay, the wheels of their chariots were suddenly jammed so they could barely drive. "Let's get away from these Israelites!" the Egyptians shouted, realizing what was happening. "The Lord is fighting for them against Egypt!"

Once all of us safely reached the other side, and the sun began to rise, the Lord told Moses to raise his staff over the sea again. When he did, the water rushed back into its original place and covered all the Egyptians and their horses and chariots. The Egyptians tried their best to escape, but the Lord swept them into the sea and drowned Pharaoh's entire army. Of all the Egyptians who had followed us into the sea, not a single one survived. When we looked back, we saw their bodies washed up on the seashore.

Pharaoh stood on the shore in his chariot in disbelief. He was ruined. Every symbol of power in his life and his country had been destroyed or lost. This included his economy, his massive slave labor force, his country's riches that those Egyptians he considered traitors had given to us, his reputation as leader of the most advanced nation on earth, and his mighty army that once conquered powerful nations. But most of all, it included his firstborn son, who was to be the heir to his throne. After being thoroughly defeated, he finally admitted that the Lord is indeed the only living God. With all humility, he raised his eyes towards heaven and acknowledged I Am. Then he turned his chariot around and headed back to his shell of a country.

CHAPTER 10

RIGHT SONG, WRONG SIDE

After that terrifying, yet remarkable exit from Egypt, we were blissfully happy to finally be free. Having seen the mighty power that the Lord had unleashed against our enemy, we were filled with awe and gratitude. Our former foe was dead and no longer a threat to us. With the wind at our backs and the sun on our faces, we had everything to look forward to.

So we came together with Moses' sister Miriam, a song-stress, and wrote a hymn of glorious praise to worship our God, who had rescued us. Accompanied by perfectly tuned instruments and beautiful voices, she led us as we sang and danced in rhythmic harmony.

The Lord is a warrior,
I Am is His name!
I will sing to the Lord,
for He has triumphed gloriously.
My strength and my song,
He has given me victory.

At the blast of your breath,
the waters piled up.
The deep waters stood straight like a wall
in the heart of the sea.

The enemy boasted, 'I will chase and catch them.
With my sword in hand,
I will destroy them.'
But you blew with your breath,
and the sea covered them.
Pharaoh's chariots and army
you have hurled into the sea.

All who live in Canaan hear and tremble.
Sudden anguish grips their hearts.
The thought of your mighty power
makes them lifeless as stone.

With your unfailing love you lead
the people you have redeemed.
By your cloud you guide us
to your sacred home.
You will plant us on your mountain,
the place, O Lord, where you dwell.

Sing to the Lord,
for He has triumphed gloriously.
He has hurled both horse and rider
into the sea.

The song with which we worshiped the Lord was beautiful and heartfelt. It was indeed the right song. But there was one problem. We sang it on the wrong side of the Red Sea.

When Moses told us while we were still in Egypt that God had promised to take us to a land that flowed with milk and honey, we were expected to trust Him to do just that. *Even when it didn't look like He was going to keep His word, we were supposed to believe Him and worship Him anyway.* Instead, some of the people panicked and doubted God when they saw the Egyptians coming after us. They had not yet learned the lesson that *the time to worship is in the midst of the problem; that God proves He is faithful to those who take Him at His word and trust Him, even before they see Him fulfill His promise.*[51] *To miss the opportunity to grow in their new relationship with the Lord was a great loss indeed.*

After a brief rest, we continued our journey. Moses led us away from the Red Sea and into the Desert of Shur. We were traumatized by what we saw when we got there. The reality of being in the desert hit us like a ton of bricks. We had lived in Egypt all our lives and were accustomed to swaying palm trees, lush, green foliage, and an abundance of water year round. The desert was the exact opposite. There was nothing there but brown sand and rocks as far as the eye could see in every direction. It was eerily quiet without a single sign of life. And worst of all, there was no water.

We traveled for three days, in silent drudgery, without finding even a drop. I was sicker than I had ever been in my life, and so were many of the others. Seriously dehydrated, our tongues and lips were swollen, and we were so weak that we

---

[51] 2 Chronicles 20:1–30 (NLT)

were struggling to keep going. Every step in the sand seemed like ten as we forced ourselves onward. There was a hollow sound in our ears that made it difficult for us to hear. Our brains were heavy which made even thinking a chore. So much effort was required to talk to each other that we scarcely tried. Though suffering like the rest of us, Ayana's emotional pain from the loss of her child seemed to make her less aware of her physical distress.

Extremely thirsty by the time we finally arrived at a place called Marah, we were elated when we saw what we thought was certain to quench our thirst.

Already out in front, Aaron was the first to see the water. He ran to it, dropped to his knees, and scooped some into his mouth with his hand. We were fast approaching him when what we saw made us stop in our tracks. Coughing and spitting, he was trying to get the water out of his mouth as fast as he could. He held up his hand to let us know to stay back and not come any closer. Fearful that he may be dying and not wanting to incur the same fate, we continued to watch him from where we stood. Having remained a few paces behind to help some of the elderly along, Moses quickly moved to the front when he saw Aaron in distress.

"Aaron, what is it?" he asked as he saw him desperately regurgitating the water, fearful that he might have been poisoned.

"This water is bad. Don't let the people drink it," Aaron begged, with his voice raspy and his face drained of color.

Moses immediately raised his hands to address the crowd who desperately needed water to revive their weak, dehydrated bodies and soothe their parched throats. The children and babies were crying. Even the animals were lowing and bleating in their distress. Before he could even speak, the doubting and complaining that had been following us like our shadows resurfaced and some of the people began to grumble.

"So what are we supposed to drink?" they growled at Moses.

Then Moses looked up and cried out to the Lord for an answer. The Lord showed him a piece of wood, and he ran and picked it up and tossed it into the water. It instantly became clean and clear, sparkling like water from a pure underground source. The bitterness had been removed.

When it was obvious that the water was different, some of the people almost trampled the others to get to it and fill their cups, drinking it as if it would be their last.

Watching them in dismay, the expression on Moses' face revealed that he understood why that place had been named Marah, which means bitter. The water had indeed been bitter and distasteful. And after seeing how most of the people had consistently demonstrated no faith in God when faced with a dilemma, he began to wonder just how unpalatable the rest of the journey with the Israelites might be. They did not yet understand that *the Lord Himself led us by the cloud to the bitter place specifically to test us and teach us a lesson. He wanted us to learn that when we encounter bitter circumstances we are to trust Him because He always has a reason for allowing them, and He always has the solution.*[52] Instead, just as they had done on the other side of the Red Sea, most of them doubted God, grumbled and complained, and failed the test again.

---

[52] James 1:2–5 (NLT, AMP)

After that frightful encounter with the poisonous, bitter water, we were all concerned about our health. We knew from what we had seen and experienced in Egypt that ingesting even a little of a tainted substance can cause the body to deteriorate rapidly. So it was there at Marah that the Lord gave us a word to reassure us and to test our faithfulness to Him. He said, "If you will listen carefully to my voice, the voice of the Lord your God, and do what is right in my sight by obeying all of my commands, then I will not make you suffer from any of the diseases I sent on the Egyptians; for I am the Lord who heals you." But obedience was a difficult concept for some of them, one that they could not seem to comprehend, no matter how great the benefit.

After leaving Marah, we traveled on to the oasis of Elim. There we found twelve springs and seventy palm trees, and we camped there beside the water. Content to have even a moment of relief from the harsh wilderness, we splashed in the water and played unhindered like children.

CHAPTER 11

A MEAL FROM HEAVEN

We arose early the next morning just before sunrise. Feeling refreshed after the night at the oasis, we were eager to continue our journey to the land of milk and honey. The camp bustled with activity as we gathered our belongings in preparation to leave. We set out from Elim and traveled to the Desert of Sin, arriving exactly one month after leaving Egypt. It seemed odd that the deserts we traveled to or camped in had different names like the Desert of Shur and the Desert of Sin because there was nothing about them that distinguished one from the other. They were all the same – barren, dry, lifeless, and void of any comfort.

After being in this new desert only a short time, some of the Israelites quickly returned to their old ways and began to complain to Moses and Aaron about not having what they needed. "If only the Lord had killed us back in Egypt," they groaned. "There we sat around pots filled with meat and ate all the food we wanted. But now you have brought us into this desert to starve us all to death."

The Lord heard their grumbling and said to Moses, "I'm going to rain down food from heaven for you. Each day the people must go out and pick up as much food as they need for that day. On the sixth day, they are to gather twice as much as they gather on the other days. This is how I will test them to see whether or not they will obey me and follow my instructions."

Moses and Aaron gathered all of the Israelites together and gave them the message from the Lord. "The Lord has heard your complaints, which are not against us, but against Him. What have we done to make you complain about us? Tomorrow He will give you bread to satisfy you. Then you will know that He is the Lord your God when He shows you His glory by feeding you miraculously."

While Moses was still speaking, an unusual sight caught our attention. We all looked out toward the wilderness where we saw a majestic looking cloud slowly approaching. Instead of being the typical white fluffy cumulus, it was perfectly round like the moon, yet soft looking and the color of a priceless pearl. It was so beautiful that gasps could be heard throughout the crowd at the very sight of it.

Bezalel and I looked at each other, speechless. There was nothing to say. We had seen the Lord perform so many miracles in the last few months that we never knew what He was going to do next. We couldn't wait to see how He was going to feed us from this awe-inspiring cloud.

When we awoke early the next morning, there was a layer of dew around the camp. After the dew dried up, thin flakes as fine as frost blanketed the desert floor. Everyone in the camp was puzzled by what they saw. We had never seen anything like it before and had no idea what it was. It tasted like honey wafers, so we named it "manna."

Moses explained that it was bread from heaven that the Lord had given us to eat. Each household was to go out early each morning and gather only as much as they needed, which was two quarts per person per day. We could grind it in a handmill or crush it in a mortar, and then cook it in a pot or make it into loaves. It was to be eaten that day, and none was to be kept until the next morning. On the sixth day, we were to gather twice as much because none would be provided on the seventh day. Only on the sixth day could we save any until the next day because the seventh day was to be a day of complete rest for us, a day set apart for fellowship with the Lord.

I was determined to have my family do exactly what the Lord told us to do. Each morning as I gathered the manna with Bezalel and the children, I entertained myself by thinking of creative, tasty ways to prepare it that would make my family's taste buds happy. I loved to cook, and I was good at it too. Using the exotic spices I brought with me from Egypt, I was able to come up with such a variety of dishes that we seldom ate the manna the same way twice. With a repertoire that included appetizers, main courses, and desserts, mealtime was always a pleasure in my tent.

Sometimes Ayana would give me the manna she had collected for herself. I would combine it with ours and cook for both families. She would join us for meals, and we always enjoyed her company. We would eat and laugh and glean something good from our time in the wilderness.

After only one week of gathering and eating the manna just as the Lord had instructed, I noticed how the Lord had blessed our obedience abundantly. Both Ayana and I began to see remarkable changes in ourselves and my family. Our appearance and overall well-being had improved. We had leaner bodies, smoother skin, shinier hair and a sparkle in our eyes. Instead of being tired all the time, we could walk long distances faster with no fatigue. We fell asleep quickly, slept more soundly, and awoke totally refreshed. Even our aches and pains had faded away. Less moody and irritable, we were better able to endure our difficult circumstances. Ayana had even healed emotionally, put the trauma of her son's death behind her, and become more of her former joyful, fun-loving, confident self. The food the Lord gave us was transforming us inside and out.

We now understood that *the Lord deliberately let us go hungry, and then fed us with food we had never seen or heard of before for a good reason. He did it to cause us to seek Him and to help us understand that food, which only satisfies our physical needs, isn't everything. He wanted to teach us that a truly abundant life comes from knowing and obeying Him, who satisfies our spiritual needs.*[53]

We also found that the Lord does not show favoritism. He gave the same blessings to the Egyptians and the people from the other nations that He gave to the Israelites, as long as they acknowledged Him as their only God and obeyed Him.[54]

While some of the people followed the Lord's instructions regarding the manna and received the benefits, others blatantly disobeyed Him. They kept some of the food until the next morning only to find that it was foul smelling and crawling with maggots. Or instead of getting up early to gather the food, they slept too late and discovered that the sun had melted it away. Some even got up early to look for food on the

---

[53] Deuteronomy 8:3 (TLB); John 6:33 (TLB); John 10:10 (NLT)
[54] Acts 10:34–35 (TLB)

seventh day and found that there was none. *They learned the hard way that the hunger of the disobedient goes unsatisfied.*[55]

Not long after that, Bezalel came to me with a special request. "I'd like to invite Moses to have dinner with us tonight if you don't mind," he said to me one morning just before we were heading out to gather manna for the day. "I want to ask him some questions about some things that have been on my mind."

"He's welcome anytime," I told him sincerely. I was eager to spend some private time with our friend too. Even though our family walked side by side with him in front of the group as we traveled through the wilderness, there were always other people around which limited our conversation. Dinner would also be an excellent opportunity to hear another one of his interesting stories.

That evening we sat around the table in our tent eating, laughing, and talking for over an hour. He entertained us with fascinating tales of his life as a prince in Egypt. When the children finally went to bed, the conversation took on a more serious tone.

"Are we making good time getting to Canaan?" Bezalel asked Moses candidly, hoping that the disobedience of the others wasn't adversely affecting all of us.

"We're making perfect time," Moses told him. *"As long as we are following I Am who is leading us* in the cloud, *we are right on schedule. It may seem like the journey is taking longer than we would like, but the Lord has a specific purpose for every place He leads us to and for the length of time that He keeps us there.*[56] *The most important question we need to ask ourselves*

---

[55] 2 Thessalonians 3:10 (NLT); Proverbs 19:15(b) (NIV)
[56] Psalm 37:23 (NLT, AMP)

is whether or not we are learning the lessons we are supposed to be learning at every stop along the way."

"Well, what do you think?" I asked Moses inquisitively. "Are we learning them?"

"A few people are, but most are not," Moses said frankly. *"Some just don't get it no matter how many times they're told. They don't understand that the Lord could have taken them to the Promised Land of Canaan by the short, easy route along the beach. But instead He is taking them through the wilderness to mature them in preparation for the land He has promised to give them. They must be spiritually ready when they get there because only the spiritually mature can take possession of the land, which means to achieve the specific purpose for which God put them on this earth. The second reason they must be ready is that they will not be able to confront and overcome the enemy that is waiting for them there if they are not. I know all of this to be true from my own personal experience. The Lord had me spend forty years in the wilderness of Midian to mature and prepare me to lead this group out of Egypt, through the wilderness, and into Canaan. I had to learn every lesson that He is teaching them. Our ancestor Joseph is another example. He spent thirteen years in a spiritual wilderness learning crucial spiritual lessons. If he had not mastered them, he would not have been prepared to become the Governor of Egypt and to save the lives of his family and many other people."*[57]

The conversation we had with Moses that evening lasted until long after midnight. It was far more enlightening than we could ever have anticipated and gave us much to think about. Like cows chewing their cud, for the next several weeks

---

[57] Genesis chapters 37 and 39–45 (NLT)

we would meditate on his words, put them out of our minds temporarily, and then bring them back and meditate on them again when needed.

Sometime later, at the Lord's command, the Israelites left the Desert of Sin and traveled from place to place. The cloud that we were following stopped at Rephidim and we camped there. But there was no water for us to drink, so once again the people complained. Moses was right when he said they just didn't get it.

"You need to find us some water!" they said to Moses confrontationally. "If the Lord is with us, why does it seem like we are out here on our own?"

"Be quiet!" Moses replied. *"Don't you know that when you quarrel with me you are quarreling with the Lord? He is the One who led us here, and He knows that we need water. We need to trust Him to provide it for us."*[58]

But all they could think of was their own misery. Parched and convinced that they were dying of thirst, they continued to argue with Moses. "Why did you bring us out of Egypt just to let us die of thirst? Because that is what's going to happen to us, our children, and our livestock if we don't get some water soon."

Frustrated with their lack of faith, Moses cried out to the Lord, "What do you want me to do with these people? Any minute now they are going to stone me." The Lord told Moses exactly what to do.[59]

"Take the staff you used when you struck the water of the Nile," the Lord said. "Lead the elders and the people to the large

---

[58] Philippians 4:19 (NIV)
[59] James 1:5 (TLB)

rock that you see in the distance and I will meet you there. You are to strike it with your staff and water will come rushing out for the people to drink." While the elders watched, Moses struck the rock and water gushed out like a dam that had just broken. The people hurried and filled their cups, jars, and pots to the brim. Unfortunately, they did not have any awareness of the seriousness of their unbelief, its potentially devastating consequences, or even a word of thanks for the Lord. Because they kept complaining and doubting God, they failed every test He had given them thus far. The Israelites consistently refused to trust the Lord even though He always proved that He loved them. He delivered them from bondage, gave them the valuable resources of the Egyptians, and drowned their enemies before their very eyes. He also kept them on the right path as He led them by a cloud, and miraculously nourished them with bread from heaven and water from a rock. *They were too focused on their discomfort and their unmet needs to understand that the Lord was with them in their adversity and that He cared about everything that concerned them.*[60]

In spite of the lack of faith of some of the Israelites, the Lord once more proved His willingness to take care of us by protecting us. The word of our amazing deliverance from Egypt had spread like wildfire throughout the people of the surrounding nations. They were afraid that they would lose their land and maybe even their lives. Rather than wait until the Israelites attacked them, the nearby Amalekites assembled for battle in the desert and sent word for the Israelites to meet them there.

Having been slaves for centuries, the Israelites were not allowed to train for battle or have their own army. In

---

[60] 1 Peter 5:7 (AMP)

anticipation of an attack, the men armed themselves as well as they could before they left Egypt by bringing various tools they had sharpened into weapons.

With no choice but to fight, Moses wanted the most skilled fighting men to go against the army of Amalek. Bezalel was one of the ones he chose and at first I was gravely concerned. I had every confidence in my husband, but I knew that while he was one of the best we had, he was still not a professional soldier. I couldn't bear the thought of him being wounded or worst yet, dying. Then Moses shared his *battle strategy* with the men, and I was confident that it would work. "I will watch the battle from the top of the hill where I will *worship the Lord* [61] with the staff that He gave me in my hand," he said.

The Amalekite army was large, well-trained, and accustomed to defending their territory. When the battle began, they came out ready to fight to the death. But the Israelites were a force to be reckoned with. As long as Moses held up the staff in his hand and worshiped the Lord, our army was winning. Whenever he lowered his hand, the Amalekites gained the advantage. As the day wore on, Moses' arms soon became so tired he could no longer hold them up. So Aaron and the elders found a stone for him to sit on. Then they stood on each side of him and took turns holding up his hands as he worshiped so that they held steady until sunset. As a result, our inexperienced army overwhelmed the army of Amalek in battle. Then the Israelites saw with their own eyes that *even when it seems as if we are at a disadvantage, I Am grants victory to His children when we worship Him.*

---

[61] Psalm 149:6–7 (NIV, AMP)

The battle with the Amalekites would be the Israelite's only war with an external enemy for a long time. *Their greatest foe and the most serious threat to their future was their inclination to doubt God and disobey Him. This very subtle internal enemy had an even greater potential to be their undoing than any external enemy. They did not know it yet, but the real battles would not begin until they were ready to possess the land. Unless they learned how to overcome the internal enemy, they would never have an opportunity to fight the external enemy and enjoy the good land God purposed for them.*[62]

---

[62] Hebrews 3:7–19 (TLB)

CHAPTER 12

FAMILY REUNION – THE GOOD, THE BAD, AND THE UGLY

The word traveled quickly throughout the region that the Lord had miraculously delivered the Israelites from slavery in Egypt and was in the process of leading us through the wilderness to a new home in Canaan. Moses' father-in-law Jethro lived in nearby Midian where he was the priest of the idol god Baal. It was there that he heard the news about everything God had done for Moses and the Israelites by bringing us safely out of Egypt and taking care of us every step along the way. Jethro had been caring for Moses' wife and sons ever since Moses was sent by the Lord to Egypt to liberate His people. Knowing that he now needed the support of his family, Jethro sent word to Moses telling him that he would be bringing them to him soon. Eager to be with them again, Moses kept an eye out for their arrival.

About a week later on an exceptionally warm desert afternoon, Moses was in the middle of a conversation with

Aaron about ordinary camp business when he saw Jethro approaching in the distance with his wife and sons. His heart began to race, and he stopped talking in mid-sentence and ran towards them. Aaron smiled with no regard for the interruption. He had not met any of them before but was sure from Moses reaction that these were the people he fondly referred to all the time. Ignoring the desert heat, Moses ran as quickly as he could.

Though he loved them all dearly, he hugged his wife Zipporah first. They both cried as they embraced each other tenderly, as though it might make up for the time they yearned for each other while apart. The boys grinned and waited their turn, happy simply to see their father again.

"I've missed you," Moses said, releasing Zipporah and reaching out for them. "You're looking well. I can see that your mother and grandfather have been taking good care of you." One in each arm, he kissed their foreheads and held them both close.

He then greeted Jethro with a hearty handshake. Moses had the highest regard for him as if he were his own father. This was the man who took him in and gave him a home when he fled from Egypt after murdering one of its own. This was the man who gave him a job and his cherished daughter Zipporah's hand in marriage, trusting him to be a good husband to her and a good father to their children. And this was also the man who imparted priceless wisdom to him whenever he saw the need.

When they arrived back at the camp, Moses introduced his family to Aaron and his sister Miriam. He left Zipporah and his sons with her so she could show them where they would be living and make them feel at home. He wasn't sure, but he thought he saw Miriam give Zipporah a look of disdain when her back was turned, and he made a mental note to address it later.

Taking Jethro into his tent, Moses told him about everything the Lord had done to Pharaoh and the Egyptians for the Israelite's sake. He also told him about how God helped them through all the hardships they encountered along the way. Jethro was delighted to learn more about this new God who had gone out of His way to be so good to His people. But he was also concerned.

"I need to be honest with you," Jethro began, as though he were deep in thought. "Everything I had heard before I got here as well as everything you have told me has forced me to reconsider my role as the priest of the god of Midian. Now I know for a fact that the Lord is the only living God. Egypt was the most powerful nation on earth, and He made fools out of their gods and rescued His people from bondage to the Egyptians. When I return home, I have no choice but to give up my position and tell the people that the Lord is the true God, and the only God they should worship. As of right now I am officially an ambassador for I Am."

Moses was elated. "This is excellent news!" he exclaimed. *"The Lord is not just the God of the Israelites. He does not show favoritism. Instead, He wants to be the God of every person in every nation who fears Him, does what's right and wants an intimate relationship with the one and only God. The Israelites are simply the people through whom He is making Himself known. As others learn about what He has done for us, the Lord's plan is that they will get rid of their lifeless gods and seek Him for themselves. And when they do, He will be right there to embrace them."*[63]

---

[63] Acts 10:34–35 (NIV); Isaiah 56:6–7 (NLT)

To make Jethro feel especially welcome, Moses threw a party in his honor and invited Aaron, Bezalel, and the other leaders. They were all very pleased to hear about the decision Jethro had made. When Bezalel came home that evening and shared the news with me, I was not at all surprised. After everything I had seen the Lord do, it made perfect sense to me that anyone who was seeking the truth would choose the only living God over a lifeless, powerless god.

The next day was business as usual in the camp. With vast numbers of people coexisting in the wilderness, disagreements and criminal activity were as common as heat and sand. Acting as judge, Moses took his seat to hear the people's disputes against each other. Because there were so many of them, they waited in line from sunrise to sunset for their cases to be heard.

When Jethro saw what Moses was doing, he asked, "Why are you trying to do this all by yourself while everyone stands around you from morning until evening?"

Moses replied, "When a dispute arises I sit as the judge. The people come to me to find out what the Lord's position is on the matter. I teach them what God's Word says about their particular disagreement and apply it to their case to decide who is right and who is wrong."

Moses' father-in-law exclaimed matter-of-factly, "*This is not the best way to handle this situation. Both you and these people who come to you are only going to wear yourselves out. This is too big a job for one person. You can't do it all by yourself. Let me give you a word of advice and may God help you to carry it out. First you need to teach the people God's laws and how to conduct their lives accordingly. Then choose capable, honest, trustworthy men from among all of the people and delegate some of your responsibility to them. These men must hate bribes and be wise enough to fear God. Appoint them as judges over groups of one thousand, one hundred, fifty, and ten based on how much responsibility they are mature enough to handle. They must always be available to hear and solve the people's smaller disagreements but will bring every difficult case to you. You should continue to be the people's representative before God by bringing their hard questions to Him to decide. This will make your job easier because they will help you carry the load.*[64] *If the Lord agrees that this is what you should do, you will be able to handle the pressure, and all these people will go home satisfied. Then there will be peace and harmony in the camp."*

Moses took Jethro's suggestion to I Am. Even though he trusted his father-in-law implicitly and his advice seemed wise, he knew that he was the one who was ultimately responsible for the people. And there was too much at stake for him to be wrong about even the smallest matter. He also knew that even a strong, competent leader could make a wrong decision on his own. Moses did not rely on his own understanding of what he thought should be done, but looked to the Lord for His wisdom instead. Therefore, the Lord gave him clear guidance by confirming that Jethro's counsel had come from Him and was to be followed.[65]

So Moses did precisely what his father-in-law recommended and the Lord confirmed. As a result, he was able to lead more efficiently because he was free to devote his time to the most important issues. He could also enjoy more time with his family who gave his life the balance it so desperately needed. Above all else, he was able to spend more time with the Lord, who was his

---

[64] 2 Timothy 2:2 (NLT)
[65] Proverbs 3:5–6 (NLT)

best friend and his source of strength, wisdom, direction, peace and everything else he needed.

By the end of the day, Moses felt lighter as if a weight had been lifted from his shoulders. The glorious sunset, exuding warmth and serenity, was in the process of bringing what had been a fruitful day to a beautiful end.

Moses took advantage of this ideal opportunity to get reacquainted with Zipporah. He looked for her and found her in their tent teaching their sons how to successfully adapt to new people and their new environment. As he stood at the entrance and listened to her, he was again reminded of why he loved her so. *Instead of joining in with the gossiping busybodies in the camp who were always eager to induct new members into their club, she spent her time constructively. When she looked up and saw him, she smiled. Anticipating that he wanted to spend some time with her and needing the same from him, she artfully ended her session with the boys. She was a master at moving between her roles of wife, mother, business owner, and daughter while ensuring that everyone's needs were met.*[66]

Throughout their years of marriage, they had established such a bond that they were able to pick up right where they left off. Giggling like young lovers, they playfully held hands as they walked out beyond the camp into the open desert. Zipporah was even more stunning this evening than he remembered. A Cushite by birth, she came from a naturally beautiful, exotic looking people, and she was the most strikingly gorgeous of them by far. But it was not just her physical beauty that made her so appealing. It was primarily the maturity and wisdom she exuded.

---

[66] Proverbs 31:10–31 (NLT)

"I am so proud of you!" Zipporah exclaimed as she beamed with admiration for Moses. "You went to Egypt and in a short time you brought all of those people out of slavery. You are my man!"

Moses blushed. Then, more interested in her than himself, said sincerely, "So tell me, how have you been?" Knowing him well, she understood just what he meant. He didn't mean the kids or the farm or her garment business. He meant her. He wanted to know how she had been.

"I've been so lonely without you," she told him honestly, emphasizing the word "you." She wanted him to know that in spite of the fact that her life was full and meaningful, not having him with her had left a void.

He studied her face carefully, and it conveyed the depth of her emotion. It said that even though they had only been apart for two months, she had missed him deeply. Only a woman, who was woman enough to love deeply, could miss a man this intensely. And it made him feel good.

"Me too," he said. "I've missed you more than you can know. You are the only woman I will ever love and I promise you, we will never be apart again. We are going to move into Canaan and begin a new life in a wonderful new place and enjoy each other's company until the day we die," he told her with certainty.

Looking into her eyes, he remembered why he wanted and needed her to be his woman for the rest of his life. Zipporah *always made him feel good about himself. She made him feel like a man is supposed to feel.* From the time he met her 40 years ago in Midian, *she encouraged him.* When he showed up at the well, ran those bullying shepherds away and watered her father's sheep, she told him how brave he was. It was just what he needed to hear because he didn't feel brave at the time. He had just run from Egypt like a coward to avoid being killed by Pharaoh. When he told her that he was homeless and had nowhere to go, instead of looking down her nose at him as another woman might, she took him home to meet her father. She convinced him that Moses had potential even though he didn't appear successful at the time. Later when he asked her to marry him, she forfeited the privileges of her position as the daughter of the priest of Midian. Instead, she chose her husband's God to be her God and diligently sought after Him. I Am, in turn, gave her the wisdom to be what Moses needed in a wife. *Prudent, she listened well and always gave sound advice. When he was faced with a dilemma and didn't know what to do, he knew he could always talk to her. She was a hard-working, responsible woman who spent her time wisely. Above all else, she respected him in spite of his imperfections. She understood that a man's number one need from his woman is to be respected.*[67] *An excellent mother, she helped raise their sons to become fine, young God-fearing men. Zipporah was indeed his helper,*[68] *and she loved him just for being him.* Because they fit together perfectly, there was no doubt in his mind that God had chosen her for him. Having Zipporah as his wife made Moses feel like a king.

His mind quickly flashed back to his encounter with Ayana in Egypt, and it grieved him to think that he let another woman cross his mind, even if for a moment. He would have been a fool to become involved with someone else and run the risk of destroying the priceless relationships he had with Zipporah and the Lord.

---

[67] Ephesians 5:33(b) (AMP)
[68] Genesis 2:18 (AMP, NLT)

Moses and Zipporah stayed in the desert laughing, talking, and reminiscing until well after dark. As they sat in the sand, side by side with her head on his shoulder, neither of them could think of any other place on earth where they would rather be.

Their romance wasn't the only one flourishing in the desert. Earlier that morning while Jethro was sitting out in front of his tent, he saw Ayana walking towards him as she was returning from gathering manna. He thought she was the most beautiful woman he had ever seen and wondered who she was. A widower, he had not entertained the idea of having a relationship with a woman since his wife died years ago. But there was something about this woman that captivated him. She was graceful, elegant, and exuded confidence. Not wanting to miss this opportunity, he spoke to her as she walked by.

"It's a beautiful day isn't it?" Jethro asked her as he stood up to let her know that he wasn't just acknowledging a passerby.

When she saw him, she stopped immediately, wondering who this mature, distinguished-looking gentleman was who had spoken to her.

"Why, yes it is," she said. "Mornings are the best part of the day in the desert."

"I'm sorry. I didn't mean to stare," he said, obviously smitten. "It's just that you are very attractive. Are you an Israelite or an Egyptian or..?" he asked as his voice trailed off, curious to know where she was from.

"I'm an Egyptian," she said, still proud of her country in spite of its current state. "And what about you?"

"I live in Midian, but I'm originally from Cush," he stated. "Moses, the man who is leading the people, is married to my daughter Zipporah. I just came here to bring her and their sons back to him."

"So, will you be heading back to your country soon?" she asked, hoping that he wouldn't.

"Not if I have a reason to stay a little longer," he told her with a look that let her know that it was her move.

"I was thinking of packing a picnic basket and going further out into the desert to watch the sunset this evening. Perhaps you would like to join me?" she asked. Jethro couldn't say "yes" fast enough.

Ayana went home in a good mood, anticipating a lovely evening with an interesting man. She used her best spices to prepare a variety of delicacies with the manna. With her basket and a blanket packed, she changed into a special dress that was becoming and suitable for an evening date in the desert.

Jethro arrived at Ayana's tent right on time, letting her know that he was responsible and conscientious. They walked out away from the camp and found the ideal spot from which to watch the sun go down. Once they began to talk, they were so engrossed in conversation that they had almost forgotten about the food she had brought. When he finally tasted it, he was even more impressed with her. By the end of the evening, they both knew that if what they saw in each other was real, they needed to find a way to be together.

After walking Ayana home, Jethro went back to Moses' tent where he was staying. Ayana left and came immediately to my tent to tell me how excited she was about having met Jethro. When she got there a mutual friend of ours named Shani, an Egyptian that I worked for sometimes in Egypt, was there too. Ayana told us everything she had learned about Jethro and how she was looking forward to seeing him again. Shani and

I were happy just to see our friend happy. At the same time, Jethro was having a similar conversation with Moses.

"Did you go out for a stroll in the desert?" Moses asked Jethro, wondering where he had been and hoping he was enjoying his stay with them.

"Sort of," Jethro said, smiling like a schoolboy in love. "I went on a picnic with a lovely woman named Ayana."

"Ayana from Egypt?" Moses asked, pondering whether this could be the same woman who worked for Pharaoh.

"Yes. She's Egyptian. Do you know her?" Jethro inquired, hoping to learn more about her from someone who knew her.

"I met her before we left Egypt," Moses told him, already planning to do some match-making. He thought his father-in-law had been alone for far too long, and this might be the ideal opportunity for him to find some companionship. "She was one of Pharaoh's advisors," he continued. "We talked a few times. I got the impression that she was serious about seeking the Lord. She's a very wise woman and pleasant too. If you're looking for a wife, you couldn't do any better. You should pray about it and see what the Lord has to say."

That was all that Jethro needed to hear. He knew Moses to be an excellent worker from when he tended his sheep, as well as an excellent husband and father. And he saw firsthand that the God of heaven had used him to bring millions of Israelites safely out of slavery in Egypt. So *he knew that Moses was a man of character, and his judgment could be trusted* when he said that Ayana would be an excellent choice for a wife. *He also knew, however, that man's judgment is limited, so he began to pray about the matter before making a decision.*[69] While he

---

[69] Proverbs 14:12 (NLT); Proverbs 3:5–6 (NLT)

was waiting for an answer he saw her every day for the next few weeks, growing even more convinced that she was the one. But there was still no word from the Lord.

Knowing that he had pressing business at home in Midian, he decided to leave and send for her later if he got the answer he was looking for. *He knew that marriage was one of the most important decisions of his life, and he had to get it right.*

The last time he saw her, he was honest and told her that he wanted to marry her though he said nothing about why he couldn't. At first he thought she wanted to say "no" because she looked unhappy. But when she told him that she had been praying about it just in case he asked, but couldn't give him an answer until she heard from the Lord, he could barely contain himself. *She too wanted what God wanted more than what she wanted.*[70] *So they agreed to keep praying, confident that if they were destined to be together, the Lord would tell them both.*

A few days later Jethro prepared to return to his country. He said goodbye to Ayana. His last words to her were, "If the Lord gives me a chance, I will love you every day for the rest of your life." Deeply touched, she cried, as she wanted that too, more than words could express. He bid farewell to his grandsons in the camp. Then Moses and Zipporah walked him out into the desert.

"Are you sure you can't stay a few days longer?" Moses pleaded, hoping they could spend just a little more time with him.

"I wish I could," Jethro told him sincerely, "but I have an urgent message to take home. Spending this time with you, hearing and seeing what the Lord has done for you and your

---

[70] Matthew 16:24 (NLT)

people, has opened my eyes. We have been worshiping the wrong god. Baal is just a wooden statue covered with gold. He cannot see or hear or think or do anything. When Zipporah married you and decided to accept the Lord as her God, she tried to tell me this. But I just couldn't see it, even though I saw her become a better person right before my eyes. I want the Lord, the only living God, to be our God. And when I tell my people about Him, I'm sure they will agree."

Moses smiled brightly. "Then I do not want to keep you," he said.

Jethro returned the smile and hugged Moses. With tears in his eyes, he said, "I thought I was just coming out here to see how you were doing and to bring your family back to you. I now know that God brought me here so that I could find Him and make Him known to my people." Then laughing he added, "And He may have even introduced me to my wife."

"I hope so," Moses said enthusiastically. "And I want you to know that I appreciate the advice you gave me about delegating to others so I won't be overburdened. And I can never repay you for giving your daughter Zipporah to me to be my wife and for taking care of my family while I was gone."

"You don't need to thank me," Jethro began. "It has been an honor. I couldn't have given my daughter to a better man, and my grandsons couldn't have a better father. You have enriched our lives tremendously."

Zipporah nodded in agreement as Jethro spoke, sincerely agreeing with everything he had just said. Moses graciously acknowledged the compliment, grateful that his family thought so highly of him.

"Listen, we're moving on to Canaan soon," Moses continued. "We'd love for you to come and spend some time with us when we get there. You're welcome anytime."

"Don't be surprised if you look up one day and see me," Jethro said as he laughed.

Before he left, Jethro hugged his daughter. After they all had said their final goodbyes, Zipporah and Moses watched Jethro walk away until he was out of sight.

The two of them walked back to the camp without speaking, each in their own reverie, enjoying the warm desert evening. Moses reminded himself how God had been so good to him. After 40 years of pain and perplexity in the wilderness of Midian, the Lord was speaking to him clearly and continuously, and their relationship had become rich and rewarding. They had become closer than he could have ever imagined. God had enabled him to lead the Israelites safely out of Egypt. We were well on the way to Mount Sinai to worship Him, and then to Canaan, the Promised Land. God had reunited him with his wife and children and his brother and sister. In spite of the fact that the Israelites were a challenging group to lead, every area of his life was showing promise.

But while Moses and Zipporah were slowly walking home, enjoying the solitude and basking in life's goodness, Miriam and Aaron were back at the camp slandering Moses.

His siblings had met Zipporah for the first time when she arrived several weeks ago. Moses had mentioned that he was happily married, and they assumed that his wife was an Israelite like themselves. When they saw that she was a Cushite, they were visibly surprised. When he introduced her to them, he saw them give each other a look that expressed their disagreement with his choice. They knew that their disapproval of her was wrong, but they wanted to keep up the appearance of being righteous to others. So they chose to malign Moses privately as soon as the opportunity presented itself, which it did that very evening in Aaron's tent.

Moses and Zipporah had just returned to the camp from the desert. They overheard Miriam and Aaron talking as they were walking past Aaron's tent on the way to their own. When they heard Moses' name, they stopped and listened.

"Who does Moses think he is?" Miriam began with contempt in her voice. "What makes him think he is the only one of us through whom God can speak to the people? Both of us are Levites, chosen to serve God, just like him." Aaron didn't speak but nodded in agreement. Neither of them verbalized the real reason for their discontent, but they both knew it was Zipporah's Cushite race.

Though disappointed, Moses was not shocked to hear his brother and sister speaking against him. Not only had he seen their disapproval in their faces earlier, but he was well-acquainted with human ugliness. From the moment he met up with the Israelites in Egypt until then, he had experienced jealousy, strife, dissension, backbiting, slander, and a host of other ills. And all of this was from the very people he was supposed to lead to the Promised Land of Canaan. So at that point in his life, nothing surprised him.

Because Moses was a very humble man, he did not feel compelled to confront Miriam and Aaron in their ignorance. He trusted the Lord to fight his battles for him. So he and Zipporah, who had also heard the entire conversation, merely looked at each other and began to move on. She knew that she was at the heart of their concern. But she, too, was mature enough to overlook an offense.[71]

---

[71] Romans 12:19 (NIV); Proverbs 19:11 (NIV)

Unbeknownst to Miriam and Aaron, *the Lord was also listening to every word they said and every word they thought but didn't say.* Immediately, before Moses and Zipporah could take another step, the Lord came down in a cloud, intervened and dealt with the issue.

"Miriam and Aaron, come outside right now," He told them sternly. They promptly obeyed, afraid of how He might deal with their disobedience.

The surprise they felt when they saw Moses and Zipporah standing there quickly turned to guilt because they knew that they both had heard them. Their primary concern, however, was what the Lord was going to do to them.

As the four of them stood there, the Lord commanded, "Miriam and Aaron, step forward," specifically calling them out. Again, they obeyed without hesitation.

"Listen to me very carefully," He began. "I, the Lord, communicate with a prophet through visions and dreams. But that is not how I communicate with my servant Moses. Of all my servants, I trust him the most. I speak to him face to face, clearly and not in riddles. He sees me as I am. So why weren't you afraid to criticize him?"

The Lord was furious with the two of them, and He left. When the cloud lifted, Miriam looked down and saw that she had been stricken with leprosy leaving her skin as white as snow. Aaron also noticed it immediately and cried out to Moses, "Please, I beg you not to punish us for this terrible sin. We were foolish to do such a thing. Do not let Miriam be like a stillborn baby coming from its mother's womb with its flesh already decaying."

So Moses forgave their folly from his heart and cried out to the Lord, "Please, God, heal her!"

But the Lord said to Moses, "Her sin has caused her to become defiled. So confine her outside the camp for seven days, and after that she can be brought back." Remorseful, Miriam cried profusely as they took her to a barren place far away from everyone in the camp and left her there.

Three days later, Zipporah went to her husband with a special request.

"Have you been to see your sister?" she asked Moses, with a genuine interest in Miriam's well-being. "She's probably feeling alone and humiliated. She might need you."

"No, I haven't seen her and I don't plan to," Moses retorted. "I have forgiven her for what she said. I even prayed for her and asked God to heal her. But I am not ready to see her just yet."

"Then let me go to her. She needs someone right now," Zipporah said imploringly.

Moses looked at her for several seconds without speaking. Her request surprised him because it was an atypical response from someone who had been insulted. On the other hand, it didn't surprise him. This was who Zipporah was – *forgiving and kind, always treating others like she wanted them to treat her, always looking for ways to be helpful.*[72]

"Of course you can go to her," Moses said with his heart brimming over with love for this woman who never ceased to amaze him. "I will pray and ask God to protect you from her leprosy."

"I already asked him," she said as she stood up and kissed him on the cheek. "It's already taken care of. I'll be back in a little while."

---

[72] Ephesians 4:32 (NIV)

Moses stood there in awe as he watched her leave the tent. He was convinced for the thousandth time that God had hand-picked and hand-molded Zipporah just for him because she was exactly what he wanted and needed. *Even though she had her own mind and her own ideas, she always asked him what he thought. She willingly submitted to his leadership as the head of their family which made him feel like a man.*[73]

She also based everything she said and did on what the Lord would have her to do. She was a righteous, praying woman who cultivated her own relationship with God. So the Lord spoke to her clearly and answered her prayers.[74]

The desert air was cool that night. Zipporah moved quickly to the outskirts of the camp where she found Miriam's shelter. And that's all it was – a structure with three sides and a roof. It was designed to be punitive and to give her minimal protection from the elements. Lighted by the moon on its open side, the only furniture in it was a bench.

As she approached the shelter, Zipporah saw Miriam on her knees praying fervently. She stood at a distance waiting for her to finish so she wouldn't interrupt her or listen in on her private conversation with God. Within seconds, Miriam stopped and listened, as though she felt someone's presence. When she turned and saw Zipporah standing there, she rose to her feet.

"I am unclean! I have leprosy!" Miriam shouted to warn her not to come any closer.

As Miriam was speaking, Zipporah noticed that the disease had already spread from her hands to other parts of her body. It was visible on her face, neck, and feet as well.

---

[73] Ephesians 5:22–24 (NIV)
[74] James 5:16(b) (AMP)

"It's alright," Zipporah assured her. "You're not contagious."

Not sure that she believed it but regretful for what she had done, Miriam said, "If you came to rebuke me for what I said, I deserve it. Since I have been out here alone, God has convicted me that I was wrong for speaking against my brother's relationship with you."

"I didn't come here to rebuke you," Zipporah said lovingly. "I just thought you might like some company."

Miriam eyed her suspiciously at first, wondering if that was her true motive. But after studying her face she realized that her reason for being there was genuine.

"Yes, I would like some company," Miriam admitted. She sat down and invited Zipporah to join her by patting the space next to her on the bench.

Miriam found Zipporah easy to talk to. She was a good listener with a quick-wit and an incredible amount of wisdom and character. Fascinated with her life and culture, Miriam hung on her every word. They chatted well into the night. Embarrassed that she had been superficial and prejudiced, Miriam knew that she needed to apologize to Zipporah.

"I misjudged you, and I am very sorry," Miriam told her sincerely. "Because of my stupidity all I could see before was your race. Now I know what an incredible woman you are. My brother is a very fortunate man. You are the best thing that's ever happened to him, and I see now why he married you. *God made every person on the face of this earth, and everyone is equal in his sight. When He creates two people for each other, His objective is for them to help each other achieve His purpose for their lives. So when two people choose to marry, He does not care about their race as long as they both belong to Him, and they marry with His objective in mind.*" Miriam paused for a moment then finished by saying, "Would you please forgive my ignorance?"

Zipporah smiled and said, "I already have."

After they'd said goodbye, Zipporah headed for home, and Miriam kneeled beside the bench in her meager shelter and prayed. *She thanked God for showing her He loved her by correcting her sins* of prejudice and backbiting, even though He used the extreme method of leprosy to do so.

Miriam was confined outside the camp for a total of seven days, after which she was healed. And the people did not move on until she was brought back.

CHAPTER 13

GREAT EXPECTATIONS

Seemingly, the day began as any ordinary day in the camp. At the first sign of daylight, some of the people gathered food for their families while others watered animals, washed clothes, cleaned tents, made repairs and performed every other normal, everyday task. Even though we were living in tents as nomads there was always work to be done. However, it was no ordinary day because there was a fervent feeling in the air that made it extraordinary.

Everyone awoke that morning with a sense of excitement and anticipation. We arrived at Mount Sinai the night before, exactly three months from the day we left Egypt, and we were halfway to the Promised Land. We were camped near the base of the very mountain where the Lord spoke to Moses from the burning bush and commissioned him to go to Egypt to secure the release of the enslaved Israelites. At that time, God told Moses that the sign that He had indeed sent him would be that we would all come to this mountain and worship Him. Doubts persisted along the journey when things got difficult or it looked like we weren't going to make it. But in spite of them, arriving at the mountain confirmed that we were right in the center of God's will. However, there was a major problem in the camp that needed to be addressed.

"Some people are going to disobey God no matter how many times you tell them that what they are doing is wrong," Bezalel said with exasperation. *"They want to do what makes them feel good and they have tricked themselves into believing that there won't be any consequences."*[75] I folded clothes and listened as he spoke, assuming that something Moses discussed with them late last night at the leader's meeting was behind his frustration. He had been appointed as one of the judges over a thousand people based on Jethro's advice. Bezalel always shared his concerns with me when he felt especially burdened.

"All of the leaders are reporting the same problems," he continued. "Sexual immorality is running rampant throughout the camp in every form imaginable. For some reason, this is one of the greatest areas of struggle for people. They are having sex with people they are not married to, with people of the same sex, and with animals. And they are looking at vile, disgusting sexual pictures they have drawn...," he said as his voice trailed off, implying that there was more, if that were even possible. *"We thought that when we started teaching them God's laws the problem would go away, but it hasn't. They know right from wrong, but they keep making bad choices."*[76]

"They must not understand that they are ruining their lives and their future," I said as I shook my head somberly and continued folding clothes. *"The devil has them thinking that*

---

[75] Galatians 6:7-8 (AMP, NIV)
[76] James 1:22–25 (NIV)

they are just enjoying themselves. But they don't realize that they are destroying their marriages, their relationships with their children, and their reputations. They just don't understand that sexual sin has even more severe consequences than other sins because they are sinning against their own bodies. They are opening themselves up to terrible diseases, and they may even wind up in bondage to the devil so that they can't stop sinning even if they want to. And if they don't repent, they will never enter the Promised Land." I stopped folding for a moment and looked up at him before continuing. *"Maybe that's what the people need to hear. Maybe they need to know more than just that sin is wrong. They need to be reminded that it has consequences that only a fool would want."*[77]

Bezalel listened and carefully weighed every word I said. Then he responded matter-of-factly, *"Then that's what I will tell them – the whole truth. The Lord put me in this position as a leader to see where the people need help and to tell them what they need to hear, not what they want to hear. I don't want anyone's damnation to be my fault, so I plan to tell them everything He says."*[78] When he finished speaking, I simply smiled, pleased that he knew exactly what he needed to do.

While Bezalel and I were discussing the problem of sexual immorality in the camp and what to do about it, Moses was in his tent praying about the same burden. The Lord spoke to him and said, *"I see what is going on amongst the people. I have great expectations for them, but they are chronically disobedient.* That is one of the reasons why Mount Sinai is the most important stop on your journey. Now that you have brought the people

---

[77] 1 Corinthians 6:9–20 (NLT, TLB)

[78] Acts 20:26–27 (NIV); 2 Timothy 4:2–5 (NIV); Ezekiel 3:17–21 (NLT)

here to my mountain, *I need to teach them some crucial spiritual lessons. And these lessons can only be learned here, deep in this dry and barren wilderness, in my School of Adversity. It is here that I will give them my laws in writing. They will develop an accurate understanding of what they mean and how their very future will be determined by whether or not they obey me.*[79] *I understand that they will sin sometimes. But I expect them to admit it when they do, and not do it again.*[80] *Sin must be the exception in their lives, not the norm. Obedience is only one of the lessons they will learn at this location. It is here that they will also learn my ways – how I use suffering and long waits to develop their faith and produce perseverance in them. This is how they become mature which means that they think and act like me.*[81] *And it is here that they will learn how to approach and worship me with sincere hearts in spite of difficult circumstances.*[82] *Once they have mastered these lessons and entered into the intimate, loving relationship with me that I created them for, I will lead them into the Promised Land. There they will reap my blessings of goodness, abundance, and purpose.* Come up to the top of the mountain later this morning, and I will meet you there."

When he finished praying, Moses looked around the tent to see if there was any work that might need to be done. He tidied up a bit so Zipporah would have less to do. Even though he was always busy with the work the Lord had given him, he never failed to make time to do what he could to make things easier for her because he loved her. He also found that *when he made her happy, she went out of her way to make him happy.*

---

[79] Deuteronomy 8:1 (NIV)
[80] 1 John 1:8–9 (AMP); Proverbs 28:13 (NLT)
[81] James 1:2–4 (NIV, NLT)
[82] John 4:21–24 (TLB)

Just as he was finishing, Zipporah returned from gathering manna. She smiled as she looked around the tent, pleased that he was thoughtful enough to help out. He quickly walked over to her and helped her by taking the containers from her hands. "I have to go up to the mountain, but I will be back as soon as I can," he told her as he put the clay pots on the table.

"Take whatever time you need," she responded understandingly. "We all want you to hear clearly from God so that you can lead us the right way." He knew that by "all" she meant not only her family, but also everyone else in the camp. And he wanted that too. *He was determined to do everything he was supposed to do in order to complete the task the Lord had given him.*[83]

Moses held out his hand to let Zipporah know that he wanted her to walk with him. She slipped her hand into his and accompanied him through the bustling camp to the base of the mountain where he kissed her goodbye. Zipporah observed from below as he climbed upward. She watched the Lord descend to the top in a majestic cloud that covered Moses before she turned and headed back.

Moses sat silently in God's presence for six days, waiting patiently to hear from Him. *He was prepared to wait as long as it took because he knew that it was only in God's presence that he would receive the instructions needed to fulfill his mission.* On the seventh day, when He was ready to speak, the Lord summoned Moses from within the cloud and invited him to come up higher.

"I want you to tell the people exactly what I say," the Lord reiterated, breaking the silence. Tell them, *'I am the Lord your*

---

[83] Hebrews 3:2 (NLT); John 4:31–34 (NIV); Hebrews 12:1 (NIV)

God, the One who rescued you from the land of Egypt where you were slaves.' *I want them first and foremost to know who I am and that they are to have the utmost reverence for me."*

The Lord continued, *"Then give them these Ten Commandments to follow. The first four have to do with their attitude towards me, and the following six have to do with their attitude towards all other people. Both are equally as important. They prove that I am their God by first loving all of their fellow human beings.*[84] *These are the commandments:*[85]

You must not have any other god but me. I am to be your first priority. Nothing and no one in your life are to be more important or even as important as me.

You must not make an idol of any kind or an image of anything from the heavens, on the earth or in the sea. You must not bow down to or worship an idol or an image because I am a jealous God who will not tolerate your affection for any other gods. If you disobey me, I will punish your children for your sin down to the third and fourth generation. But if you prove that you love me by obeying me, I will show you that I love you by blessing your children down to a thousand generations.

You must not misuse my name. When you speak my name from your mouth, it must be with the utmost reverence, not casually or with profanity. I will not let you go unpunished if you misuse my name.

You must observe the Sabbath, the seventh day of the week, by keeping it holy. It is to be a day of rest dedicated to me. You have six days each week to do your ordinary work. On the Sabbath day, no one in your household is to do any work including you,

---

[84] 1 John 4:20 (AMP, TLB, NLT)
[85] Exodus 20:1-17 (TLB)

your sons and daughters, your male and female servants, your livestock, and any foreigners living among you.

You must honor your parents, both your father and your mother. Then you will live a long life that is rich in every way in the land I am giving you.

You must not intentionally take the life of another person, which is murder, unless you are defending yourself or your family, or you are at war with another nation.

You must not commit adultery which means to have sexual relations with someone other than your wife or husband. If you look lustfully at anyone other than your wife or husband and even think about having sex with them, you are sinning just as if you had committed the act. If you are not married, you are not to have sex at all or even think about having sex.

You must not steal which means to take anything that does not belong to you.

You must not lie which means to say anything that is not true. And you must not say that anyone else said or did anything that is not true.

You must not secretly desire what belongs to anyone else including their house, wife or husband, male or female servant, ox or donkey, or anything else that belongs to them. This desire can lead to many other sins such as murder, adultery, theft, lying, jealousy or deceit. Instead, you must be content with what you have, trusting me to take care of your needs."

Then the Lord continued, "These commandments are just the first part of what I expect from the people. The second part is a Tabernacle, which is a portable home for me that they will build in the middle of the camp. Once it is finished, I will come and live there amongst them. They will use it to draw near to me in the way that I will require. I will tell you more about this later."

When the Lord finished speaking, Moses continued to sit there for a while, just enjoying being in His Presence. *He now understood why the Lord had called him up to the top of the mountain. He could have just as easily given him the commandments for the people in his tent. But being on top enabled him to see the massive assignment before him from God's perspective. It also gave him the extra strength and wisdom he needed for the challenging tasks that awaited him at the bottom of the mountain.*

Later that day when he arrived back at camp, Moses summoned the people. At the sound of the trumpet, they left their chores and quickly assembled at the foot of the mountain. They stood silently before him as he recounted everything the Lord had told him. Hanging on every word, they seemed eager to learn what was required of them.

"Do you fully understand our purpose for being here at Mount Sinai and everything the Lord expects of you?" Moses asked them.

With the exception of one man, they shouted, "Yes," in unison.

The man raised his hand, stepped forward, and asked a question that others may have had but were not bold enough to ask. "Are you saying that for the rest of my life, the only person I can have sex with is my wife?" he inquired, with disbelief in his voice.

"That is exactly what the Lord is saying," Moses told him definitively. He put an emphasis on "the Lord" so everyone would understand that they would be accountable to Him if they chose to disobey His command.

"That doesn't seem fair. Even if a man loves his wife, sometimes he wants a little variety," he said while some of the other men in the crowd snickered in agreement. The looks on the women's faces revealed that they didn't think it was funny at all.

"You need to understand that all of the Lord's laws are designed to protect you and others," Moses explained. *"When you disobey them, you bring ruin and destruction into your life and the lives of others. When you choose to sleep with a woman who is not your wife, and it becomes known, it will destroy your relationship with your wife and your children, thereby ruining your family and your reputation. And you can rest assured that it will become known because the Lord will make sure that it does. Whatever sin you commit in the dark, He will expose in broad daylight.*[86] *And not only will you and your family be affected, but your relationship with the Lord will come to a grinding halt. Until you repent, the Lord will not hear or answer any of your prayers.*[87] *You can forget whatever good plans He had for you. You will be on your own, which is a dark and dangerous place to be."*

Some of the men looked disheartened. They believed what Moses said, but they hated the thought of giving up this sin that was so dear to them. Seeing this, Moses finally said, *"So let's all make wise choices. You can either choose to obey the Lord and be blessed or disobey Him and be cursed. It's that simple."*[88]

Moses had requested that the scribes among them record the Ten Commandments as he spoke them. He encouraged the people to place an order for their own copy which would be written on a papyrus scroll. *They were to read it to themselves and their children morning and evening to ensure that everyone in the family knew the commandments and obeyed them.*[89]

---

[86] Numbers 32:23(b) (NLT, TLB)
[87] Psalm 66:18–21 (NIV); Proverbs 28:9 (AMP, NLT)
[88] Deuteronomy 28:1-68 (NIV)
[89] Deuteronomy 6:6-9 (AMP)

When he later inquired of the scribes how many orders they had received, he was not surprised by what they told him. Bezalel and I were among the many people who were serious about doing what the Lord required of us, so we were eager to get our own copy of the Lord's commandments to meditate on daily. But many others were not. They had no intention of obeying God in spite of everything they had just heard.

CHAPTER 14

Any "god" Will Do

The last time the Lord invited Moses to come up to Him on the mountain he remained only a short while. This time, his stay lasted forty days and forty nights because I Am had more to tell him. But it wasn't just the length of time he was gone that made the Israelites as irritable as teething babies. It was being stuck in the wilderness for over a month with no movement. As long as they felt like they were going somewhere they were content, even if the cloud only led them five miles. It was the sitting still with no indication of progress that was wearing them thin.

"Did Moses tell you when he'd be back?" I asked Bezalel one evening while we were having dinner with the children.

"I have no idea, and he probably doesn't either," he said sincerely. "He'll stay until the Lord finishes telling him whatever he needs to know for now."

"It's boring out here!" our son Shemaiah exclaimed. "How are we ever going to get to this Promised Land if we keep sitting here?"

"I was wondering the same thing," his sister Mychal chimed in.

Bezalel and I looked at each other, surprised to hear such questions and comments from our own children. We had been trying so hard to teach them that *every stop in the wilderness serves a specific purpose in our lives.*[90] But they were merely echoing the sentiments of many of the others in the camp including some of the people under Bezalel's own leadership. So he gave our children the same counsel he had given them.

"We will get to Canaan right on time," their father reassured them. Even though that wasn't much information, they accepted it because they trusted him.

In the meantime, Moses was in God's presence on top of the mountain receiving detailed instructions on how to build a sanctuary – a home for Him called a Tabernacle. It was the means by which the Lord would live with us. Through it we could approach Him and worship Him. *He* showed Moses a pattern and *told him exactly what He wanted to be done, who would do it, and where the resources would come from,*[91] even though it was not yet time to build it. Moses found that *sometimes the Lord gave him information before he needed it to give him ample time to prepare himself mentally for what was to come.*

While Moses was there, the Lord took the two stone tablets Moses had been told to bring with him. With His own finger, He engraved the Ten Commandments He had verbally given to Moses the last time he was in His Presence on the mountain. The stone tablets were always to remain with the Israelites.

---

[90] James 1:2-4 (TLB, NIV, AMP)
[91] Exodus chapters 25–31:11 (NLT)

They were to remind us how important it was to always obey God's Word.

But forty days and forty nights was too long for most of the people. Moses was in the Lord's presence receiving instructions on how we would ultimately receive everything God had for us. At the same time, the people were in the desert under Aaron's supervision, ready to abandon God, His Word, and Moses.

Just as the Lord finished giving His directions to Moses and handing him the two tablets that contained His laws, He looked down and saw the Israelites rebelling.

"We are tired of sitting around in this desert doing nothing and going nowhere," the leader of the malcontents shouted to Aaron. "We have been here too long. That man Moses promised to lead us to a land that flows with milk and honey. So where is he? He has been gone for forty days. I know because I have been counting. How do we know that he is ever coming back? The way I see it, we can stay here in this desert and wait on him like stupid idiots or we can make a god who will take us to that good land."

Like the others, Aaron too had become impatient. He was supposed to help the Israelites understand that God was using the long wait to test us to see if we would continue to obey and trust Him. Instead, he failed the test and led the people to fail this test of faith also.

"I don't know where my brother is, and I am sick of this place too," Aaron stated emphatically. "We can make a god with some gold, just like we used to do in Egypt. Tell the people to take off their earrings, necklaces, nose rings, ankle bracelets, and anything they are wearing made of gold."

The leaders put the word out, and the people eagerly responded. They too wanted out of the wilderness and were ready to go along with any idea that might work. Men, women, and children came forth in large numbers with their contributions.

Aaron, a goldsmith, took what they had given and made a large golden calf with an altar in front of it. When he presented it to the people, they were amazed. Seeing that they were pleased, he enthusiastically pointed to it and said, "This is the god who brought you up out of Egypt! Let's have a festival in his honor."

The Israelites bowed down, worshiped the calf, and sacrificed animals to it. Then they threw a wild party in celebration of their new god with the expectation that it would guide them to the Promised Land and provide everything they needed along the way.

My family was astonished as we watched the idolatrous festivities from the door of our tent. Speechless, we wondered how things had deteriorated so badly in spite of everything the people had been taught. It was as though they had short attention spans that couldn't stay focused on God for more than a few minutes at a time.

Unbeknownst to the wayward Israelites, the Lord was watching them and listening to them the entire time.[92] While He was speaking with Moses on the mountain, He was aware of their every move.

The Lord said to Moses, "We are done here for now. You need to go back down to the camp because those people you brought out of Egypt have become corrupt and failed my test.

---

[92] Psalm 33:13–15 (TLB)

They have quickly turned away from me and my commands.[93]
I told them I am to be their only God. But because they cannot
see what I am doing on their behalf, they assume that I am not
doing anything. *They do not understand that real faith has the
confidence to believe that I will do what I have promised even if
they cannot see it yet.*[94] So they made themselves an idol in the
shape of a calf. They bowed down to it and sacrificed animals
to it. Then they said, 'This is the god who brought you up out
of Egypt.' If they do not want me to be their God, then I won't
be. They are on their own. Let them see how far they get. I
have watched them since the day they left Egypt, and they
are stubborn and rebellious. *They have abandoned me, so now
I will abandon them.*[95] Now leave me alone so I can kill them
all. Then I will make a great nation from you and your family."

But Moses pleaded with God not to kill them. "Lord," he
said. "You are the One who brought these people out of Egypt
with great power and mighty miracles. *They cannot survive
without you – they just think they can.* These are your people,
and your reputation is at stake. If you kill them, the Egyptians
and the people from the surrounding nations will hear about
it. They will say that you are evil and that you lured them into
the wilderness just to destroy them. Part of your plan is to
draw people from other nations to you by showing them how
faithful you have been to the Israelites. Why should you abort
your plan just because of their foolishness? I know that they
have sinned against you. But remember, you promised your
servants Abraham, Isaac, and Jacob that you would make their
descendants, these same Israelites, as numerous as the stars

---

[93] Luke 8:13 (NIV, AMP)
[94] Hebrews 10:35–39 (NIV, NLT)
[95] 2 Timothy 2:12 (b) (TLB, NIV)

in the sky. And you said you would give them the land you are taking them to as their inheritance."

The Lord thought about what Moses had said and acknowledged that it was true. "You are right," He said. So He relented and did not destroy the Israelites.

Moses left the Lord's presence and walked down the mountain carrying the tablets. As he approached the camp, his heart sank when he saw the calf idol that the Lord had spoken of. He stood and witnessed the people dancing and behaving wildly. Outraged that the Israelites had so quickly lost their faith in God, he threw the tablets on the ground in sheer anger and broke them into pieces at the bottom of the mountain. Seeing with his own eyes how they had fallen away, he finally understood the depth of God's fury.

Moses knew he had to take charge of this situation that had spiraled so badly out of control. To punish the Israelites for their folly, he took the calf idol, burned it in the fire, ground it to powder, scattered the ashes over the water, and made them drink it. He then turned to Aaron to find out why he had allowed this to happen.

"What on earth did these people do to you to make you go along with this nonsense?" Moses asked him angrily.

"Don't be upset," Aaron began his weak defense, knowing that he was in serious trouble. "You know how unstable these people are. When you stayed gone for such a long time, they thought you were dead. So they brought me their gold jewelry, and I threw it into the fire and out came this calf."

"That's ridiculous," Moses exclaimed. "The truth is that you are as unstable as they are. *You say you trust God with your words, but your actions say you don't. As soon as the road gets a little too rough, or the wait takes a little too long, you are ready to walk away from I Am and bow down to another god, or to anything else you think will meet your needs. Any god will do for you and most of them, even if it is not real. You are still spiritually immature. You have yet to understand that the Lord gives us a promise and then tests our faith by making us wait for Him to keep His word. He does this to teach us how to endure during the hard times so that we can become mature, fully developed spiritually, and well prepared to achieve His purpose for our lives. Then we can receive all the good things He has planned for us.*[96] *Furthermore, as a leader you are supposed to be on your guard at all times because the devil targets leaders. He knows that if he can get one leader to fall into sin, not only can he discredit the leader, but he can cause many other people to fall as well. Don't you know that most people are only as strong as those who are over them? They need constant guidance or they, like sheep, will wander away from God.* Now look at how the people have backslidden. Not to mention that we are a laughingstock to our enemies who are watching us at all times."

Aaron was seized with remorse. He knew he deserved the verbal thrashing and that everything Moses had just said was true. Having no words with which to redeem himself, he looked at Moses with a look that asked how he could fix the wrong that he had committed.

With a specific plan in mind, Moses stood on a hill above the camp and said, "Whoever is for the Lord, come to me." All the men from the tribe of Levi, including Aaron, rallied around him.

"The Israelites have committed a grave sin today," he told them. "According to the Lord's command, each of you is to take

---

[96] James 1:2–4 (AMP, NLT)

your sword and go throughout the camp killing those who are not for the Lord. We cannot move on until we eliminate the evil sin from our camp." Led by Aaron, they followed His instructions without hesitation. About three thousand people would die that day.

My family and I were listening along with the other Israelites when Moses told the Levites what to do. The slaughter began so quickly that we had no time to seek shelter in our tent. With swords slashing and blood splattering all around us, we knew it was pointless to run. So we stood still and prayed. And because we refused to bow down to the calf but trusted the Lord instead, we were all still standing, without a scratch, when the mayhem was over.

The next day Moses was still grieved. The three thousand deaths had not begun to atone for the idolatry with the golden calf. So Moses went back to the crowd and reminded them that they had committed a horrendous sin, lest they delude themselves about how much trouble they were still in.

Hoping there was something he could do to make atonement for the people, Moses climbed Mount Sinai again to speak to the Lord. Once in His presence Moses confessed, "Lord, these people have committed a terrible sin. They made a god for themselves out of gold, even though that is the first thing you told them not to do. Please forgive their sin. But if you won't, then remove my name from the book you have written – the book of life that contains the names of everyone who will spend eternity with you."

The Lord replied to Moses, "No. You cannot take the punishment for anyone else. *The person who sins against me is the person whose name I will take out of my book.*[97] Now go and lead the people to the land I promised to them, and I will go with you. However, when the time comes for me to punish, I will definitely punish them for their sin."

And the time came quickly. The Lord struck the people with a plague because they worshiped the calf Aaron had made. By the time Moses arrived back at the foot of the mountain, those destined for death were already dead.

---

[97] Exodus 32:30–33 (NIV); Revelation 20:15 (NIV); Revelation 21:1–27 (NIV)

THE TABERNACLE

CHAPTER 15

HE LOVED US ENOUGH TO COME LIVE WITH US

After the unfortunate fiasco with the golden calf idol was over, it was time to get the people and the plan back on track. So the Lord summoned Moses saying, "Cut two stone tablets like the first ones that you broke so I can write the Ten Commandments on them again. Have them ready by tomorrow and bring them to me on Mount Sinai."

Moses chuckled as he envisioned himself throwing the tablets on the ground. In retrospect, it seemed impetuous and even childish, but he admitted to himself that he enjoyed every second of it. Usually self-controlled, it had been decades since he had let himself be so reckless. Knowing that God had a sense of humor, Moses even thought he heard a bit of amusement in God's voice when He mentioned that he had broken them.

Early the next morning Moses climbed the mountain and met with the Lord. While he was there, they spent time together enjoying each other's company. Moses desperately needed the hiatus and this peaceful time with God. *He found that shepherding humans was harder than shepherding sheep because humans were more difficult, and they sapped his energy. Most of them were slow to learn God's ways if interested in learning them at all. They were just along for the ride, wanting only their own personal gain. They only wanted the Lord to bless them, protect them, and meet their needs. Getting to know Him was the last thing on their list of priorities. Plus, they were constantly being disobedient and complaining about one thing after another. Spending time with the Lord helped Moses to remember his role and to see the people as He did, as those He loved who simply needed help getting to the level of spiritual maturity that He was trying to take them to.*[98]

God again showed Moses the detailed plans for the Tabernacle, the home where He would live among us and through which we would draw near to Him. The fact that He gave him the same information twice emphasized to Moses how important it was that the Tabernacle be made correctly. At that time, the Lord also inscribed the Ten Commandments on the new tablets with His own finger while Moses watched.

"Be sure that you build the Tabernacle and its furnishings exactly like the pattern I showed you," the Lord commanded. "And when you have completed it, you will place the tablets in it."

When Moses returned to the camp, *he immediately transferred the plans* for the Tabernacle to a papyrus scroll. *He had been given a wealth of information and knew better than to rely on his memory.* Even though he thought of himself as

---

[98] 2 Timothy 4:2,5 (NIV, TLB)

an eighty-year-old man with the mind of a forty-year-old, *he knew that he was prone to forget some things.*

Then he sent someone to bring Bezalel to his tent along with a man named Oholiab, son of Ahisamach. It was time for Moses to make the plan known to those who would be involved.

"Have a seat my friends," Moses said heartily when they entered the tent as he motioned to two chairs. Bezalel was glad to see him and eager to hear what he wanted to share, but Oholiab sat down tentatively, having no idea why he had been summoned. He hoped it was good news.

"The Lord has given us a phenomenal task. We are to build a Tabernacle here in the desert," Moses told them. He could see from the look on their faces that they had no idea what a Tabernacle was, and neither did he at first. He unrolled the papyrus scroll on which he had drawn the details that God had given him.

"A tabernacle is a portable home for God where He will live among us in the very center of our camp," he said as he pointed to the drawing on the table. "It will be sectioned into three areas. The first area will be an outer court with a bronze altar. The altar will be used by the priests to sacrifice animals as offerings to the Lord to atone for the sins of the people. It will also contain a bronze water basin. The priests will use it to wash themselves before they approach the altar to offer the sacrifices, and before they enter the second area, the inner court. They must wash because *everyone must be pure before approaching the Lord.*[99] The second area, the inner court, also known as the Holy Place, will contain three items. They are

---

[99] Psalm 24:3–6 (NLT); Psalm 15:1–5 (NLT)

a golden lampstand to provide light, a table that will hold twelve loaves of bread that will be replaced regularly, and an altar that will be used to burn fragrant incense throughout the day and night. *The lampstand represents God's guidance and direction,*[100] *and it also lights the path into His Presence. The bread represents His unfailing physical and spiritual sustenance,*[101] *and the incense represents the unceasing prayers of the people which keep them in touch with the Lord at all times.*[102] The third and most important area will be the Most Holy Place, the place of God's Presence, where I Am will live. It will be located next to the Holy Place and will contain the Ark of the Covenant. The Ark is a gold covered rectangular chest with two gold angels on the lid, and the Lord will be enthroned between the two of them. The Ark will hold the two stone tablets with the Ten Commandments inscribed on them which we have agreed to obey. I will stand before the Ark, as needed, to talk to God and hear from Him for the people. Aaron and his sons, the priests, are the only other people allowed to enter the Most Holy Place. They will go in once a year with the blood of a sacrifice to make atonement for their sins and the sins of the entire community."

As they listened intently, Moses went on to explain the other details that God had given him. They included the dimensions of the structure, its contents, and what materials would be used to build it. He also shared the designs for the linen clothes the priests would wear as they performed their priestly duties, and the formula for the fragrant incense that would regularly be burned on the incense altar.

---

[100] Psalm 119:105 (NIV)

[101] John 6:35 (NIV)

[102] 1 Thessalonians 5:17 (TLB); Ephesians 6:18 (TLB)

Bezalel and Oholiab asked many questions that not only gave them the clarification they needed to complete the tasks correctly, but also confirmed to Moses that they had the proper skills for the assignment. Lesser skilled individuals would not have even known what to ask.

Oholiab's face showed that he had grasped the vision and was pleased with it. As an afterthought, he asked, "Where did God tell you the material would come from to build this place that He will live in?"

"From the people," Moses told him. "Before we left Egypt, the Lord told us to ask the Egyptians for gold, silver, and other valuables. He gave us favor with them, and they gave us everything we wanted. Everything we need to complete the Tabernacle is in our possession right now."

"This is a big job. How many people will be helping us?" Bezalel asked, realistically assessing the task at hand.

"You will be the lead craftsman," Moses said as he pointed to Bezalel. "Oholiab will be second in command and God has assigned several other highly skilled men and women to work with the two of you. We have one year to complete this task. I am going to give you these specifications to review now while I send someone to gather the rest of your team so you can start planning."

Shortly after that, Moses met with the community and asked them to bring an offering to the Lord so the workers would have what was needed to build the Tabernacle. Once he explained to them what it was and what purpose it would serve, as he did to Bezalel and Oholiab, they were more than happy to contribute whatever they could. God touched their hearts, and they gave so generously that Moses had to ask them to stop. They brought gold, silver, bronze, precious stones, fine linen, blue, purple and scarlet yarn, oil, and many other materials in abundance.

The work began right away. The male and female craftsmen assembled under the direction of Bezalel, who had honed his skills in Egypt making items of the finest quality for Pharaoh. He shared all the details of the plan with them. Once they had a thorough understanding of what to do, they worked tirelessly day and night inside of the enclosed area that would soon contain the finished Tabernacle. They melted metals, made molds, took measurements, spun yarn, cut and nailed wood, and wove cloth, meticulously performing every task.

At the end of each long day, Bezalel came home exhausted. I always had a delicious meal and a back rub waiting for him which relaxed him and brought his productive days to a pleasant end. I listened intently as he gave me a first-hand account of the work he was doing.

"I feel privileged that the Lord chose me to make His sacred items and build His sanctuary," he said with tears in his eyes. "I feel so close to Him while I'm working, like He's right there with me helping me."

In awe of what he was telling me, I hung on every word.

"Now I understand how special we are to Him," he continued, obviously moved by what he had come to know. "What other God cares enough about His people to show them exactly how to draw close to Him? There isn't one. The Tabernacle is strategically designed to lead us into His Presence. That includes us, the people, not just the priests. We can't physically go into the Holy Place and the Most Holy Place, but we can still draw near to Him. *When we go into the outer court to bring our best animal to Him as a sacrifice for our sins, we also need to offer our hearts and minds as living sacrifices, wholeheartedly devoted to Him.[103] Then we have to let the light of His commandments guide and direct us. We must also pray so that we can stay in touch with Him at all times, and look to Him to sustain us and meet our needs in His way and His time. When we do these things that are represented in the Holy Place, He will allow us to enter His Presence spiritually. Then we will hear from Him with clarity and commune with Him, just as Moses physically comes into His Presence, hears from Him, and communes with Him."*

As I listened to Bezalel, I was overwhelmed with gratitude. I was grateful that the only living God, I Am, had provided a way for me and every one of us, whether Israelite, Egyptian or other, to have a close relationship with Him. It was true that no other god cares for His people as our God does, and I loved Him for that. Both Bezalel and I went to bed that evening totally at peace.

The next day the project resumed. No one but the workers and Moses could see the work in progress. All of the tribes surrounding the area could hear the construction of the Tabernacle taking place behind the closed-in structure. And we eagerly awaited the completion of the place where God would live.

Several months later, all of the individual components of the Tabernacle were completed. Even though he had carefully supervised their construction, Moses went over every inch of them a second time to ensure that they had been built exactly like the ones the Lord had shown him on the mountain. And every detail was perfect. The workers had done everything just as the Lord commanded Moses.

---

[103] Romans 12:1 (NIV, NLT)

Exactly one year from the day we left Egypt, the Lord instructed Moses to set up the Tabernacle. Following His instructions to the letter, he erected it by setting down its bases, inserting the frames, attaching the crossbars, and setting up the posts. Then he spread the coverings over the Tabernacle framework and put on the protective layers.

He took the stone tablets inscribed with the Ten Commandments and placed them inside the Ark. Then he attached the carrying poles to the Ark, set the Ark's cover on top of it, brought the Ark into the Most Holy Place, and hung the inner curtain to shield it from view.

Moses then brought the items into the Holy Place. He placed the table just outside the inner curtain and arranged the bread on the table. He set the lampstand across from the table and lit the lamps. He also placed the gold incense altar in front of the inner curtain and burned the fragrant incense. Then he hung the curtain at the entrance of the Holy Place.

Next, Moses completed the outer court. He placed the bronze altar near the Tabernacle entrance and burned an offering on it. The bronze water basin that the priests would use to wash their hands and feet was filled with water and placed between the bronze altar and the entrance to the Holy Place. Moses then took the anointing oil and anointed every single item in the outer court, Holy Place, and Most Holy Place, to make them sacred and devote them to the Lord.

Moses brought Aaron and his sons to the Tabernacle entrance, washed them with water, dressed them in the sacred priestly garments, and anointed them, thereby consecrating them to serve as priests. Once anointed, Aaron's descendants were set apart for the priesthood for all generations.

Finally, Moses formed the courtyard by hanging curtains around the bronze altar, bronze washbasin, Holy Place, and Most Holy Place. He also hung the curtain at the entrance to the courtyard.

At last, Moses finished the work, and the Tabernacle was ready for the Lord to move in and live with us. Then the cloud descended, and the awesome glory of the Lord filled the Tabernacle.

Later that day we heard the trumpet sound that summoned us to meet at the base of the mountain. We eagerly gathered to hear what Moses had to say. It felt like we had been in the wilderness for an eternity, even though it had only been one year. The rumor spread that the Tabernacle was completed. Bored and impatient, some hoped it was true because they were ready to move on.

"I have some very good news for you," Moses said enthusiastically, knowing that they were restless and wanting to encourage them. "The Tabernacle has been finished according to God's design and His schedule. We are privileged to have the Creator of heaven and earth, the one and only God, come and live with us. I am proud of everyone who generously gave from their resources to help build the Tabernacle. I am also proud of the workers who labored tirelessly building it and did an exceptional job. The Lord will reward you all." He paused before continuing. "We are making good time on our journey to the wonderful land the Lord promised us. We left Egypt exactly one year ago, and we are right on schedule. So *this is a good time to make an honest assessment of what we need to do differently if we are going to finish our journey.*"

Moses noticed that the word "if" in his last sentence got their attention, just as he had planned. So he continued. "*We need to have a candid conversation about how serious God is about us keeping His commandments. He is not playing with us. He expects us to obey Him, and He will not take us to the Promised Land until after we have proven to Him that we will trust Him and do what He says.*[104] Instead of being grateful for everything He has done for you, you all have been murmuring and complaining about every little obstacle and hardship since we left Egypt. This proves that the Lord is not truly your God because you don't believe He can be trusted. When we were almost at the Red Sea, you turned and saw Pharaoh and his army behind us. Then you said, 'Was it because there were no graves in Egypt that you brought us to the desert to die? It would have been better for us to serve the Egyptians than to die in this wilderness.' When we arrived at Marah after traveling for three days in the desert without finding water, the water we finally found was bitter. Because you were thirsty, you grumbled and asked, 'What are we to drink?' After we left Elim, you were hungry, so you complained again and said, 'If only we had died by the Lord's hand in Egypt. There we sat around pots of meat and ate all the food we wanted, but now you have brought us into this desert to starve us all to death.' When we got to Rephidim, there was no water, so you quarreled again saying, 'Give us water to drink.' And then you really strayed off course. While I was on Mount Sinai with God for forty days and nights receiving instructions on how to build the Tabernacle so the Lord could come and live with us, you became impatient because of the long wait. So you lost hope and made another god for yourselves. It has also come to my attention that many of you are breaking the other commandments too."

Then Moses went on. *"You must understand that I Am uses hardships and suffering to teach us His ways and to cause us to*

---

[104] Deuteronomy 8:1 (NIV, NLT)

draw close to Him. Sometimes He deliberately causes us to hunger and thirst, to go without what we need. He does this to teach us that we need more than physical food and physical water. More than these physical necessities, we need Him, the bread of life [105] *who meets our spiritual needs. So He withholds these physical necessities to make us seek after Him.*[106] *He also makes promises to us and tells us what He is going to do for us. Then He uses long delays to test our faith to see if we trust him to keep His word and to firmly establish our faith in Him.*[107] *In addition to long waits, suffering is also part of His plan to develop perseverance, also known as patience, in us. Patience is that quality that allows us to go through anything with hope, no matter how difficult it is because we know that He loves us and is using our circumstances to mature us.*[108] *The wilderness is the place where He develops us in preparation to enter the Promised Land. Once we are mature, He draws us into the close, intimate relationship for which He created us, and He brings about His good purpose for our lives."*

The people were dumbfounded. They knew they had broken many of the commandments and had been disobedient by complaining and not trusting God. But they felt justified in their sin because they were bored, and their hardships had been so severe. *Somehow they had deceived themselves into believing that they were going into the Promised Land to receive all the good things God had for them whether they obeyed Him or not.*[109] This long overdue verbal thrashing gave them the wake-up call they needed.

---

[105] John 6:35 (NIV)

[106] Deuteronomy 8:2–3 (NLT)

[107] Romans 4:18–21 (TLB)

[108] Romans 5:3–5 (NIV, TLB); James 1:2–4 (NIV, NLT)

[109] James 1:22 (NIV)

"You're right," one of them exclaimed remorsefully before others agreed that they too had sinned. *"So what do we have to do now to undo the wrongs we have committed?"* they asked.

Moses smiled, pleased that they wanted to start afresh. *"It's simple. Just stop doubting God and disobeying His Word. Have your mind set on trusting Him no matter what you are facing, and do what He tells you to do at all times.* You can begin by regularly bringing an animal without defect to the Tabernacle as an offering to the Lord. This will serve as an act of worship and an outward expression of your inner devotion, commitment, and complete surrender to God. It will also atone for your unintentional sins and restore you to a right relationship with Him. Then *you will find that when you choose to draw close to Him by obeying Him and spending quality time with Him in prayer, He will draw close to you."*[110]

Shortly after that, the people who understood the utmost importance of what Moses had said began to bring their offerings to the Tabernacle and to seek the Lord with all their hearts. For others, the message was short-lived. Many of them walked away and disregarded it, as though it had never even been said.

We remained camped at Mount Sinai until shortly after the Tabernacle was completed. When the cloud rose from it, we set out and followed it, continuing our journey. With precision, the priests disassembled the Tabernacle and carried it with them until the cloud stopped at our new resting place. There they reassembled it, and the Presence of the Lord filled it again.

---

[110] James 4:8(a) (NLT)

CHAPTER 16

FROM BAD TO WORSE

One night I awoke from a restless sleep as I felt Bezalel get out of bed for the third time. I had slept next to him every night for the twenty plus years of our marriage, and I knew him well. Once he curled into the fetal sleeping position that he favored and closed his eyes, he usually didn't stir until early the next morning. I tried to remember how long he had been suffering from these bouts of disturbed sleep and recollected that they started about three months earlier.

"Are you ok?" I asked him with concern in my voice.

Without answering me, he quickly ran outside to the latrine. His bladder was full, and he had a strong urge to urinate. When he tried to relieve himself, he found the pain to be almost unbearable. Knowing that he would be miserable whether he kept it in or let it out, he endured the pain and forced his bladder to empty itself.

As soon as he left, I got up, lit a lamp, and sat at the table to wait for him. For some time I suspected that something was seriously wrong, but shrugged it off out of fear that I might be right. I had a hunch that he might have even had the same concern. While I waited, I bowed my head and humbly prayed, "My Lord, please help us. Heal my husband's body. Make him well again."

When he came back into the tent, he was pale and sweating with a grimace on his face. He made his way to the table and sat down, knowing that I was worried and wanted to talk.

"Let me get you some water," I said as I reached over to get the pitcher and a cup from the other side of the table. I poured the water and handed it to him, watching him as he gulped it down. When he finished, I took the cup from him, put it down and held his hands in mine.

"Talk to me," I entreated him as I carefully studied his face and eyes.

"I'm not well," he admitted, with a weak voice and beads of sweat on his forehead. "I'm not myself. Something is not right."

"What do you mean?" I asked, not quite sure what "not right" meant.

"I've been in a lot of pain for some time now," he told me as he winced from his aches. "My lower back and hips hurt and my legs get numb and tingle. I didn't say anything about it before because I thought it would just go away. But it's gotten worse. Then I started having to urinate all the time, especially at night, and it hurts badly when I try to go."

My mind quickly flashed back to a party that Ayana threw when I worked for her in Egypt. Because Ayana and her husband were wealthy and well connected, they knew everybody who was anybody. The best doctors in the country were there that evening, and I overheard them talking. They mentioned seeing an increase in an illness that I did not remember the name of, but the symptoms were the same as those of Bezalel.

"I think you need to see a doctor," I told him with a definitive look that let him know he couldn't talk his way out of this. "Now that you've mentioned it, I've noticed some things too. You've been eating the same amount of food, but you seem to be losing weight. And you're tired all the time. I thought it was just because you haven't been sleeping through the night, but now I'm not sure."

"You know how I feel about doctors," he complained. "I've been sick before and I've gotten over it every time. I just need some rest and a little more time to heal."

I knew that it would be fruitless to belabor the point with him. He hadn't been to see a doctor even one time since we had been married. And he was right in saying that he had been sick before and gotten over it every time. But he was also right in saying that something was not right this time. So in spite of his aversion to doctors, I knew that for his sake and that of mine and the children, I had to ensure that he saw one anyway.

"Well then, I'll let you get some rest," I assured him while gently patting his hand. "You just stay in bed today. The children and I will do the chores." I helped him into bed, tucked him in, and kissed him. He fell asleep quickly, tired from being up most of the night. Since it was now daybreak, I put out the lamp, quietly roused the children and headed out with them to begin the activities for the day.

So as not to disturb Bezalel, the children and I did not return to our tent after we gathered the manna for the day. Instead, Mychal and Shemaiah went to tend to the animals, and I went to visit my friend Ayana. Both busy with everyday life, we hadn't seen each other in a while.

Ayana was sitting outside, grinding her manna in a mortar when I walked up. "Good morning," I said cheerfully. "And what are you cooking today?"

"One of your recipes," Ayana exclaimed. "Sit down and join me. I can use some company. Listen, it's my turn to cook anyway. Let me prepare your manna with mine, and you all can join me for a meal later. I don't know if my version of your recipe will be as good as yours, but I think you'll like it anyway."

I was very pleased to oblige her. With all the other chores the children and I had to do while Bezalel was out of commission, eliminating even one helped me immensely.

"Thank you so much," I said gratefully, before Ayana took my pots of manna and scraped them into the mortar. "At least let me help you mix some spices or do something else while I'm here."

"Don't be silly," Ayana replied. "You're my guest. Now just relax and fill me in on what you've been doing since the last time I saw you."

My mood immediately became serious, causing Ayana to stop grinding and focus her full attention on me. "What's the matter?" she asked, honestly concerned.

"Something's wrong with Bezalel," I began. "He has been in pain for months and he can't sleep through the night without having to get up and urinate," I said before continuing. "Do you remember the big party you had about a year before we left Egypt?"

"Yes, yes I remember," Ayana said after thinking back. "It was my annual New Year's Day party. But what does that have to do with Bezalel?"

"While I was helping serve dinner at the party I overheard a group of doctors talking about an illness with the same symptoms that he has. Do you know if any of those doctors left Egypt with us?" I asked, hoping that at least one of them had.

"As a matter of fact, they did," Ayana told me. "All of the educated, professional people left. They didn't want to forfeit years of education and the opportunity to use their hard-earned skills. When we get to Canaan, they plan to re-establish their practices and do what they do best. I know how to reach them. We all stay in touch with each other."

"I'm sure they're all good at what they do, but is there one that you would recommend over the others?" I asked, wanting to find the one who could best help my dear Bezalel.

"Dr. Imhotep is the one you want," she said assuredly. "He has been teaching and practicing medicine for more than forty years. People used to come from all over Egypt and other parts of the world just to be treated by him. He knows what he is doing, and he has an excellent reputation. If you give me half an hour, I can go find him and bring him to see Bezalel in your tent."

"Oh thank you, Ayana," I said with profound gratitude, pleased that I was making progress towards getting some help for my husband. "I'll meet you back at my place in a little while." Then I left.

Ayana grabbed her shawl and threw it over her shoulders before heading out for the part of the camp where Dr. Imhotep lived. When she arrived, it didn't surprise her to find that he was sitting outside enjoying the sunrise and reading medical scrolls.

His face lit up when he saw her, and he stood to greet her. "To what do I owe the pleasure of your visit," he asked as he kissed her on each cheek. She gracefully refused the seat he offered her, preferring to state her business quickly and take him to see the ailing Bezalel. Because they were friends, they could always find time to engage in idle chit chat.

"An Israelite named Chaya, who used to work for me in Egypt, has a sick husband," she explained. "Would you please come and take a look at him? Just name your price. I'm sure that whatever you ask will be fair."

"I wouldn't think of taking money from you or your friend," he stated. "I am only too happy to help out where I can. I don't need any money. If I do not make any more gold in my life, I'll be just fine. Now take me to this young man so I can see what I can do to help him." Just in case he would need it, he went inside and grabbed his medical bag before they left.

When they arrived at my tent, I was sitting on the bed beside Bezalel, applying a cool, wet cloth to his forehead. I turned around when I heard them at the entrance. Immediately recognizing Dr. Imhotep as one of the doctors I had seen at the party, I got up and went to greet him.

Ayana formally introduced the doctor to Bezalel and me then excused herself to give us the privacy we needed.

"Tell me how I can help your husband," Dr. Imhotep asked me as he watched Bezalel shift himself to another position to try to relieve some of his pain.

I described Bezalel's symptoms while Bezalel listened. Even though he was not partial to doctors, he understood that I had sought one out because I loved him and was concerned about him. And he was in enough discomfort that he was ready to entertain any suggestions the doctor might have.

"Is there anything you want to add to what your wife has shared with me before I examine you?" Dr. Imhotep asked Bezalel as he walked over to the bed.

He remembered one thing that he had not yet told me because he had just noticed it. "I saw something red in my urine today. It looked like blood, but I wasn't sure," Bezalel declared.

Dr. Imhotep made a mental note of the red substance, pulled the covers back and thoroughly examined Bezalel through his bed clothes. Using the tools he brought with him, he poked and prodded and pressed all over his body as I watched. The doctor noticed that Bezalel was experiencing the most pain in his lower back, hips, upper thighs and legs.

Suspecting that he knew what the problem was, he needed to inspect one last area before making a final diagnosis. "For the last part of the exam, I need you to lift up your night shirt, turn on your side, and bring your legs up to your chest so I can perform a rectal exam," Dr. Imhotep candidly informed Bezalel. There was something about this part that all men hated no matter what nation they were from. And Bezalel was no exception.

When he fully understood what the doctor had said, his eyes widened as if this couldn't possibly be true. No one had ever done such a thing to him before, and he found the very thought to be abhorrent. He looked over at me, and I was equally as surprised by the doctor's instructions. If I had known that this was what the doctor was planning to do, I would have at least had some time to emotionally prepare Bezalel for the intrusion.

"Dr. Imhotep, can you give me just a moment with my husband," I asked. "He'll be ready for the rest of the exam in just a moment," I assured him.

"I understand," he told me, truly comprehending my dilemma. "You can take whatever time you need. I'll just have a seat outside until he's ready."

Sitting on the side of the bed, alone with my husband, I logically explained what Bezalel did not want to hear. "Honey," I said soothingly as I held his hand. "I need you here with me for as long as possible. The children need you too. I can't even think about life without you. That's why Dr. Imhotep is here. He is one of the best doctors in the world. If he can figure out what's wrong with you, he can probably fix it. Then you will be well again, and we can go back to enjoying our life together. But first, you need to let him finish your exam. If it makes you feel better, I'll hold your hand the whole time."

Bezalel thought about everything I said. And because he wanted to get better and enjoy life with his family again, he reluctantly agreed. "Alright, tell him I'm ready," he said, getting his nerve up.

When I called Dr. Imhotep inside, he went over to Bezalel, who had already done as the doctor had asked. With his knees pulled to his chest, and his bottom exposed, he felt more vulnerable than he cared to feel. I held his hand from one side of the bed while the doctor explained what he was going to do to him from the other side.

"Just relax," Dr. Imhotep said as he applied some lubricant to his finger that he had taken from his medical bag. "There is a walnut sized gland known as the prostate that is located below your bladder. I am going to insert my index finger into your rectum and feel it for anything abnormal such as bumps or hard spots. This may be a little uncomfortable, but try to relax."

Bezalel had no idea what the doctor was talking about. A craftsman by trade, with a body that had been perfectly healthy until recently, he had no medical knowledge, nor had he ever needed any. He just wanted this "uncomfortable" experience to be over.

"I'm relaxed," Bezalel told him, stretching the truth a bit. "Just do what you need to do." Then he closed his eyes and prayed while he tightly squeezed my hand.

The doctor gently inserted his finger and moved it around until he found the prostate. He took his time, carefully analyzing its size, shape, and firmness. I searched the doctor's face, but it remained neutral, giving no indication of what he was thinking. When he finished the exam, he brought the stool he had been sitting on around to the other side of the bed and sat down so he could face Bezalel and me.

"Based on your symptoms and my exam, you have what is known as cancer of the prostate," Dr. Imhotep told Bezalel plainly but gently. "As you probably know, cancer is a malignant tumor or growth caused when cells multiply uncontrollably, destroying healthy tissue. Prostate cancer is the second most common form of cancer in men. I am familiar with it because I saw thousands of cases of it in Egypt, though rarely in men as young as you are. Unfortunately, your cancer has metastasized, which means that it has spread from your prostate to other parts of your body."

We were both numbed by the diagnosis. Our thoughts were muddled, and we could not think clearly. Even though we had both been healthy for most of our lives, illnesses were common in Egypt with the natives, foreigners, and the Israelites. So we knew what cancer was. We just never expected it to visit our immediate family.

In anticipation of the question he thought we would ask next, Dr. Imhotep said, "There is no treatment for this cancer. Once it has spread outside of the prostate, it can't be cured. Therefore, it would be cruel and pointless to subject you to the rigorous demands of surgery. It will not prolong your life and may even make the rest of it worse."

Not wanting to believe what he was hearing, Bezalel asked with desperation, "Are you sure the surgery won't help? I remember hearing about men having this kind of surgery in Egypt, and they lived for many years afterward."

"Trust me, son," Dr. Imhotep began as he placed his hand on Bezalel's knee to comfort him. "The men who received the surgery and lived did not have an aggressive cancer in an advanced stage like you do. Egyptian doctors are the best in the world. We have the skill, tools, and anesthetics needed to successfully remove the prostate and heal the patient, as long as the cancer is confined to the prostate. Once it leaves that gland, the patient needs a miracle in order to recover."

The doctor paused for a moment to give Bezalel a chance to comprehend what he had just said before continuing. "Realistically, you have about one year to live. If you would like, I can give you an opiate for pain so you can function and do the things you need to do."

Bezalel and I looked at each other, still reeling from the worst news we had ever received in our entire lives. We both knew that opiates were mind-altering drugs. Without hesitation, Bezalel said, "No, I don't want anything for the pain. I need to be able to think clearly so I can hear from the Lord and be here for my family." I beamed at him, proud of his decision.

"Well, if you change your mind or if you need anything, anything at all, day or night, don't hesitate to come and get me," the doctor said as he stood to leave. I thought of something, but I waited until Dr. Imhotep and I were outside of Bezalel's hearing range to mention it.

"Doctor, this may be nothing but I have not had a period for the last two months," I began. "This has happened before when I was under a lot of stress. With Bezalel not feeling well and not sleeping through the night, I have not been relaxed either. Do you think it's nothing or...?" I asked, letting my voice trail off without finishing my question.

"Or what?" he inquired, quickly pondering the implications of my suspicion. "Do you think you might be pregnant?"

"I hope not," I replied dejectedly. "It is possible. But the timing couldn't be worse. My husband is sick, and he needs my help. He may be dead soon so my child would be fatherless. My son is over twenty so he could die at any time. It has been so long since I had a baby I don't even know how to do that baby stuff anymore. And even if I did, it's hard raising a child in this desert. I know. I've watched many women try to do it, and it's hard."

"Let's put first things first," the wise, elderly doctor said to console me. "You might be worried about nothing. Take a pregnancy test. It might just be negative. You know what to do. Get some barley seeds and some wheat, put them in separate containers, and moisten both of them with your urine every day. If you are pregnant, one of them will sprout in three to four days. If the barley sprouts, you will have a boy, and if the wheat sprouts, you will have a girl. You are not pregnant if neither of them sprouts. This test is highly reliable even though you may only be in the earliest stage of pregnancy."

When the doctor left, I went back inside. In the corner of the tent, we kept the items we brought with us from Egypt that we would need to start our new life in Canaan. Amongst them were the barley seeds and wheat that I needed for the test. While Bezalel slept, I followed the doctor's orders and moistened them both with my urine. Then I hid the containers that held them on a shelf behind some jars so no one would find them, praying all along that they would not sprout.

Bezalel had not gone to the Tabernacle to take an offering to the Lord in almost a month. While this was the responsibility of the head of the household, it was understood that if he were unable, another family member could bring it in his place. So I went outside to the pen and chose our best lamb, a perfect one without a spot or a blemish. I lightly tied a rope around its neck and led it to the Tabernacle entrance. A priest met me there and led me inside to the altar. There I put one hand on the head of the lamb and cut its throat with the other. The priest caught the sacrificial blood in a basin and sprinkled it on the altar. Then he dismembered the lamb, washed it and burned it on the altar as a sweet savor to the Lord.

By participating in this ritual, I worshiped the Lord, expressed my devotion and complete surrender to Him, and atoned for me and my family's sins by transferring them to the lamb. Restored to a right relationship with God, I was now able to receive the Tabernacle benefits of those who choose to draw near to Him – His presence, guidance, provision, and assurance of answered prayer.

I went home immediately after offering the sacrifice. With nowhere else to take the pain of my dilemma, I took it to the Lord. On my knees in my prayer corner, while my husband slept soundly, I sought the face of the living God whom I desperately needed. Not just His miracles and His power to fix the broken places in my life, I needed Him – His Presence, His comfort, and His friendship. And He met me there. He flooded my heart with His love and His peace, and I knew that, come what may, I could count on Him to be with me and to help me.

Before I finished praying, I made two specific requests. I asked the Lord to heal my husband and not let me be pregnant. For the first time in my life, I clearly heard Him speak to me. His answer to my requests was, *"My grace is sufficient for you. My power works best when you are weak. I am with you, and that is all you need."*[111] Though His response puzzled me, I knew that in time it would make sense.

Over the next few days, Bezalel took a turn for the worse. He completely lost his appetite and thereby his strength. Bedridden, he could do very little except watch his body succumb to the illness that had begun to ravage it. I spent most of my time meeting his needs and trying to make him as comfortable as possible.

I always found the time, however, to moisten the barley seeds and wheat with my urine. Eager for the results, I checked on them regularly, sometimes several times a day. On the fourth day, the results came back. To my disappointment, the barley seeds sprouted. I was expecting a baby boy.

Surprisingly, after I prayed, my circumstances went from bad to worse.

---

[111] 2 Corinthians 12:9 (AMP)

CHAPTER 17

TIME TO DIE

When I first found out that I was pregnant, I experienced a myriad of emotions from depression to fear. So I kept the news to myself for over a week because I didn't want to talk about it, and I was afraid it might make my already dying husband even sicker. We already had two children and the very notion of more responsibility, by itself, cast a shadow over my mood. And the thought of having to raise a child on my own took me to an even grimmer place.

For a split second, the idea of having an abortion entered my mind. Egyptian doctors were able to concoct a special tea made of herbs that were sure to terminate a pregnancy. And if that didn't work they had many other techniques, one of which would undoubtedly eliminate the problem. Fortunately, *I was able to capture that thought and send it away as quickly as it had come.*[112] Many of the Israelite women among us were choosing this way out, but I knew it was not for me.

---

[112] 2 Corinthians 10:5(b) (NIV)

I remembered that the Lord had promised to be with me and to help me. *If I sinned against Him by taking the life of my child, it would mean that I did not trust Him to work the situation out for my good;*[113] *that instead, I preferred to handle the matter myself, in which case He would stand back and let me do so. But I was wise enough to know that left on my own, without His help, I had the capacity to make a terrible mess out of my life. So I wrapped my mind around the fact that I was going to have a baby* and carefully chose the time when I would tell my husband.

One evening after dinner, while the children were out with their friends and Bezalel was sitting up in bed reading, I scraped up the nerve to broach the subject. "Have you noticed that as quickly as the men in the camp are dying off, the women are turning up pregnant?" I asked him, hoping to sound as though it was just an observation.

He thought about it for a moment before answering. "Now that you mention it, I have seen a lot of pregnant women. We don't have to wonder how those men were spending their time before they died," he remarked with a chuckle, making light of an otherwise serious topic.

"But think about how hard it will be for those women to raise their children without fathers," I said, still probing him. "That can't be what those men wanted."

Always pragmatic, he replied, "This thing is bigger than any of us. In order for the Lord to preserve our people, there has to be a birth for every death. I know the men don't want their wives to have it hard any more than they want to die early. But *sin has its consequences.* When we had a chance to trust

---

[113] Romans 8:28 (TLB, NLT)

God and go into the land He promised to us, we complained and didn't believe Him and even spoke against Him. So the punishment is that the men are cut down in their prime, and the women have the burden of raising the next generation of children alone. That's just the way it is."

"Well, what if that were to happen to us?" I came out and asked him, after not having received any insight into his feelings from what he had just said. "What if we were to have a baby?"

Knowing that something was amiss because I continued to press the issue, he asked, "So who is this really about? Is this about other people or is it about us?"

"It's about us," I told him frankly as I sat down on the bed facing him. "We're going to have a baby boy in about six months."

After I had spoken, I watched his face carefully as he processed what I had just said. I could see the wheels turning in his mind. Finally, he broke the silence with a response that was not what I expected. "This could be one of the best things that ever happened to us," he exclaimed, visibly pleased with the news. "Don't you see? Our son Shemaiah will die here in the wilderness. Until now we had no male heir to carry our family line into the future. Now we do. This is a blessing from God!"

Not quite sure I saw it that way yet, I said, "But the doctor only gave you one year to live. And your health is already beginning to fail. That means that most of the responsibility will fall on me while you are alive, and all of it will fall on me after you're gone."

"You know I would give anything for things to be different right now," he told me lovingly. "I wish we were in the Promised

Land in our own home in a green valley with bountiful crops, flowing springs, and herds as far as the eye can see. I wish we were expecting a baby there and not here. And I wish that I was perfectly healthy so I could raise him to be a man and play with his children and his children's children. But none of that is going to happen."

My eyes began to tear up as I envisioned the life he described. With all of my heart, I wanted that too. He reached over and wiped my tears. Holding my face in his hands he said, "We may never get there, but we can have an abundant life right here. *As long as we are faithful to God, He will make this desert fruitful for us. The Lord can demonstrate His faithfulness here in the wilderness just as well as there in the Promised Land. We were sentenced to come back here because we didn't learn what we were supposed to learn the first time. Well, I do not want us to waste this opportunity. I want us to get it right this time. No matter how hard it gets, we have to remember that this is just a test. If we respond to it the right way, God will bring some good from this wilderness experience.*"[114]

I shook my head in agreement, as more tears poured from my eyes. Everything Bezalel had said deeply touched my heart.

"Don't you worry," he told me with conviction. "I'm not going to just lay here and die. While I've been stuck in the bed these last few weeks, I've been doing a lot of praying. And I've been doing even more listening. *The Lord has an excellent plan for our family, and He is beginning to share His vision with me. I am going to spend whatever time I have left seeking His face and doing exactly what He tells me to do.*"

---

[114] Deuteronomy 8:16 (AMP, TLB)

I couldn't have asked for more. The Lord had promised to be with me and to help me in my weakened state. And He was already beginning to show His faithfulness. While I was praying to Him, He was speaking to my dying husband and working through him to fulfill His purpose for our family. Even though the Lord did not keep me from becoming pregnant and had not healed my husband, I could already see that *He had something greater in mind.* Things had not gone from bad to worse, as I had thought, but from bad to much, much better. With my heart now filled with hope instead of despair, *I couldn't wait to see the Lord's plan unfold.*

Just as Bezalel and I were finishing our conversation, Shemaiah and Mychal came back from their ball game with their friends. We knew that it was the right time to share the news with our children.

"Did you all have fun?" I asked them as they sat at the table.

"Yeah, our team won," Mychal bragged, pleased that her team had finally beaten her brother's team at stickball.

"Are you alright Dad?" Shemaiah asked as he looked over at his father. "You've been resting a lot lately."

"It might not look like it, but I am very well," Bezalel exclaimed. He slowly lifted himself up from the bed and made his way to the table to have a conference with the family. When I tried to help him, he motioned to me to let him do it by himself. *I smiled to myself* as I joined them at the table, *happy that my husband,* in spite of his illness, *was boldly walking in his place of leadership as the head of our household. When he was like this, he made me want to submit to him and follow his lead.*[115]

---

[115] Ephesians 5:21–28 (NLT, TLB) and verse 33 (AMP)

"Guess what?" Bezalel asked the children. Instead of responding they just looked at him because they were too tired to play the guessing game.

"Ok, we'll tell you," he said, eager to share the news. "Our family is going to have a baby!" It took a second for it to sink in but when it did, they were elated.

"When is the baby due, Mom?" Mychal asked with excitement.

"In about six months. And I'm going to need your help," I told her, looking forward to this task that would give she and I an opportunity to spend more quality time together.

"I'm happy for us Mom," Shemaiah said. "Are we having a boy or a girl?" I liked the way my son said "we" and "us." It let me know that he saw our family as a whole unit where what affected one of us affected all of us, just as Bezalel and I had taught them.

"We're having a boy," I told him.

That must have been exactly what he wanted to hear because he grinned from ear to ear. Then suddenly his countenance changed, and he said, "I'm glad it's a boy so you will have someone to take my place when I die."

I was speechless, stunned by his comment. Bezalel, however, knew precisely what to say.

"Son," he began. *"We are all going to die someday. And only the Lord knows when that day will be for each of us.*[116] *You never know. He may choose to give you many more years. But no matter how much time He gives you, the important thing is that you use it wisely;*[117] *that you spend it getting to know Him and doing what He put you on this earth to do. Then when you breathe your last breath,*

---

[116] Hebrews 9:27 (AMP, NLT)
[117] Ephesians 5:15–17 (NLT, TLB)

your life will have counted for something here, and you will wake up and see Him face to face.[118] *It doesn't get any better than that."*

Shemaiah's actions spoke louder than any words could have. He got out of his chair and went over and hugged his father for a long time. Mychal and I watched the love expressed between the two men, and it warmed our hearts, making us all feel even more like a family.

"Now, let's talk about how we are going to come together as a team to make this thing work," Bezalel expressed to us as we settled down and looked to him for direction. "If each of us carries our share of the load, this will be easier for everyone." He looked at each of them as he told them what their responsibilities would be. "Shemaiah, you will continue to train with the army and shepherd the sheep. Make sure that they are fed and watered every day. Check their pen regularly. Mend the fence if necessary to be sure that it is secure and that none of them get out. Take care of them so that they stay healthy because our sacrifices must be perfect, without a spot or a blemish. Once a month, on the first day of the week, you are to take the best one to the Tabernacle and offer it to the Lord on behalf of our family. Mychal, your brother, will help you gather the manna each morning, and you will grind it so all your mother will have to do is cook it. You are to wash the clothes, clean the tent, and go to school every day that it's in session."

Then he asked, "Do either of you have any questions?"

Not out of disrespect, but out of a desire to spend time with his father, Shemaiah inquired, "What will you be doing Dad? Will you be helping me?"

---

[118] Psalm 17:15 (NLT, TLB)

Bezalel had not yet told the children that he was dying of cancer and had only been given one year to live. They knew that he hadn't been well. It was obvious that he was losing weight, and it was not like him to stay in bed, but they had no idea how dire his prognosis was. But he still did not believe it was time to tell them. For all he knew, the Lord might intervene and give him more time to die.

"Yes, son," he replied. "I haven't been feeling well lately, but I'll help you with the sheep when I can. I want to stay close to home so I can be here for your mother when she needs me."

That was the truth, and Shemaiah seemed content with that answer. When he had the strength, Bezalel would gladly do more. He wanted to spend as much time as he could with each of them so that he could bless their lives in ways they would remember long after he was gone.

As the weeks moved on, my pregnancy became more noticeable. But long before I began to show, my body confirmed that I was expecting. Green with the nausea that came with morning sickness, vomiting was almost a daily routine. Even though I made myself eat so that I could nourish my developing fetus, I rarely kept my food down. I prayed that the Lord would give me a healthy baby anyway.

On the days that I wasn't sick, I went with the children to gather manna in the morning. I especially enjoyed that time as it gave us a chance to talk.

"Mom, when you were my age was there a boy you liked?" Mychal asked me while Shemaiah was gathering further away. *I kept the lines of communication open between myself and my daughter primarily for opportunities just like this one. I wanted her to feel comfortable talking to me about anything. Only then could I know what was going on in her head and her life and have any influence.*[119]

I thought about it for a moment before answering. "Yes, there was," I responded, as though a pleasant memory had come back to me. "His name was Gabriel and I thought he was very cute. Our parents were friends, so we saw each other whenever our families got together. But eventually we got older, and we both moved on. I met your father and Gabriel met the woman he married, and things turned out just like they were supposed to." I paused before continuing. "Are you asking me about this because you've met someone you like?" I asked her playfully.

Mychal's face lit up like the sunrise as she talked about her new love interest. "There's this boy in my class at school. He's nice-looking and smart. And he's very good at stick ball. He even plays on Shemaiah's team with the older boys. Whenever I look up in class, I see him looking at me. I hope he comes over and talks to me because I want to get to know him."

"Then I hope you have a chance to talk to him," I told her. "You are too young for marriage right now but you'll be old enough soon. I was only seventeen when I married your father. Perhaps it's time for you to start thinking about what you should be looking for in a husband."

Thankful that I understood how she felt, Mychal embraced me and then asked, "So *what should I be looking for in a husband?*"

"Well," I began, all too happy to tell her. "*First of all he needs to be a man who wants with all of his heart to know God and is determined to obey Him, no matter what. He finds out from the Lord what He put him on this earth to do, and he works at it*

---

[119] Proverbs 31:27 (NLT)

diligently. Because he is a man of character and integrity, when he has to choose between doing right and wrong, he chooses to do the right thing every time. Second, he must be loving and kind towards you and other people. A hard-working and responsible man, he must take care of his family and pay his debts. And third, he must understand the importance of sexual purity, both yours and his. God has determined that sex should only take place between a man and a woman who are married to each other. Sex outside of the Lord's boundary lines is dangerous because it ruins lives in many ways. If these three things are not evident in a man, he is not the one for you."[120]

Following our mother-daughter talk, we finished filling our jars with the manna, caught up with Shemaiah, and returned home to our tent. After grinding the manna, Mychal grabbed her language scroll and left for school, and Shemaiah headed out to care for the animals.

Once we were alone together, I felt compelled to discuss with Bezalel what Mychal told me about the boy. When I broached the subject, he sat up in bed, very interested in what was going on in his daughter's life.

"So who is this boy?" he asked with a father's concern. "Do we know his family?"

"I don't know much about him except that she likes him," I said, as I mixed some exotic herbs into the manna. "I don't think she knows much yet either. We had a nice talk about what she needs to look for in someone. She's a smart girl. I'm sure she'll be fine."

"It's not her that I'm concerned about," Bezalel exclaimed. "I know she's smart. And so are predators that prey on innocent

---

[120] Ephesians 6:4 (TLB)

fifteen-year-olds. There are some questionable people in this camp, and I want her to be safe."

"I do too," I told him plainly. *"But we can't make her stay in this tent day and night. All we can do is teach her right from wrong, which we have, and then keep our eyes open. And most importantly, we need to keep both her and Shemaiah in prayer.*[121] *The Lord can protect them better than we can."*

In the meantime, Mychal arrived at the school. Instead of a building, it was merely rows and rows of tents that were open on all four sides in the middle of the desert. Various subjects were taught at different levels from the lowest to the highest. The mandate for everyone under the age of twenty to be educated was gladly welcomed. It gave the children something constructive to do besides chores to keep their minds from wandering into mischief. Since they were well-supervised by the schoolmasters, their parents knew what they were doing, at least during that half-day block of time.

Mychal enjoyed school. She loved learning new things and getting to know other teenagers her age. Most of all, she liked the cute boy across the room. When she took her seat on the bench next to her girlfriend, she glanced over to see if he was there yet. He was standing up gazing out into the desert with his back facing her. She didn't want him to see her looking at him, but she wasn't fast enough. When he turned around, he caught her before she could look away. But she was glad that he did because he smiled at her and waved. Educationally, that day was a complete waste because Mychal was so smitten by the good-looking boy that she heard nothing the schoolmaster said.

---

[121] Ephesians 6:18 (NLT, TLB)

After class was dismissed, Mychal and her friend went outside and caught up on girl talk. To her total dismay, the nice-looking boy walked up to them and introduced himself.

"Hi, my name is Benjamin," he said confidently, shaking both of their hands. Mychal thought he seemed very sure of himself and maybe even a bit conceited. But that didn't matter. When he told her that he noticed how smart she was in class and that he needed some help with his reading homework, she was only too willing to offer her assistance. Reading was her best subject, and she enjoyed helping other students understand it.

"I could tutor you sometime after class if you need me to," Mychal volunteered.

"Yeah, yeah, that would be great," Benjamin said. "What about this evening after dinner. You can come to our tent, and you can even meet my parents."

Something about going to his tent didn't sit right with her, but she let the thought that his mother and father would be there overrule her concern. She was even flattered that he wanted her to meet them.

"Ok," she agreed, still a bit reluctantly. "Just give me some directions and I'll be there right after dinner."

After he told her how to get there and left, her friend Dalia immediately hit her with a barrage of questions. "What are you doing? Don't you think this is moving kind of fast since you just met him? Are your parents going to let you go to his tent to help him?"

"Stop," Mychal said, interrupting her. "Just stop and listen to me. I'll tell my parents that I'm going to help a friend with their homework and if they ask me who, I'll tell them that it's you." Dalia just stood there and looked at her with her mouth open in disbelief.

"I'm not planning to do anything wrong," Mychal continued. "Plus, his parents are going to be there. This will give me a chance to get to know him and to see what kind of family he comes from," she said, justifying her decision. "So if anybody asks you, I need you to say that I was with you."

"*If you are so sure that what you're doing is alright, why do you feel the need to lie about it?*" Dalia said, trying to reason with her.

"I have to go," Mychal told her abruptly. "Please, just back me up on this." Mychal's friend nodded with reservation before Mychal walked off.

Dinnertime was fun that evening. I prepared everyone's favorite foods. *Bezalel and I always made sure that the family ate at least one meal together every day so that we would remain close. This time was especially important because it gave us an opportunity to take advantage of teachable moments as the children shared the details of their lives.*[122] The four of us laughed and talked and enjoyed each other's company while we ate. Afterward, we played an entertaining Egyptian board game called Senet.

"Mom, Dad," said Mychal as she looked at both of us when the game was over. "We have a reading lesson due tomorrow, and I would like to go over to Dalia's to help her out if it's alright with you?" she asked. "I promise to be back before dark."

Bezalel immediately thought that was odd. He had met Mychal's friend before because *he and I made it our business to*

---

[122] Ephesians 6:4 (TLB)

know who our children spent their time with.[123] But never before had Mychal requested to leave home after dinner without her brother. She knew that she always had permission to spend time with her friends during the day, but that for safety reasons she could only go out in the evening with Shemaiah.

"You couldn't have helped her after school?" Bezalel asked her inquisitively.

"No," she told him. "Remember you gave me some more chores to do so I had to come straight home to finish them. Please, dad. Dalia really needs my help."

"Fine," Bezalel said. "But take your brother with you."

Both Mychal and Shemaiah looked shocked. Since it was still early, she hoped this would not be her father's response. This would totally ruin her plans. And Shemaiah's too. The last thing he wanted to do was spend his free time listening to his sister tutor her friend in Reading.

Mychal looked at me in desperation and gave me that "please don't let him do this to me" look. And it worked. I turned to Bezalel and said imploringly, "Dalia lives right around the corner, and she won't be gone long."

Her father thought about it for a moment. Then because he could never say no to me, he gave in even though it was against his better judgment. "Just be sure that you're back here before dark," he cautioned her before she left.

With the help of a staff, Bezalel walked outside and sat facing the setting sun. He closed his eyes, enjoying its warmth on his face. *He wasn't sure why, but he suddenly felt compelled to pray. This happened to him from time to time. When it did, he always started with his family, asking the Lord to protect us*

---

[123] Proverbs 31:27 (NLT)

from harm and danger and to keep us in the center of His will for our lives. Then he prayed for all of the other Israelites, the foreigners with us, and Moses, our leader.[124]

Meanwhile, like a kid who had just been given her favorite candy, Mychal skipped off, not to Dalia's house as she had told us, but to Benjamin's instead. He met her at the entrance as if he was waiting for her. Seeing him again, she was sure that he was the best looking boy she had ever seen. "You came!" he exclaimed as he ushered her inside.

To her surprise, there was no one else there. She felt naïve as if she had been duped. Seeing the concern on her face and afraid that she would leave, he quickly offered an explanation. "My parents just left. They went to check on my sick grandmother, but they'll be back in a little while." She wasn't sure if she believed his story, but she did want to stay.

They sat at the table across from each other while she explained what the schoolmaster taught that he didn't comprehend. Then she drilled him to be sure that he had understood it, and he had. She thought to herself that he was either a very quick learner, or he didn't really need a tutor anyway. In which case, she wondered if he had some other motive for inviting her.

When the tutoring session was over, he brought his chair over and sat down right next to her. They were so close that their shoulders were touching. He quickly changed the subject from school to her. "You are so smart and so pretty," he told her flatteringly. "I've been watching you since the first day of school." By this time, he was so close that she could feel his breath on her face. And she liked the closeness. She knew by

---

[124] Ephesians 6:18 (NLT, TLB); Philippians 2:13(b) (NIV)

now that something was amiss, but she couldn't bring herself to move. He leaned a little further in and gently kissed her lips. Her mind was saying "leave" but her body was saying "don't." She was afraid that she had stayed too long and passed the point of no return. When he saw that she responded to his kiss, he caressed her thigh. Now she was in an entirely different place, near the point of no return, and open to the idea of whatever might come next. Then out of nowhere, she saw my face in her mind and heard the very words I had spoken to her that morning. I had told her, *"He must understand the importance of sexual purity, both yours and his. Otherwise, he is not the one for you."*

Without hesitation, she pulled herself away from him, pushed back her chair, and headed for the entrance. Benjamin looked startled and disappointed as if his prey had just escaped from his paws. Running the entire way, she arrived home within minutes. There she found her father sitting out in front with his eyes closed. He opened them as he heard her approach, wondering what she was running from. She fell into his lap and burst into tears. He let her cry until she was done before asking her, "You didn't go to Dalia's house, did you?"

"I'm sorry Dad," Mychal confessed, still traumatized by the experience she had just had. "I lied to you and Mom. I went to a boy's house, and he tried to get me to have sex with him. I almost did but then I didn't because I saw Mom's face, and I remembered that she warned me about that this morning."

Bezalel suddenly realized that God had compelled him to pray just in time to keep his daughter from making a grave mistake. He knew, in fact, that he was praying at the very moment she was getting ready to fall. *He reminded himself not to ever ignore the Lord's inner prompting to pray.*

He held her close and said emphatically, "I love you, and I am so proud of you. You were wrong for lying, but you listened to your mother's advice and left before anything happened. Now tell me. *What did you learn from this incident?*"

Mychal thought for a moment before easily recounting what that near-fiasco had taught her. *"I should never lie to you and Mom again. I should never go anywhere I am not supposed to be. I should carefully pick the people I spend my time with because I am more likely to do things I shouldn't do if I hang around the wrong people. And I should not have sex or even get close to it until I am married."*[125]

"That's my girl," Bezalel said. "Before you go I want to tell you something. Even though you didn't help Dalia tonight, I know that you really do like to help people understand things. You like to teach because you are destined to be a teacher. One day you will teach people what God's Word says and how to apply it to their lives. Now go on and go to bed so you won't be tired tomorrow."

After she had gone inside, Bezalel sat quietly, overwhelmed with gratitude. He looked up to heaven and said, "Thank you, Lord. You saved my daughter tonight. You warned me by putting it on my heart to pray, and you pulled my child out of the lion's mouth. You could have taken me home by now, but you haven't. You have given me time to die so that I can put my house in order and make sure that my family is on the right path. *To the faithful, you show yourself faithful, and to the blameless you show yourself blameless.*[126] And I am forever grateful to you."

---

[125] Ephesians 6:1–3 (NLT, TLB)
[126] Psalm 18:25 (NIV)

I had been listening from inside the tent. I heard Bezalel's entire conversation with Mychal but did not interrupt them. *He was teaching her a priceless lesson about forgiveness and unconditional love that a girl needed to learn from her father. This lesson would produce a bountiful harvest in her life by making her a better person, one who forgave others and loved them even if they didn't always do what she wanted or expected.*[127] I also heard his prayer to the Lord and felt exactly what he felt, and would have prayed the same words. I too was glad the Lord had given him time to die, for his sake and ours.

By my seventh month, I was very pregnant and very miserable. I had gained twenty pounds and felt like I was carrying a moving boulder with me everywhere I went. No matter what I did, I just couldn't get comfortable, night or day. My pregnancy was simply a lesson in endurance.

But while I was growing larger, Bezalel was growing smaller. Looking gaunt and skeleton-like, he had lost two pounds for every pound I gained. My physical body was full of life, and his physical body was obviously dying.

It was during this phase of my life that *I reminded myself daily of the words the Lord had spoken to me* when I prayed that I wasn't pregnant. *He said, "My grace is sufficient for you. I am with you, and that is all you need because my power works best when you are weak."*[128] And He had been faithful. There is no other way I could have dealt with being pregnant while raising two children and caring for a dying husband.

And during this phase of his life, *Bezalel was focused on what he knew was most important – spending quality time*

---

[127] Ephesians 4:31–32 (TLB)
[128] 2 Corinthians 12:9(a) (NLT)

with God and spending quality time with his family. He rose early to pray, prayed throughout the day, and went to sleep praying every night. With his imminent departure in mind, his objective was to draw intimately close to the Lord for himself and his family. *He wanted to leave us with God's vision for our future so our time on earth would be spent productively.* So whenever either of his children wanted to talk to him, Bezalel went out his way to be available.

Shemaiah came to him early one morning before he went out to tend the animals. "Dad," he began. "A couple of the sheep seem to be sick. Can you come out and take a look at them?"

"Of course I can, son," Bezalel told him, glad that he had asked. With the help of his staff, he slowly lifted himself out of the chair where he had been sitting in front of the tent. Shemaiah supported him as they walked out back to the pen and entered the gate. Like a true shepherd, Shemaiah was able to quickly make his way through dozens of sheep and find the two that needed help. When he brought them to his father, he inspected them carefully.

"This one's leg is bruised but it's not broken," Bezalel informed him. "It should heal on its own. Just keep an eye on him. And this other one just needs a little salve for his wound. Bring it here, and I'll put it on." Shemaiah got the salve from the tool box in the pen and gave it to his father. He watched him as he meticulously applied it.

Without looking up from the sheep, Bezalel said, "The sheep will be just fine. But how are you doing?" Because Shemaiah was a seasoned shepherd, Bezalel knew that he could have easily addressed those minor ailments. He suspected that Shemaiah called him out there so that he could talk to him without the risk of being interrupted by me or his sister.

"I'm not happy, Dad," Shemaiah told him solemnly, getting straight to the point. "I hate this wilderness, I hate waiting to die, and I hate that I can never marry or be a father. I don't have anything to look forward to. I just want to end this right now."

"End what?" Bezalel asked him as he looked up, obviously alarmed.

"My life," Shemaiah responded sadly. "I just don't want to be here anymore."

Bezalel put the salve down, went over and held his arms out for his son. Shemaiah embraced him tightly, needing comfort at that moment that only his father could give him.

"Son, let's talk," Bezalel said as he led him outside the pen where they sat on the ground. "I am pleased that you felt you could talk to me about this. First of all, *Don't ever let a dangerous thought like that remain in your head.*[129] And second, *sometimes we need to redefine happiness. We have this idea in our minds about what we think will make us happy. When those things don't happen, we tend to become discouraged. The truth is that we may have been looking for happiness in all the wrong places to begin with.* As far as this desert is concerned, none of us like it. God never meant for us to stay here. We were supposed to learn to trust and obey him here, and then move on. This second stint in the wilderness is the price we have to pay for not getting it right the first time. But that doesn't mean we can't turn this wilderness into a place that benefits us if we properly define what happiness is."

Shemaiah gave his father a look of perplexity as though he was speaking a foreign language. So Bezalel tried to state his point better.

---

[129] 2 Corinthians 10:5(b) (NIV)

"Yes, you are going to die, and quite possibly sooner rather than later," he informed him. "No, you will never marry or be a father. If you did, you would only complicate other lives by leaving a widow and a fatherless child behind. *The truth is that not everyone is supposed to marry, and not everyone is supposed to be a biological parent. But everyone is expected to find out what God put them on this earth to do, and find their happiness in that. Then you will have something to look forward to.*"

Shemaiah just sat there, not knowing what to say. He needed some time to absorb this new concept of happiness.

"So Dad are you happy?" Shemaiah asked, wondering if his father had truly redefined his own happiness.

"Yes son, I am," Bezalel responded without hesitation. "I left Egypt with an entirely different set of expectations. I thought we would walk through the wilderness in a few days, go straight into the land of milk and honey, and live there happily ever after as a family. I expected to grow old there with your mother on a nice piece of land and help you and Mychal raise your children. But that all changed after we disobeyed the Lord and He sentenced our generation to die in the desert. Now I am a sick man with only months left to live and a pregnant wife who is carrying a baby that I will not have the pleasure of raising. So I could be discouraged too because my life is not going to turn out the way I planned. But, I have redefined my happiness. *Happiness is seeing my life from God's perspective, which means knowing that earth is only my temporary home. It means understanding that the most important thing is not that I enjoy every minute of my life, but making sure that what I do here positively affects the lives of others forever.* Happiness is God not taking me right away as He has done to thousands of others. Instead, He has given me time to die so I can draw close to Him, and it has been wonderful. *Happiness is being given the time to teach each of you how to obey Him and find Him for yourselves. Happiness is having Him tell me what His purpose is for each person in our family, and making sure you are all on the right path* before I die. *Happiness is knowing that my God is faithful to keep you on that path and protect each of you* after He calls me to be with Him. *Happiness is being confident that one day I will see you all again.* That, my son, is happiness."

Shemaiah smiled as though a light had just come on in his head. "I get it Dad," Shemaiah acknowledged. "Now I just need to figure out what my purpose is and what happiness is for me."

"Ok, let's *start with what you like doing and what you're good at*," Bezalel began, encouraging Shemaiah to discover for himself what the Lord had already conveyed to his father.

"Well, I like coaching the little boys stickball team," Shemaiah told him. "Not just because I like the game. I like being with them, and they like me too. Most of their fathers are already dead, and they treat me like I'm their father."

"I noticed that when I've come to your games," Bezalel stated. "You have real compassion for those kids. They can tell that you care about them, and they look up to you. *With so many of them fatherless, you could become a mentor to them. You could do the things for them that fathers do like take them places, teach them right from wrong, and just listen to them. You would be helping them and their mothers, who are doing the best they can but desperately need father figures for their boys.* And while you are helping other mothers raise their sons, you will take my place and become a father to your brother. This, my son, is your purpose."

When their father-son talk ended, Shemaiah had a new perspective on life. *He understood that it was not just about him, but also about what he was destined to contribute to the lives of others.*

The next few months were a real test of faith. Bezalel was rapidly dying, and I was being stretched beyond my limit. Totally bedridden, he was unable to do anything for himself. He didn't have the strength to get up and go to the latrine, bathe, or even lift a spoon to his mouth. So I did for him what I would later do for our newborn infant. Because he weighed as much as I did, lifting him was very difficult. But somehow, I diapered, changed, washed, and fed him. Though the children could help me feed him, they were unable to do more because it was immoral for them to see their father's nakedness. Lying next to him at night, I rarely slept because I constantly listened for his cry for help. The burden of taking care of him during his final days had fallen almost entirely on me.

But I wasn't the only one under tremendous strain. Bezalel, too, felt that he could take no more. His pain was unbearable and never-ending. He hurt whenever I touched him, turned him, changed him, or moved him. His body smelled like that of a dying man and the noxious odor only added to his misery. All he could do was lie there and pray. Confident that he had achieved his purpose for this life, he was ready to leave. However, his final request was that the Lord would keep him alive long enough to see the face of his legacy.

My friend Ayana had been with me through the entire ordeal. When I needed to vent, she listened. When I needed to cry, she cried with me. She came by frequently to support me and help out in any way she could. And then it was time for her to leave.

One day Ayana brought me some news that made me both elated and disappointed. God had confirmed to both her and Jethro that He approved of their marriage. Jethro was coming for her, and she would be leaving soon. I knew that I would never see Ayana again this side of eternity. I would miss her friendship but wished her a long, happy life. This time it was my turn to laugh and cry with her.

The day before Ayana left, the children and I attended the fabulous wedding that Moses and Zipporah threw for her and Jethro. Many people were there because Ayana had scores of friends and Jethro brought a large entourage with him. The bride and groom were radiant while Moses performed the ceremony. Watching the couple reminded me of the bliss that I felt on my wedding day. When the fanfare died down, I bid them a heartfelt farewell before they left.

As time wore on, I knew that the baby could come at any moment. I wondered how on earth I would keep up with the demands of a newborn and Bezalel too. The strain of taking care of him was killing me physically and watching him die was killing me emotionally. Completely drained, at my wits end, and unable to do anymore, I prayed more than I had ever prayed in my life. I even found myself asking for something I thought I would never request. I asked the Lord to take Bezalel home to be with Him. And then a peace came over me.

The next twenty-four hours transpired as if they were orchestrated from above. Bezalel mustered the strength to sit up, and the children went in and sat with him. He blessed them and admonished them to fully obey the Lord and carefully keep all of His commands so they would be successful everywhere they went and in everything they did. I then sat next to him and put his hand on my stomach. In spite of his pain, feeling the movement of the baby made him smile, which warmed my heart.

Bezalel took advantage of that special moment and shared with me one last thing that God had spoken to him earlier while he was praying. "You have been put on this earth not just to find the Lord for yourself but to show others the way to Him," he told me as he watched my face for a response.

My smile lit up the room. "Those were the same words He used when He told me," I said, pleased that the Lord had used my husband to give me the confirmation I needed.

Then all of a sudden, a labor pain tore through my body, knocking me to my knees. While the children ran to get the midwife, the contractions kept coming. When she arrived with the birthing stool, they remained outside, eagerly awaiting the new addition to our family. The midwife helped me onto the stool while Bezalel watched. I was not in labor long. Within minutes, the new baby was born. After washing him off and wrapping him in a soft linen blanket, the midwife handed him to Bezalel, who kissed him gently on the forehead and spoke to him. "You will be called Nathaniel which means "God gave," because God has given me an heir to continue my name on this earth. May He bless you and make you a blessing to others." Then Bezalel closed his eyes for the last time. Within twenty-four hours from the time I asked the Lord to take him, Bezalel was gone.

After we buried him, *I reflected on what I learned from that experience. I realized that the Lord used the pain* of a dying husband and an unwanted pregnancy *to cause me to seek Him so He could prove that He is faithful in every way. He proved that He is always there in the time of need and provides His strength when mine runs out. He proved that He cared* enough *about my family* to give my husband time to die so he could prepare us for the future before his departure. *He proved that He loved me* by taking Bezalel to be with Him when I couldn't take anymore. *Above all else, I learned that it is during the dark and difficult times that God best proves His trustworthiness and draws us close to Him.*

CHAPTER 18

NOT GONNA TAKE IT ANYMORE

Unlike my family, not everyone had made peace with the inevitability of the wilderness. Some just hated and endured it. Others, like Ahira and Eliab, decided to pursue other options because they had simply reached the end of their rope.

Their father Ammiel was one of the twelve men who went in to explore the land of Canaan over two years ago. He was also one of the ten men who came back and spread a bad report about the land, causing all the others to doubt God and lose their inheritance. Their father, a widower, was one of the first to be killed. His death left them distraught and directionless. Awaiting their own deaths, they felt like men caught between two bad worlds. One was that barren, lifeless wilderness full of dying, misery, and nothingness. The other was eternity in Sheol, a dark place they'd only heard about that held even less promise.

Restless by nature, the desert proved not to be a suitable place for the twenty-four-year-old twins. They found the laws, rules, regulations, and structure of the camp to be too restrictive. Accustomed to sleeping until noon, they preferred to steal food from others instead of getting up early to gather manna. Always in search of some desperate, weak-willed woman to meet their sexual needs, the Ten Commandments were of no interest to them. Preferring to keep their best animals for themselves, they had no intention of sacrificing them to the Lord or to anyone else for that matter. And waiting for the cloud to move before they could move just wasn't working for them.

Everyone in the camp knew about the two wayward young men. They played stickball on Bezalel's adult team and a mean game of it at that. The people tolerated them only because the camp loved a good ball game, and the twins usually led their team to victory. This sport was the only thing in their lives that gave them any real satisfaction and relief from their hopelessness.

One evening while still on the field after a winning game, Eliab decided to share an idea with his brother that he had been pondering. "Why are we hanging around in this desert waiting to die?" Eliab asked, as though only the foolish were still there.

"What do you mean?" Ahira responded with suspicion. "You're not thinking about leaving here are you? You know I know you like the back of my hand."

"That's exactly what I'm thinking," Eliab told him frankly. "Almost all of our friends have already died. We can stay here, be miserable, and wait for death, or we can go to Canaan and enjoy that land of milk and honey. Do you remember how Dad described it to us before God killed him? He said it was everything he thought it would be and more. So what do you think? Are you with me or not?"

"Not without a good plan," Ahira fired back, knowing firsthand how impetuous his older brother could be. "Canaan is over a hundred miles from here across nothing but desert. The manna we would need for food does not fall outside of our camp. The rock here is the only source of water from here to Canaan. Without that cloud to cover us, the days will be too hot and the nights too cold. And I know you think you can fight, but if some bandits decide to attack us we could have a problem."

"Come on brother, you know me," Eliab said. "Have I ever started anything I couldn't finish? I already planned the whole thing out. Just listen."

In spite of the fact that they were alone, Ahira leaned in closer as if he were about to hear a secret. He knew he needed to understand every step of this plan to be sure he didn't follow his brother into a hole, as he had done more times than he could count.

As Ahira listened, Eliab explained in detail how they would get to the Promised Land. It would take approximately one week to complete the journey if they walked twenty miles a day. For food, they would slaughter an animal, cook the meat, and ration it into equal portions. They would carry water in wineskins, and bring what they needed to defend themselves if need be. The route was an easy one to remember as it was the same one they had taken the first time they were headed for Canaan. The plan sounded thorough enough to Ahira that he was ready to go.

Eager to put some real distance between themselves and that horrid camp, the twins started prepping for their journey that very day. They roasted a stolen animal and begged some skins for water off their neighbors and filled them. Finally, they gathered the weapons they were most skilled at using.

The two of them packed everything carefully, including their sleeping mats, a change of clothes, and some gold, and divided the load between them.

As soon as the camp settled down for the night, they set out. Once they walked far enough to be out from under the cloud of fire, the moon lit up the desert. Its light was pleasant, and they took it as a sign that their journey would be blessed.

The first night was uneventful. A large caravan of men riding camels laden with goods to sell in Egypt strode by them. Like strangers headed in opposite directions, neither of them acknowledged the other. They kept walking and later came across a shepherd watching over a flock of sheep. When they were too exhausted to go any further, they laid down and slept for hours before going on.

Their luck ran out the second night. Asleep on his mat on the ground, Eliab thought he heard a noise that was atypical of the normal night sounds of the desert. Without opening his eyes, he undetectably moved his hand over and touched his brother. Ahira instinctively knew what that meant. They both opened their eyes in time to see four men approaching them. Quickly rolling onto their feet, they pulled their knives out of their scabbards and assumed a fighting stance. Even when caught off guard, they were adept at defending themselves.

The four men ran towards them, clearly intent on inflicting some damage. But they were no match for the twins who were skilled at fighting as a team. Within a few minutes of sparring, it was evident that the four had picked the wrong two men to attack. The twins toyed with them at first and then mercilessly killed them and stripped them of their valuables. Alive and unhurt, they assumed that this too was a sign that their journey would be blessed.

They made good time over the next few days and arrived in Canaan according to schedule. The land was magnificent, just as their father had described it. They saw the same bountiful crops, clear, flowing streams, beautiful walled cities, and affluence that he saw. They also saw those giant-sized people, the Nephilim, carefully observing them. But they were determined not to be afraid, surmising that they were only staring at them because they knew from their appearance that they were from somewhere else.

At first they wondered why they hadn't done this sooner. How foolish they had been to stay in that vile desert waiting to die when they could have come back here a long time ago. The fact that they had arrived there unscathed must have meant that either the Lord had not seen them leave, or He did not care that they left. It was quite conceivable to them that He had his hands full just dealing with those millions of wayward Israelites.

Once inside the large metropolitan city of Hebron, their first order of business was to find somewhere to stay. They came to a lovely, posh inn and went inside to rent a room. Eliab took out some gold and placed it on the wooden registration desk. Then he said, "We would like to rent a room for the week, with a view of the courtyard, if you have one available."

The innkeeper looked at Eliab's hand in fear and shook his head from side to side to tell him "no." Baffled by the man's response, Eliab looked down at his hand and saw that it was white with leprosy. He gasped in horror, wondering where it came from and why he hadn't noticed it until then. Ahira too was speechless, thinking about the implications of his brother having the worst disease on earth. Then he remembered something the Lord had told Moses to tell them. He said that if they would carefully obey Him, He would not inflict any of the diseases on them that He inflicted on the Egyptians; that He would heal them instead. But they had done the opposite and disobeyed. He suspected that was the reason his brother had leprosy. No sooner than he completed that thought, Ahira looked down and saw the disease on his own hands. The twins looked at each other, both convinced that this was not a mere coincidence, but God's judgment. And the innkeeper was equally as certain.

Running from behind the desk and out into the middle of the street, the innkeeper waved his hands and shouted, "Unclean, unclean! The two men inside are unclean!"

The people poured into the streets from the shops and houses, some carrying long sticks. Ahira and Eliab were alarmed, wondering what the people were getting ready to do. They didn't have to wonder long because the innkeeper led the crowd inside. They surrounded the twins and prodded them with the sticks until they moved out of the inn and into the street. They thought of trying to defend themselves but knew that would only make matters worse, as they were badly outnumbered.

"Who are you?" the people shouted loudly as they shook their sticks at them. "How dare you bring this sickness into our city? Who are you and why are you here? If you lie to us, we will kill you and leave your dead bodies here in the street."

Ahira and Eliab were petrified. If they told a lie, they might get caught in it, and if they told the truth it could be worse. As they were wondering what to do, the size of the mob grew rapidly. An official looking man pushed forward from the back of the crowd, spoke briefly to the innkeeper, and then demanded silence. The twins figured that he must have been important because the noise stopped immediately, and the people turned their eyes to the man.

"I am the chief magistrate of Hebron, and it's my job to keep order here," the man began, establishing his authority. "We don't have any lepers in this city and we don't want any. Now I'm going to ask you one time and one time only. Who are you and what are you doing here?"

There was no doubt in the twin's minds that he meant "one time only." Though quiet, the people in the crowd looked like rabid dogs, ready and eager to attack at the first signal. Hoping to save their lives, Ahira spoke up out of sheer fear.

"We are Israelites," he told the mayor. "Our people are camped in the desert and we just came here to get away for a little while." It was the truth, just not the part about how long they planned to be gone.

The magistrate thought about it for a moment before responding. "I know exactly who you are. Your people came here from Egypt some time ago and spied out our land because you were planning to take it. Then something happened, you messed up with your God, and He sent you back out into the desert to die. Isn't that the truth? Don't lie to me."

"Yes, yes, that's what happened," Eliab admitted reluctantly. "But we did not come here to spy on you or take anything. We just came here to get out of that desert and live in peace."

"Well you lepers are not going to live here!" he snarled at them. For one, we know what that disease can do to a community. Our citizens are clean, and we plan to keep it that way. And the way that leprosy showed up on both of you all of a sudden means that your God is trying to tell you something. We've heard about what He did to those Egyptians and what He did to you all. And we don't want His judgment to come down on us because of you. So you need to take your stuff and get out of here."

Ahira and Eliab didn't have to be told to leave twice. Grateful that they weren't killed or skinned alive, they gathered their belongings and headed for the city gate under the watchful eyes of the magistrate and the townspeople. They had no food, but too scared to ask if they could buy any before they left, they chose to take their chances with the desert. In preparation for the long journey ahead, all they could do on their way out of town was fill their empty skins with water from a nearby stream.

"So now what?" Ahira asked his brother as they prodded along in the desert heat. "They'll probably find some reason to stone us if we go back home. If nothing else, they'll make us live outside the camp with the other lepers. So it makes no sense for us to go back there."

"Who said anything about going back?" Eliab asked, more as a statement than a question. "Canaan is not the only country over here. We could go to Moab or Edom or even Midian."

"Which one is the closest?" Ahira inquired. "I'm not up for another long trip on foot.

"Edom is the closest," Eliab told him. "And I've heard good things about the place. "It's got some of the best looking women on earth. So what do you say? Should we try Edom next?"

"Edom is as good a choice as any," Ahira said, so thrilled to be alive that he didn't much care where they went. "We just need to get somewhere soon so we can find some food. If we only drink what we need, our water should last a few days. We will also need to wear our gloves to hide this leprosy so we won't get run out of there too." In the meantime, they cooked and ate whatever animals they found dead in the desert.

Several days after leaving Hebron they finally saw other human life. A caravan of camels was approaching from the distance. Waving their arms wildly, they got the attention of the leader. When he stopped, those behind him followed suit. Eliab walked up close to the man who looked down at him with curiosity from the height of the camel.

"Good evening, friend," Eliab said to him, hoping to seem friendly enough that they would want to help them. "We are on our way to Edom and we could use some food and a ride. We have the money to pay you."

The man motioned to another man on a camel, and he quickly came over to him. They spoke a few words and the other one went to the back of the caravan and brought a camel with a light load but no rider.

"We are going all the way to Midian but you can come with us as far as Edom," the man told him. "Both of you can ride on this extra camel. Help yourselves to the skin of water and dried meat in the pouch on his side. You can pay me when we get there." Eliab was relieved that the man didn't ask them to pay right then because he dreaded having to remove his gloves. If the people in the caravan were going to find out that they were lepers, it needed to be after they got to Edom, not before.

With the help of the other man, they climbed on the camel. Never having ridden one before, they weren't accustomed to its jerky movements. If they didn't know better, they would have thought that the beast was trying to throw them to the ground. But they endured the unpleasant ride because it was better than walking.

Hours later the caravan stopped for the night. One of the camel drivers came over and made the twin's camel kneel so that they could climb down. The first order of business for everyone was bodily relief. They all went off in separate directions to do what they needed to do.

Ahira and Eliab were within a few yards of each other. When they removed their gloves to free their hands, they were both terrified. In the short time since they joined the caravan, their fingers had become severely deformed and were gnarled down to the first knuckle. Their fingertips and fingernails were completely gone. They both immediately remembered the words the mayor of Hebron spoke to them when he said, "your God is trying to tell you something." While looking over his shoulder to be sure that no one else was coming, Eliab hurriedly put his gloves back on and ran to his brother.

"Let me see your hands," Eliab demanded in a whisper. Still dazed, Ahira held out his hands to let Eliab inspect them. Eliab carefully looked over every inch of them on both sides. Then he took his gloves off and did the same to his own.

"Do you know what this means?" Eliab asked, angry that their plans for a new life had been ruined. "We've seen leprosy before. We saw it all the time in Egypt and the camp. It does not progress this quickly."

"No, it doesn't, Ahira responded with a blank look on his face. Then he turned and stared directly at his brother and continued. *"This is a warning from the Lord. He saw us leave, and He has been watching us ever since.*[130] *We should know that we are in dangerous territory, dead and lost when we are out from under the cloud of His will.*[131] If we don't get back to the camp, this leprosy is going to eat us up. We're lucky He hasn't killed us yet."

---

[130] Psalm 33:13–14 (NIV)
[131] Luke 15:11–32 (NIV) especially 24(a), 32(b)

"Now wait a minute." Eliab began, not ready to entertain the idea of returning to the life he hoped he would never see again. "The Lord is merciful. He understands that we are only human, and we need to enjoy ourselves sometimes. If we pray, He'll forgive us and heal us from this leprosy so we can get on with our lives."

Appalled at what he had just heard, Ahira retorted, *"Stop it. You are deluding yourself. You want to believe that God understands your sin and looks the other way so you can feel comfortable remaining in it. But it isn't true.*[132] Just think about what you've already seen Him do. He warned Pharaoh many times, and when he refused to obey Him, God utterly destroyed his country. When we left Egypt and came into the desert the first time, the Lord warned us to stop disobeying and doubting Him, but we didn't. Therefore, He killed our father along with nine other men. Then He sentenced us back into the desert where He is still killing off all the men of our generation. *He does punish disobedience. It's time for us to stop fooling ourselves and take Him seriously."*[133]

For the first time in his life, Eliab was remorseful. He knew what he had to do. First, he reached into the inner pocket of his cloak and pulled out a small wooden idol covered with gold. He gazed at it, wondering how he could ever have thought it could help him. It had eyes but could not see, ears but could not hear, a nose but could not breathe, a mouth but could not speak, and hands but could do nothing. It was a worthless man-made object that had no life or power. With no regret, he threw it on the ground and stomped it with his foot.

---

[132] James 1:21–22 (AMP, NIV)
[133] Galatians 6:7–8 (NIV, AMP, NLT)

"Does this mean we're going back to the camp?" Ahira asked, smiling.

"Yes, we're going home," Eliab said, knowing beyond a doubt that he was making the right decision. *"The Lord is fair. However He chooses to punish us* for leaving, *we deserve it.* We were men enough to walk away, so we need to be men enough to go back and face the music. Let's stay here tonight and head out first thing in the morning."

They rose early just as the men in the caravan were stirring about. Eliab paid the leader for the use of their camel while they were with them and for food and water for their journey. Then they set out on foot.

With a new perspective, the things they discussed on the way home were entirely different than the ones they talked about when they left. No longer preoccupied with getting their needs met by whatever means necessary, their conversation turned to what lessons they had learned and how much better their lives would be once they started doing what they were supposed to do.

"Remember those Ten Commandments that Moses read to us that day?" Ahira asked.

"I remember being there that day but I wasn't listening," Eliab responded honestly.

"Well, I was listening," Ahira began, as though getting ready to share something he had been seriously thinking about. *"I didn't want to hear it because I was doing everything the commandments said not to do. And I did not want to give any of those things up. But now that I think about it, none of that bad behavior was worth it. I always had an empty feeling inside of me, I had a bad reputation, and nothing I ever tried worked out like I wanted it to. I just thought I was getting away with sinning against the Lord, but I wasn't. He was watching me the whole time and waiting for me to come to my senses and give up my meaningless life so He could make it worthwhile."*

"When did you figure all this out?" Eliab asked, thinking that he had never seen this side of his brother before.

"When that leprosy came down on us all of a sudden in Hebron but we got out of there alive!" Ahira exclaimed. "Then we kept going the wrong way, and the leprosy got worse. That's when I realized that the Lord could have killed us to punish us for running off and for all our other wickedness. But instead He afflicted us just enough to get our attention and to drive us back to Him. Only a good and merciful God would do something like that."[134]

"I believe you," Eliab said. "I don't know how much longer the Lord is going to let me live, but I'm going to spend the rest of my life walking with Him.

After what seemed like a journey that would never end, they finally saw the camp in the distance. It was near sundown, and some of the shepherds were out letting the sheep graze. Before Ahira and Eliab could get close enough to recognize anyone, Shemaiah recognized them. He left the sheep and ran to welcome them.

"I knew you'd be back," Shemaiah said assuredly, as if they were best friends. "I just knew it." Ahira and Eliab were surprised to receive such a warm welcome because they thought that everyone in the camp hated them.

"We're glad to be back," they said, meaning every word of it.

"So has our team been winning since we left?" Eliab asked, quickly changing the subject before Shemaiah asked them any

---

[134] Hosea 6:1–2 (AMP, TLB); Psalm 119:75 (TLB)

embarrassing questions about where they had been. They had decided to change their ways, but they still wanted to reserve the right to discuss what they had been through in their own time.

Discerning their wishes, Shemaiah didn't press them but merely said, "We've won every game. But we can talk about that later. Let's take you back to your tent so you can get some rest."

When they got there, the twins were surprised to find that it was still standing and that their neighbors hadn't torn it down. They also noticed that it was neat and organized as though someone thought they were coming back and kept it for them. And whoever it was had even been looking after those sheep they had refused to sacrifice to the Lord.

Shemaiah couldn't wait to tell me that Ahira and Eliab were back. We had prayed for them daily since the evening Shemaiah saw them take off across the desert in rebellion. Because of the pain we experienced from Bezalel's long illness and death, my family vowed to do whatever we could to alleviate the discomfort of anyone in need. We were also determined to help restore their fellowship with the Lord.

When I heard the good news, I packed some leftover dinner and dessert and took it to the twins while Shemaiah watched the baby. They had previously only known me as the mother of one of their stickball teammates. But they readily welcomed me because I gave them a sense of belonging they hadn't felt before. While they ate, I talked to them as though they were my own sons. I encouraged them to take the next step and go to the Tabernacle with their best offering so they could worship and draw near to the Lord.

I never told them it was I who took care of their tent while Shemaiah cared for their animals. All they needed to know

was that *God worked through others to show them that He loved them.*

They followed my advice and early the next morning, after gathering manna for the first time, they went before the Lord with their best sacrifice. *They praised Him and thanked Him for forgiving them and for using their painful circumstances to lead them to Himself.*

When they showed their leprous hands to the priests at the Tabernacle, they had them quarantined separately outside the camp, according to the Lord's laws. In their loneliness and solitude, they prayed as never before. God healed their disfiguring disease and gave them back the hands of their youth. At the end of their period of separation, they came out of confinement with a new agenda and purpose.

Addressing the entire community, they confessed their crimes and offenses and asked for forgiveness. They made restitution and compensated their neighbors for everything they had taken from them. When the people saw that they were changed men, they welcomed them back into the fellowship of the community. And *out of gratitude to the Lord for the love and mercy He bestowed upon them, they committed themselves to teaching other young men His ways.*[135]

---

[135] Psalm 51:12–13 (TLB)

CHAPTER 19

A DESPERATE ATTEMPT

It was a magnificent morning. The sky was a rich, crystal blue, and not a cloud was in sight. Warm inviting air from the plain blew over the balcony and into the king's chamber stirring him from his slumber.

Balak opened his eyes and lay there, thinking of all the items that were on his agenda for the day. A meeting with the commander of his army to discuss Moab's military readiness was first on the list. He knew that no country was ever completely safe from attack. A foreign nation, any foreign nation, could come in over the plain at any time and go to war with him for his land. In fact, the Moabite king that preceded him warred with the Amorites and lost a good share of their territory. And he didn't want any more of it to be lost on his watch.

A soft, coded knock on the door signaled that his bath was ready. "Come in," he said, knowing that it was his private servants who took care of all of his personal needs. As he got up, one of them carried a fresh chamber pot that he exchanged with the one located behind an elegant curtain. The other one wheeled in a large wooden bathtub filled with steaming water.

"What royal robe would his majesty like to wear today?" one of them asked him as the other began to make his bed. "I don't care. You pick something," he told him. He knew that all of his robes were kingly. Not only that, but what he wore that day was the least of his concerns.

His scouts and spies had been keeping him informed about a large group of people who had miraculously come out of Egypt years ago. According to the story, their God had destroyed Egypt in the process. They spent two years in the wilderness on their way to conquer a nearby land called Canaan. But when God gave them an opportunity to trust Him to give them that land, they didn't. So He sent them back into the wilderness to stay until every male twenty and over died off. And die they did – already by the hundreds of thousands. But they were reproducing and replenishing their numbers just as quickly, and those who had been under twenty were growing older. Their young, new army was being trained daily in preparation for the time when they would be ready to go back and take Canaan and any other nation along the way. So Balak knew he needed to be prepared in case they set their sights on Moab.

Balak snapped out of his reverie and began his morning routine. Even though the hot water in the tub felt splendid, and he wanted to linger there, he bathed and dressed quickly. He viewed his reflection in the full-length mirror and as usual, was pleased with the distinguished look that he saw. It was obvious why the ladies loved him.

When he got to the dining room, Hasan, the commander of his army and his military council were already there, prompt as usual. Hasan was a dependable man, and he liked that about him. Methodical by nature, he carefully weighed every decision along with its pros and cons. Those from whom Hasan took advice were equally as wise, discerning every possibility for victory. He did not manage the army from afar. A rugged man, he had no fear of blood but enjoyed the thrill of an engaging battle.

He greeted the king, bowing before him as he approached, as did the others. Once seated, they began to discuss the issue at hand. They would eat later as the king could think better on an empty stomach.

"What news do you have for me?" Balak asked Hasan, eager to know what threat he might be facing.

Hasan was candid. "The Israelites captured all the cities of the Amorites, who live near us, and occupied them, including Heshbon and all the settlements that surround it. Then they turned and went up along the road towards Bashan where they killed the king, his whole army and all of the people. They left no survivors, and they took possession of their land. They are moving towards us and could be here in a few weeks."

Balak was terror-stricken but tried not to let his face give him away. His attempt to hide his fear was of no use as he could see in their faces that they knew he was afraid.

Hasan spoke quickly in an effort to reassure the king. "Our army is larger, well-trained, and ready to meet them. We should catch them by surprise and ambush them somewhere while they are on the way here. If we wait until they get here, we will lose the advantage."

Balak carefully considered what Hasan had just told him. Under ordinary circumstances, he may have been right but this was different.

"You are right. It would be best for us to catch them off guard and destroy them along the way. But we can't be sure that will work. The Amorites used that very same tactic, and they were still wiped out. We need to be realistic. If an army as powerful as theirs could not beat them, we have no reason to believe we can defeat them, no matter how prepared we are. I have another idea. We need to get someone to put a curse on them. If they have sinned against their God in some way, the curse will defeat them."

Hasan and his military advisers were speechless. They had never heard of such a thing. They were developers of military strategies and warriors. Sometimes their approach was wrong. The king of the Amorites had taken half their territory when they served Moab's former king. But sometimes they were right. They fought hard and were able to keep half of their land. But right or wrong, all they knew was traditional warfare.

Hasan tactfully broke their silent stupor, knowing that it would be fruitless to contradict the king. "Your highness, we are at your service," he said as he bowed. "What would you have us to do?"

"There is a man named Balaam who lives north in the city of Pethor on the Euphrates River. He calls himself a prophet of I Am, but he works both sides of the fence. For the right amount of money, he will do the devil's bidding and curse anyone he is paid to curse. I know this for a fact because I have used his services before." Unbeknownst to all of them, Balak had hired Balaam to curse the former king of Moab so that Balak could take over his kingdom. And it worked.

"But your highness, won't we bring a curse on ourselves by cursing someone else?" asked Hasan.

"No, you won't. You and your men will be faultless because you are just following my orders," Balak assured them.

"But what about you? Won't you be bringing a curse on yourself?" one of the advisors who had been silent asked, out of genuine concern for the king.

"I will cross that bridge when I come to it. Right now I need to do what I need to do to save all of our lives," replied Balak, comfortably justifying his sin. They all suspected that the life he most wanted to save was his own. "You are to leave immediately to find Balaam and bring him here. Take with you two bags of gold which is double the fee for divination. He's a greedy, heartless pig who would kill his mother for the right price." Balak then pretended to spit on the ground to show the disdain he felt for Balaam.

After leaving Balak's presence, Hasan and some of the other members of the military council summoned the best guide. Then they packed the supplies they would need for the journey and went in search of the Balaam, the man the king hoped would save his country.

When they arrived, they found that Pethor was a booming metropolis, more modern and progressive than most of the other cities in Mesopotamia. Their guide was the only one in the group who had been there before. The others had only heard tales of this city. Oddly enough, it was not far from Ur. Ur was the city from which God had called Abraham, the ancestor of the very Israelites Balak was hoping to have Balaam curse.

Once they entered the gates and were well into the city, the guide asked two different shop owners who were located some distance from each other where he could find Balaam, son of Beor. Apparently he was well known in the city as both of them told him that he could be found in the temple of Baal in the center of town.

Not long afterward, they arrived at the colossal, imposing structure that made their temple in Moab look small and insignificant. They each secretly wondered if this meant that the god of this temple was bigger and more powerful than their own. They circled the structure twice, looking for an entrance. When they found one, the guide moved into the background and Hasan, the negotiator, took over. He got off his camel, walked up to the intricately carved door and knocked.

After what seemed like an eternity, a shadowy figure of a man in what looked like priestly attire opened the door and suspiciously asked, "Who are you looking for?" It was obvious from his demeanor and tone of voice that seldom did anyone other than priests come there and only then when they urgently needed to get in touch with one of the temple servants.

"I'm looking for Balaam, son of Beor," he told him.

"I am Balaam, son of Beor. And who are you?" the man responded, again with suspicion.

Hasan tried to hide his surprise. He had heard about this so-called prophet who allegedly heard from and spoke for the God of the Israelites, but would turn around and curse anyone for the right price. This man had taken low to a new high. He was a priest for Baal, the god of Pethor and a prophet of the God of the Israelites at the same time. He couldn't possibly have had any real fear of or regard for either god. Even Hasan knew that a wise man picks one god and stays with him because gods are like men. They don't like it when one claims to be committed to them yet shares their affection with another.

"My name is Hasan from Moab. Balak, the king of Moab, has sent me to you to tell you this – 'A large group of people came out of Egypt not long ago and they are taking over all the countries around me. I want you to come and put a curse on them because I know they are too powerful for us. Then I will be able to defeat them and drive them out of the land. I know for certain that whoever you bless is blessed, and whoever you curse is cursed.'"

Hasan then held out the bags of gold with which he hoped to entice Balaam. Balaam pondered the request for a moment, remembering all the things he was able to buy the last time Balak had generously compensated him. Then Balaam gave an answer that did not surprise Hasan at all.

"Let me go and ask the Lord what He wants me to do," he said as he greedily eyed the bags of gold. "You and the men who must have come with you can spend the night in the city, and I will give you God's answer in the morning."

Hasan knew well what that meant. *A man should know his God well enough to know the answer to some questions without even asking.* It was obvious that *Balaam wanted to ask God under the pretense that he wanted an answer. But he was hoping that God wouldn't say anything so he could do what he wanted to do* – to curse the people and take the money.

"We'll come back at dawn. If your God says "yes," be prepared to leave with us right away," Hasan said as he played along with Balaam's game.

Balaam was just about to close the door behind him then turned abruptly and said to Hasan, "How much money did you bring with you in those bags? You know that my services are expensive."

Hasan, who was halfway down the steps, smiled to himself and turned to Balaam and said, "Balak sent double your usual fee for divination. If you decide to assist us, you will get the money when you finish the job."

The very thought of that much gold made Balaam's sinister face beam with glee. "Good, good. Until tomorrow then," he said hungrily. Then he closed the door.

Balaam's reaction only confirmed what Hasan had already surmised about him. For the right amount of money, there was nothing he wouldn't do. He didn't even have to negotiate with the greedy degenerate. The gold did the talking.

Once inside, Balaam went to his room and mused as he sat by the window looking out over the city. The fee for divination was sizable and could definitely improve the quality of his life. But double the fee could totally change his life. He was tired of being a poor prophet. In fact, he hated it. That was why he became a priest for Baal, the god of Pethor. He deserved to live well and needed resources to do so. Plus, the pretty women liked men who could take care of them and buy them nice things. And he was partial to pretty women. So he decided that he would go with them first thing in the morning.

Knowing that Balaam had definitively made up his mind without consulting Him, God spoke to Balaam and said, "Who was that man that just came to see you?"

Balaam replied, "Balak the king of Moab is worried because the Israelites are camped near his country. He is afraid that they will attack and conquer it. So he sent those men to have me come to Moab and put a curse on the Israelites. He hopes that after they have been cursed he can defeat them."

But God said to Balaam, "I have blessed those people, so you are not allowed to put a curse on them. You are to go with those men tomorrow but when you get to Moab, only say what I tell you to say."

Balaam got up in the morning and saddled his donkey. Then he and some of his men went with the Moabite officials.

When Balak heard that Balaam was on his way, he went out to the edge of his territory to meet him. Balak smiled as Balaam got off his donkey and walked up to him. "I am so glad you decided to come, my dear friend," Balak said to Balaam as he shook his hand and patted him on the back. His disdain for Balaam had not waned even a little bit, but he knew that being pleasant would increase the odds that he would get what he wanted.

"I am at your service," Balaam replied, wondering how he was going to get his hands on the money without cursing the people as he was summoned to do. "I have to tell you though that I can't say whatever I want to say. The only words I can speak are the words that the Lord puts in my mouth."

"Good, good," Balak said, not really listening. "Let's get on with what you came for."

Balak took Balaam to the top of a nearby mountain so he could see the outskirts of the Israelite camp and understand the severity of the problem.

"My scouts have been keeping an eye on them," Balak told Balaam. "They showed up over there a few days ago. Any minute now they could attack us and kill us all. So go ahead and do what you came here to do."

Balaam closed his eyes and stood perfectly still as though he were listening to God's voice. Balak and his officials watched him with their eyes open, convinced that he was not one to be trusted. In the back of Balak's mind was the thought that he didn't want that vile Balaam to stay in his presence or even in his country one second longer than necessary.

When Balaam opened his eyes, he looked as though he was in a trance. In a loud, clear voice he said, "These are the prophetic words of Balaam, son of Beor. My eyes see clearly, I hear the very words of God, and I have been given this vision from the Almighty:

Balak brought me from Pethor,
the Moabite king from the eastern mountains.
'Come and curse the Israelites,' he said.
'Come and condemn them for me.'
But how can I curse
those God has not cursed?
Because the Lord, their God, is with them,
no curse can touch Israel.
Nor does any sorcery
have any power over them.
God brought them out of the land of Egypt.
He gave them the strength of a wild ox.
They devour every nation that opposes them
and break their bones in pieces.
They will soon become a nation.
Their kingdom will be exalted.
Now it will be said of Israel
'See what their God has done for them!'
Those who bless Israel be blessed,
And those who curse Israel be cursed."

When Balaam finished speaking, Balak and his officials looked at each other, astounded. They knew they were right in thinking that Balaam couldn't be trusted. Balak said angrily, "What have you done? I brought you here to curse my enemies, but all you've done is bless them. Even if you couldn't curse them, you shouldn't have blessed them. It would have been better if you hadn't said anything at all!"

Balaam answered, "Didn't I tell you that I have to do whatever the Lord tells me to do. Must I not speak the words the Lord puts in my mouth? He gave me a command to bless them. They have been blessed, and I cannot do anything to change it."

At that very moment, Balak wanted with all his heart to kill Balaam. His official's expressions told him they were all on the same page and would be more than happy to let that mountain be Balaam's final resting place.

But Balak didn't want to waste their energy on that vermin. He had more pressing issues to deal with. "You need to leave this country right now," he told him sternly. "I promised to pay you well but you did nothing, so you earned nothing. Now get out!"

"That's fine," Balaam said, as though this wasn't the first time he had been told to leave somewhere. "I'm leaving. But before I do, let me warn you. One day, these people will destroy this country." And then he left.

CHAPTER 20

IT WORKS EVERY TIME

Balaam had ridden about ten miles from Moab when he had an epiphany and urgently felt the need to go back. Motivated primarily by financial gain, the thought of returning to Pethor empty-handed turned his stomach. The Lord wouldn't let him curse the Israelites, but he needed and wanted that money badly. So he thought of a way to get the Israelites to bring a curse upon themselves. He knew that *an undeserved curse would not fall on them, but a deserved curse most assuredly would.*[136]

Balaam stopped his donkey abruptly, and his men did the same, thinking that he needed to take a break to relieve himself.

"We're going back to Moab," he told them. They looked at him curiously. "I have an idea," he continued. If it works, I get paid and so do you. If we go home now, we go home with nothing."

---

[136] Proverbs 26:2 (TLB, NIV)

"We've been with you for years, and we have never come up short, so we trust your judgment," said one of them as he motioned with his head towards Moab. Without saying a word, the others nodded in agreement. They traveled quickly and arrived back in Moab sometime later.

When they arrived at the palace, Balak was meeting with his military council. Having faced the hard reality that they were going to have to fight, they were discussing every possible strategy they could think of to defeat the Israelites. One of Balak's servants knocked and walked in, interrupting the session. Balak, knowing that it must have been urgent, ushered him further in.

"Balaam has returned and needs to see you," he said as he bowed.

Balak's eyes widened and his countenance changed as he hoped that Balaam was ready to take the money and curse his enemy, the Israelites. The men in his council also looked encouraged, not wanting to risk their lives in battle if they could avoid it.

"Send him in. Don't keep him waiting," Balak said quickly.

Balaam walked in, bowed before the king and immediately explained why he had returned. "God will not let me curse the Israelites. But there is something you can do to get them to make God curse them Himself. It should not matter to you how they get cursed as long as they are no longer a threat to you," Balaam reasoned.

Balak eyed Balaam suspiciously. "Keep talking. I'm listening," he said.

Balaam continued, "God hates sin."

Before Balak could catch himself, his face showed that he didn't see how a vile hypocrite like Balaam could know or care how God feels about sin.

Balaam saw the visual slight, ignored it and continued. "The Israelites are strictly forbidden to participate in any form of sexual immorality or to eat meat that has been sacrificed to an idol. If you can trick them into engaging in one or both of these sins, God will surely punish them. Hopefully, they won't be in any condition to attack you afterward."

Balak was listening intently and pondering in his mind whether this might work. "How would we get close enough to them to trick them?" he asked.

"We will trick them by appealing to their weakness and catching them off guard. Their men are like all men. They like beautiful women. And Moabite women are some of the most stunning on earth," Balaam said.

Balak nodded in agreement to this irrefutable fact, apparently intrigued by Balak's plan. "Keep talking," he told Balaam.

Balaam continued. "The Israelite soldiers practice for battle and do military exercises every day in the open plain. You should find your most beautiful, seductive shepherdesses and have them pretend to shepherd their sheep nearby. When they get close to the men under the guise of bringing back wandering sheep, they can invite them to a festival. These men have been wandering in the wilderness for years, doing nothing but burying their dead, eating the same disgusting food, and getting ready for the next war. They are bored and ready for something interesting to do."

Balak liked the idea. "Brilliant!" he said emphatically to Balaam. "I believe this plan will work. I will get on it right away. Thank you for your help. I will definitely keep you in mind should I need your services in the future." Somehow, he didn't hate Balaam as much as he had before.

After telling his servant to pay Balaam and show him out, Balak immediately went to work implementing the plan. His chief wife was told to assemble the best-looking shepherdesses in the kingdom. He had never seen them before but when they arrived, even he was captivated by their beauty. He could see how a man caught off guard would jeopardize his own well-being for an opportunity to get to know one of them. To be certain that nothing got lost in the translation, he personally explained to them that they were on a mission to save their lives and their country. He knew that if they had some skin in the game, they would put all of their efforts into making sure the plan worked.

"Our kingdom will be under attack soon, and all of our lives are in jeopardy," he began as he saw the alarm in their faces. He knew they had seen the tents of the Israelites in the open plain but wanted them to know that the Moabites were in immediate danger. "The enemy has just moved next to us. They have conquered every nation around us that they have fought. They have killed the people and taken their land. We cannot let this happen to us. I have chosen you to trick them into coming to one of our festivals and then seducing them. When they succumb to your charms, they will sin against their God and bring a curse on themselves, and we will save our nation."

Balak watched their varied reactions. Some were pleased to be able to help, and others were less enthusiastic about the prospect of being intimate with strangers. But like the idea or not, they all knew that this task was mandated by the king and therefore not optional. Balak then put them in the care of his chief wife who would tutor them in the art of seduction and prepare them to do what was needed to save the kingdom.

Shortly after that, the king's plan was put in place, and it took two days to accomplish. The first night they had an "enticement festival" in the plain near the Israelite camp. It was designed to pique the interest of the male Israelites. Just after dark the Moabites lit torches and assembled for revelry. They put on their most colorful clothes, danced to their most exotic music, ate their fill of tender, succulent meats grilled over open flames and drank wine well into the night. Just as Balak had planned, the Israelites peeked out of their tents with intrigue. They were captivated by the sounds of music and laughter and the delicious smell of foods that most of them had heard of and craved but never tasted. And the word spread amongst them that the Moabites were a people who knew how to have a good time.

The following day, the men came out into the plain, as usual, to practice their military exercises. They trained with swords, spears, and an assortment of other lethal weapons. So engrossed were they in their drills that they did not initially see several sheep wander into their midst.

On cue, the shepherd girls ran in after the sheep, immediately catching the attention of the soldiers. Some wanted to kill them because they were suspicious of their motives. They questioned why foreign women would risk their lives by coming into their camp to retrieve a few sheep. But some of the other soldiers took the bait. They were taken by the women's beauty and even offered to help them round up their sheep. The women pretended to be shy and innocent, so the soldiers thought they were harmless. When they invited them to join them at the festival to be given later that evening, the soldiers didn't hesitate. They were sure that no harm could possibly come of it. Even my son Shemaiah was tempted to go at first. But something told him to go home instead and spend his time constructively, with his family. Little did any of the soldiers know that this night's festival would be different from the one they watched from a distance the evening before.

The word spread quickly throughout the camp that the Moabites were throwing a party, and any man who wanted to come was invited. Just as the king of Moab had predicted, the men were bored with the wilderness and eager for some fleshly indulgences.

When the shepherd girls returned to their city, they reported to the king and his wife that the ruse had worked. The Moabites immediately began preparation for the evening. They sacrificed the meat that would be eaten that night to their god Baal. They even brought him from his temple to the festival area so the Moabites and their guests could bow down and worship him. The beautiful shepherd girls who were shy and unassuming earlier now became seductresses with painted faces, flowing hair, clothes that emphasized their femininity, and come-hither attitudes. The stage was set.

As soon as dark fell, and the music began to play, the male Israelites eagerly walked across the plain in large numbers to join the Moabites. They were each welcomed by a beautiful woman, some of whom were the shepherdesses who had invited them earlier. Immediately the wine began to flow freely, and the men drank the fruit of the vine, goblet after goblet after goblet. They gorged themselves on the delicious meat that had been sacrificed to Baal, without giving a thought to where it had been.

After the Israelites were full, drunk, and incapable of reasoning, the Moabites wheeled Baal into the center of the room. Each of the women walked the man that was with her up to Baal, and the two of them knelt before him. She told him what words to say, and he repeated them. He did not know that he was uniting himself with the Baal of Peor and causing the Lord's anger to burn against all of them for worshipping an idol god.

After enticing the men to worship the statue, the women took the men to their private quarters to engage them in sexual immorality. *The men easily succumbed, not because they were inebriated, but because that is what they were hoping would happen in the back of their minds all along.*[137] *The alcohol just made it easier for them to do what they already wanted to do.*

Most of the men snuck back into their camp during the night after their revelry was over. They thought that their absences had gone unnoticed except to their wives, who were powerless to say or do anything, no matter where they suspected they had been.

What they didn't know was that the Lord had been carefully scrutinizing their every move and was deeply grieved.[138] He alerted Moses to the sin that was taking place in the camp and gave him specific instructions on how to address it. "Tell the men you put in place as judges to go and get all of the leaders who sinned against me," the Lord told Moses. "They are to kill them and expose them for everyone to see. This is their punishment because they committed sexual immorality and bowed down to Baal, another god."

Most of the men who sinned the night before tried to creep back into the camp. But one of them, a leader of a tribe, brazenly walked in at daybreak just as the Israelites were

---

[137] James 1:14-16 (TLB); Proverbs 31:3 (NLT); Proverbs 5:1-23 (NLT)
[138] Psalm 33:13–14 (NIV)

collecting the last of the manna they would need for the day. Everyone, including me, stopped and stared in disbelief as he took one of the Moabite women right past us all and into his tent. I wondered to myself if the man was coming from that Moabite party Shemaiah told me about but had sense enough not to attend.

Totally fed up with the blatant disregard for Him and His commandments, the Lord did not wait until the leaders were publicly executed but dealt with the matter by His own hand. Seemingly out of nowhere, a strong, powerful wind from heaven swept through the camp carrying a deadly plague. All the men, both leaders, and non-leaders, who had slept with the Moabite women and bowed down to the Baal of Peor, turned a deadly gray. They quickly began dropping like flies, in massive numbers, right where they were. *They thought their secret sins had gone unnoticed by the Lord. But they were gravely mistaken.*[139]

One of the priests had seen the leader take the woman into his tent. When he saw how rapidly the men were dying, he thought they would all be dead within minutes if someone didn't do something. Grabbing a spear, he quickly went into the man's tent and drove it straight through the man and the woman, killing both of them instantly. The Lord's anger calmed and immediately the plague stopped. But not before twenty-four thousand men died for the sins the Israelites committed against God.

---

[139] Numbers 32:23(b) (NIV); Galatians 6:7-8 (AMP, NLT)

CHAPTER 21

ONE IS NOT ALWAYS A LONELY NUMBER

Balaam was right. When the Moabites enticed the Israelite men to sin, they brought a curse on themselves, their families, and the entire community. Twenty-four thousand men died, twenty-four thousand women were left alone, and more than twenty-four thousand children were left without fathers, all in one day.

After Bezalel passed away, I suffered from a severe struggle with loneliness. Nothing prepared me for the void left in my soul by Bezalel's death. Even though I had the company of a newborn baby and two other children, I missed the presence of the man I had loved so dearly for so long. I discovered that loneliness had nothing to do with being around people, but about not having the companionship of a human being with whom your soul connects.

When twenty-four thousand men in the camp died, many of the women suffered the same fate as I did. They were alone, which was challenging enough all by itself. But they had children to raise which only added to their distress. It was true that this was not the first time this misfortune had fallen upon the Israelites. Thousands of men died years ago when the Israelites were first sentenced back into the wilderness for their sin. And men were slowly dying off every day. But it wasn't until after Bezalel died that I really understood being alone and raising children without a father. Having personally experienced what they were going through enabled me to understand their dilemma and help them navigate their way through it.

Knowing that I had firsthand knowledge in this area, my friend Shani came to me with a special request.

"How's my baby doing?" Shani asked as she walked into my tent and scooped the baby up off the floor. He squealed and laughed as she kissed him all over his face.

I stopped folding clothes and put my hands on my hips. "That boy really loves you," I said, grateful that my friend had established such a close bond with my son. "Would you check and see if he's wet?" I asked her. "It's probably about time I changed him."

Shani checked his diaper and said enthusiastically, "I can do it." She loved doing even the simplest things for Nathaniel. I handed her a diaper then took another towel out of the basket and folded it while Shani changed him.

"I have a neighbor whose husband just died recently with those men who snuck into Moab that night," Shani began, sounding somber. "She's nine months pregnant with her first child and the baby is due any day now."

I looked up from my folding and gave Shani my undivided attention. I knew that *she was not a gossip, so she never told me anything about anyone else unless she had a good reason.* "The woman is not doing well," Shani continued. "And she's not the only one. This last plague hit the women in the camp almost as hard as it did the men. It was one thing for the men to be dying a few at a time. We had gotten used to that. But twenty-four thousand deaths on the same day were just too many. The women are worried about their future. They feel hopeless, and they need some strong encouragement."

"I'm sure they do," I said, wondering where Shani was going with this. "Are you asking me to go and visit your neighbor and talk to her? I would be happy to do that if you think it would help. I do know a little something about being alone and raising children by myself."

"Yes, it would be great if you could go and see her," Shani told me appreciatively. "She needs someone to talk to who understands how she feels. By the way, have you ever delivered a baby?"

"Uh, no I haven't," I responded, not at all sure how the conversation went from me visiting someone to delivering babies. "Why do you ask?"

"Because the midwives can't keep up with the demand, Shani told me. "A lot of the wives of those men who just died are pregnant and the babies are coming every few days. The midwives need some help. You can come with me and watch the next birth. Then I can walk you through one of your own. You already know more than you think you know because you were there three times when your children were born. This is new to me too. I was never a midwife in Egypt. I just learned it from the Egyptian midwives since we've been here in the wilderness."

I wanted to help, and I felt confident that I could learn anything. I just wasn't sure I wanted to help in that way. Surely there must be something else I could do, I thought.

Sensing my apprehension, Shani said, "Just think about it. We can always come back to this later. If you have the time, I can watch Nathaniel and finish your laundry while you have a word with that young woman I was telling you about."

After finding out the woman's name and where she lived, I headed out. Though I loved my son, I was glad to get out of the tent for a while. Every mother needs some time away from the mundaneness of her family responsibilities. I felt blessed to have a friend that I could trust enough to leave my home with.

When I arrived at the young woman's tent, she was sitting outside with her feet on a stool. "I'm Shani's friend Chaya," I said with a friendly tone of voice. "You look like you're going to have that baby any minute now," I continued, trying to make her feel at ease.

"I don't want to have this baby at all," Brielle said matter-of-factly. "This is not what I planned."

I pulled up a chair and sat across from her to listen intently so I would know what advice to give her. "Do you mean you didn't plan to raise a baby by yourself?" I probed gently, to better understand what she was thinking.

"Yes, but that's not all," Brielle exclaimed angrily. "I didn't plan to have a baby by a man who cheated on me. God killed my husband because he slept with another woman. And he got just what he deserved. I hate my husband for what he did, and I don't want this baby. If I wasn't so far along I would go and see one of those Egyptian doctors and get rid of it. But I can still leave it in the desert after it's born."

This was not at all what I expected to hear. I came emotionally prepared to share my experience with loneliness and single parenthood, hoping that it might provide some encouragement. But the young woman's primary concern was her husband's unfaithfulness. This issue of infidelity was so painful for her that it was foremost on her mind and almost nullified the other issues. I somehow knew that, for the first time in my life, I had to tell someone my story.

"My husband cheated on me too," I told her plainly. She had been looking away as though she was too consumed with her grief to be engaged in our conversation. When I shared my secret, the woman suddenly turned and looked directly at me.

"When I first got married back in Egypt, I was silly in love," I said as I reminisced. "We were both slaves, but we didn't care because we were so happy. At least that's what I thought at the time. My husband worked as an apprentice to a craftsman who custom-made jewelry and other things for Pharaoh. Sometimes he would have to work long hours to finish a job. Well, the craftsman had a daughter who also worked in the shop during the day, cleaning up and keeping the books. One evening it was getting late, and I knew my husband must have been hungry. So I packed some of his favorite foods, put our new son on my back, and went to the shop to surprise him. When I got there, the door was locked but I didn't think anything of it because it was late, and they weren't expecting any more customers. I knocked on the door, but no one answered, which seemed odd. I went around to the back door and found it slightly cracked, so I opened it and went inside. There were no lamps burning, but the setting sun provided just enough light through the windows that I could see. I heard a familiar noise in the back room that made me suspicious. Instead of calling my husband's name, I tiptoed towards the room and peered inside. I will never forget what I saw."

"What did you see?" Brielle asked, now sitting straight up in her chair, enthralled by the story.

"I saw my husband having sex with the shop owner's daughter," I told her, with the image of that scene still fresh in my mind. "I was horrified," I continued. "It felt like my life as I knew it had just unraveled before my eyes. I had a new baby, and his father, the man I loved with all my heart, was having sex with another woman right in front of my face."

"So what did you do?" she asked, eager to hear the rest of the story.

"I couldn't move," I said. "I just stood there as if I was in a trance and watched them. But they were too engaged to even notice I was there. Then the baby began to cry, and my husband looked up and saw me standing by the door. He was even more horrified than I was. He jumped up, put on his clothes and came over to me with a guilty look on his face. By this time, the shop owner's daughter had dressed and walked towards the door as if she was going to leave. But before she did she stopped and said to me, 'Don't be mad at him. This was all my fault. He's a nice-looking man, so I approached him. He kept telling me that he was married, but I kept at him until he finally broke down and gave in. I'm sorry. I never planned to hurt anybody.' Then she left. My husband was standing there, afraid to say or do anything, hoping I believed her. She seemed sincere, but she did not understand that *when people do things they shouldn't do, other people still get hurt even if that's not the plan.* I did believe her, but that didn't change anything. He still cheated on me and ruined my trust in him. Anyway, to make a long story short, we went home, and I didn't speak to him or let him touch me for a week. Then *I finally realized that not forgiving him was destroying me emotionally and spiritually because I was angry and bitter.*[140] *It was also jeopardizing our future. I knew that if I wanted to save my family I had to forgive him, wipe the slate clean and move on."*[141]

"Are you still married to him?" the woman asked, wondering how the story finally turned out.

"We were happily married for over twenty years until he died a few months ago," I told her. *"I can tell you for a fact that it is possible to forgive someone no matter how badly they've hurt you. It doesn't mean you forget what they did. It just means that you choose not to hold it against them or to let it come between the two of you. And you may have to make that same choice every day for a long time."*

"But your husband was sorry for what he did," Brielle told me. "My husband never apologized to me. He just came home in the middle of the night, smelling like some other woman's fragrance. When I asked him where he had been, he wouldn't answer me. He just got in the bed and went to sleep. Then the plague struck him, and he died later that morning."

"Even if my husband hadn't been sorry for what he did, I still had to forgive him for my own well-being," I explained. *"We can't wait for the other person to regret what they did. Sometimes they do regret it, but sometimes they don't. And sometimes they don't even know they hurt us.* In your case, *sometimes they die before the problem even has a chance to be fixed."*

---

[140] Hebrews 12:15(b) (TLB); James 1:19–20 (TLB)
[141] Colossians 3:13 (NIV, TLB)

Brielle sat there for a moment, not saying anything. I waited, giving her a chance to absorb what I had just said. Then she smiled. I could tell that her heart had changed because her face softened.

"So what have you decided to do?" I asked her, wanting to hear her say it from her own mouth.

"I'm going to forgive my husband and keep my child," the woman said with conviction, as though she had made peace with what she knew she had to do.

"Good," I said as I leaned over and gently squeezed her hand. "And there's one more thing. *You need to see this child not as just an obligation, but as a gift from the Lord.*[142] *He has entrusted this life to you, and He wants you to raise him or her to know Him and obey Him from an early age.*[143] *I know that this sounds like a lot of responsibility. But just remember that if you seek Him with your whole heart, He will be a father to your child and a husband to you as well. Make sure that you spend time with Him every day, talking to Him and then listening to hear what He wants to say to you. And be sure that you obey Him in everything.*[144] *Then you can count on Him to give you the guidance and direction you need for every decision.*"[145]

"Thank you for helping me," the young woman said with sincerity. "I feel like my life has just started over. If you have some extra time, I have a couple of friends who need your advice."

"I'll make the time," I promised. "You tell them they can come to me whenever they need to, day or night. I'll always be available."

---

[142] Psalm 127:3 (NLT)
[143] Genesis 18:19 (TLB)
[144] Psalm 68:5 (TLB); Hosea 2:16 (NLT)
[145] Proverbs 3:5–6 (NIV, TLB)

I got up to leave and remembered that Shani had encouraged me to become a midwife because of the great need for them. Seeing the very pregnant woman in front of me and knowing that she could go into labor at any moment convinced me to do what I could to help.

"When you're ready to have that baby, you send for me," I told Brielle, who seemed very pleased. "I want to help you bring this new life into the world."

As I walked home, I realized that my life, like Brielle's, had also just started over; that I had just begun to fulfill my purpose. When Bezalel fell ill, the Lord told me that He put me on this earth to find Him and to lead others to Him. Not sure exactly what the Lord meant at that time, I kept what He told me to myself. But before Bezalel died he told me the same thing God had told me, confirming that that was what I was called to do. I now knew that I was to teach women how to develop an intimate relationship with the Lord and live a life that pleases Him.

Within no time, the women started coming to me for guidance. First two at a time, then five, then more than my tent could hold. I developed a reputation for providing wise counsel. When I asked Moses if we could make use of the school tents in the evenings when the children were not there, he gladly agreed. He was thankful for every opportunity the women had to learn how to walk in the Lord's ways.

They came to the sessions with many questions, longing for information that would make their lives better. They were concerned about not having a man in the house to teach their boys how to be men. They worried about dealing with wayward children who misbehaved at school and were disrespectful and disobedient at home. The burden of having to be both a mother and a father, responsible for everything in their lives and their children's lives with no one to help them, was seemingly impossible. It was surpassed only by the challenge of their loneliness.

Never wanting to give the wrong advice, I always prayed before I spoke so that I would be sure to tell them exactly what the Lord wanted them to hear. I wanted my counsel to be His counsel and not my opinion.[146]

Some of the women would spend the rest of their lives in the wilderness while others were young enough and would live long enough to go into the Promised Land. Some of those might even remarry. *My advice to them was what I had personally lived by after my husband's infidelity. Even though I trusted the Lord to maintain what belonged to me, I knew that my own actions also played a role in keeping my marriage thriving and impenetrable. So I was wise enough to nurture and affair-proof my marriage. To do so, I respected my husband at all times, publicly and privately.*[147] *When a decision had to be made I offered my opinion, but always yielded to him, letting him be the leader of our household. If I questioned his judgment, I took my concern to the Lord and trusted Him to broach the issue with my husband.*[148] *I showed an interest in his work and hobbies. And I was always available to talk to him, listen to him, and do whatever else I could to enrich his life and help him achieve his God-given purpose.*[149] *Knowing that men appreciate physical attractiveness, I kept myself up and went out of my way to be*

---

[146] Job 12:13 (TLB, NIV)
[147] Ephesians 5:33(b) (AMP)
[148] Ephesians 5:22–24 (NIV, AMP)
[149] Proverbs 31:12 (AMP), Genesis 2:18 (AMP, NLT)

appealing at all times.[150] *As a result, our home was the place where he wanted to be.*

But no matter what their circumstances were, I taught them that they must learn to be content in order to be at peace.[151] *My ultimate advice to them was simple. If they would only seek the Lord's face with their whole hearts and obey Him in everything, He was eagerly waiting to be a father to their children and a husband as well to all in need.*[152] *They would find that one is not always a lonely number.*

[150] Proverbs 31:22(b) (TLB, AMP)
[151] Philippians 4:12–13 (TLB)
[152] Psalm 68:5 (NIV); Hosea 2:14–16 and 20 (TLB)

CHAPTER 22

THE INSURRECTION

Moses knew that many of the Israelites hated not only the wilderness but him as well. They were naysayers who opposed his every move. Always dissatisfied with one thing or another, they kept the pot of strife stirred up. He had felt some dissension brewing for a while. It was not so much the blatant actions of some of the leaders as much as the obvious changes in their attitudes. What he did not know, however, was that they were planning an outright mutiny.

Out of the twelve tribes of the Israelites, God chose the Levites to serve Him. They had the awesome responsibility for the Tabernacle, its contents, and the sacrifices that were offered on behalf of the people. However, only Aaron and his descendants were allowed to minister before the Lord as priests in the Holy Place and the Most Holy Place.

Korah, a Levite, and well-known community leader was frustrated and had been ever since the people were sentenced back into the wilderness. He was always jealous of Moses' position as leader of all the Israelites and his relationship with the Lord. The thought of having to submit to Moses until the day he died was more than he could bear. He was always resentful that God had not chosen him instead. After all, he was a descendant of Abraham, just as capable a leader, and just as knowledgeable of the laws, or so he thought. It also irked him that his clan of the Levites was not allowed to serve as priests in the Holy Place. *He was not wise enough to know that God in heaven assigns each man's work and that He alone chooses who will lead His people and in what capacity.*[153] So out of his ignorance and envy, he set out to move Moses out of power.

Surmising that the leaders would be in the best position to overthrow Moses, Korah thought of whom else he knew who hated Moses as much as he did. Dathan from the tribe of Reuben immediately came to his mind. He had seen the way he watched Moses during the meetings Moses regularly held with the leaders. Though he nodded when Moses spoke, he was only pretending that he agreed with him. The look on his face portrayed the disdain that he secretly felt.

One evening Korah went to see Dathan, the most respected and highest ranking leader of the tribe of Reuben. Dathan heartily welcomed him in, thinking that this would be one of their usual social visits. After the customary questions about family, health and overall well-being, Korah asked Dathan a question designed to elicit the exact response he was looking for.

"How would you like to put that disgusting manna aside and eat choice steaks for the rest of your life?" Korah asked with a look of assurance on his face.

---

[153] John 3:27 (TLB, AMP)

"Of course I would," Dathan replied suspiciously. "But the only people who can eat the animals after they have been sacrificed to the Lord are Levites like you.

"Right," Korah said, eager to set the record straight. "We get to eat the meat. But my clan still has to do the nasty grunt work in the Tabernacle. Eating better food does not make up for this. I am a Levite with as much right to enter the Holy Place and Most Holy Place as Moses and Aaron. I'm sick of them. The only reason Moses is in charge is because he put himself in charge. If we can come together as leaders, we can bring both of them down. Then you and the leaders from the other tribes get to sacrifice the animals and enjoy the meat along with us. And all the Levites can wear the priestly garments and perform the priestly work in the Holy Place and Most Holy Place. Don't you see? With them gone, we all come out ahead."

Dathan thought about it for a moment. It was true. He never did like Moses, and it would be nice to eat some meat for a change. He had been tired of eating that manna since the first time he tasted it. It didn't seem fair that only Aaron and his sons could go into the Holy Place and Most Holy Place and do whatever it was they did in there. He was fed up with being treated like a second-class leader with no recognition and no benefits. He was sure the other leaders felt the same way.

"Let's do it," Dathan said as he smiled. "My friend Abiram has as much clout with the leaders of the tribes as I do. I know I can get him to go along with us. Then we'll go to the rest of the leaders. They'll fall in line for sure. And the ones that won't, well that's their loss."

Korah extended his hand to Dathan to solidify their agreement, and he shook it. Then Dathan put his arm around him and walked him out of his tent. As Korah left he muttered to himself, "What an idiot! *You can get a weak and discontented man to go along with just about anything.*" Little did he know it, but the devil was thinking the same thing about him.

Dathan did as he promised and met first with Abiram. Once he was on board, they both went to all the other tribal leaders. Some of them agreed to help overthrow Moses, but others did not. *They understood that God in heaven appoints each person's work. Even if they were not completely satisfied with the duties assigned to them by the Lord, they were wise enough to accept what they had been given or to at least be afraid to participate in the insurrection.* They saw how the Lord promptly killed the ten men who explored the land then came back and spread a bad report, and the twenty-four thousand who committed sexual immorality and worshiped the idol god Baal. So *they did not dare cross Him.*

That very day Korah, Dathan, Abiram and hundreds of other prominent leaders of the community met up and went as a group to remove Moses and Aaron. The two of them were standing outside at the entrance to the Tabernacle when they saw the large group coming. They looked at each other, knowing that trouble was on the way. "We want you to know that we are not happy with your leadership," Korah walked up to them and said. "First of all, you brought us out of Egypt, a land flowing with milk and honey, promising to take us to a better land. But you haven't delivered. All you did was bring us into this wilderness and get us killed. Our men are dying every day because of you."

Moses was appalled at their illogical reasoning. Egypt may have been a land of milk and honey, but it definitely wasn't for them. They must have forgotten that they were slaves there whose daily lives were full of hard work and misery. Rather than see that they were the cause of their own inability to go into the Promised Land and enjoy it, they preferred to blame him.

"Second of all," Korah continued, "We are all Israelites and the Lord is with every person here. So what makes you think you have the right to act like you are more important than the rest of us?"

Moses didn't even bother to respond to their stupid question. *To keep from opening his mouth and saying something he would later regret, he immediately* fell to his knees and *prayed for direction on how to handle the insurrection.*[154] Once the Lord told him what to do, he stood up and spoke to Korah and the other Levites. "Why isn't it enough for you that God has chosen you out of the whole Israelite community to be near Him doing the work in the Tabernacle and offering the people's sacrifices to Him? He has already given you a very special ministry, so why do you want to serve in the Holy Place and the Most Holy Place too? *You need to understand whom you are rising up against. It's* not me and Aaron, but *the Lord Himself.*"[155]

Korah, as though he didn't understand the significance of rising up against the Lord Himself said, "We are tired of doing the grunt work in the Tabernacle. All we do all day is skin animals, cut them up and burn them on the altar. We're sick of the smell of blood and smoke. Then when it's time to move on, we have to take that Tabernacle thing apart, pack it up and carry it to the next place. Then we have to put it back together when we get there. Now how special a ministry is that?"

---

[154] Proverbs 3:5–6 (NLT)
[155] Acts 26:14 (AMP)

Moses knew that *it was fruitless to continue to try to reason with fools*.[156] He had received the Lord's instructions on how to crush the revolt, so he proceeded to put the matter to rest. Addressing Korah and all the rest of his followers, he said, "The only people who can come into the Lord's presence, into the Holy Place and the Most Holy Place, are the ones He selects. Therefore, we will let Him choose. Tomorrow morning all of you are to come here to the Tabernacle entrance. You must put burning coals into an incense burner, light the fire and place incense in it. Aaron will do the same. Then you will all present yourselves before the Lord. We will see whom He chooses to come near to Him. If He chooses you all, so be it. Aaron and I will accept whatever decision He makes."

The insurrectionists looked at each other as if that was easier than they imagined it would be. Since Moses and Aaron did not put up a fight to keep their positions, they thought the Lord was ready to put a fresh face on the priesthood. It was only fair, they reasoned, since Moses and Aaron had occupied those jobs since that Tabernacle thing was built anyway.

Moses was mentally exhausted when he got home that night. He sat down at the table and held his head in his hands, wondering how much more of those people he could take.

Zipporah walked over to him and put her arm around him. Knowing that he must have had one of those days, she asked, "Do you want to talk about it?" He removed his hands from his head, looked up at her and shook his head to say "yes." *She* sat down across from him and *studied his face and body language as he spoke, looking for clues in what he said and didn't say that would help her understand what he was facing.*

---

[156] Proverbs 12:15 (NLT)

Only then would she be able to give him the wise counsel he so desperately needed.

"Hundreds of the leaders came out today to try to overthrow me and Aaron and take over our positions," Moses began. "I tried to rationalize with them but their minds were made up before they got to us. These people have been a problem since before we left Egypt. Sometimes I want to just walk away from all of this."

Zipporah could see that Moses was at his wits end and needed to redirect his thinking and get back on track. She reached out and gently touched his hand and said, "When you talked to the Lord about this, what did He say?"

"He told me to tell them to come back tomorrow, and He would show them who He has chosen," Moses stated. "And I'm sure He will. I know that He has put Aaron and me in these positions, and He will keep us here as long as we obey Him. But what about next week? And the week after that? These people are going to bump heads with us until the day they die. I just don't know if I want to keep going through this. I'm not sure it's worth it."

"Moses," she said softly. "You may be right. These people may oppose you until either they die or you die just because they are contrary and they want to be in charge. But God is not going to give them another leader until He is ready to do so. However, *He will do what He has promised and make it clear to them that He is behind you one hundred percent.*[157] *You're tired right now because you're trying to face this enemy with your own human strength. You need to ask the Lord for His supernatural strength, the kind that will enable you to handle this situation*

---

[157] Exodus 14:5–31 (TLB); Exodus 19:9 and 16–19 (NIV)

and anything else that comes your way successfully.[158] *Now about whether or not this is going to be worth it. You can rest assured that the Lord sees everything you do for Him, and He will compensate you generously in this life and in the next one."*[159]

Moses looked at Zipporah with the utmost admiration and respect. As far as he was concerned, she was the best compensation God could give him this side of heaven. *"Would you please pray for me?" he asked* her. He was too tired to pray for himself, but *confident that she would pray for what he needed and that her prayer would be answered.*

She prayed a sincere, heartfelt prayer, like one he would have prayed. When she finished, his mind was flooded with a perfect peace, and he knew for sure that everything would be alright. That night he slept as soundly as a baby.[160]

The next morning Korah, Dathan, Abiram and hundreds of the leaders who were following them showed up at the Tabernacle entrance. As instructed, they brought their incense burners with them, already lit, releasing a fragrant smell into the air. They had also stirred up the rest of the community against Moses and Aaron so that everyone else was present to watch what they thought would be the changing of the leadership. While they all waited, the glorious presence of the Lord appeared in a cloud for the entire community to see.

Then the Lord said to Moses and Aaron, "Tell everyone to get away from the tents of Korah, Dathan, and Abiram, the leaders of this insurrection. I am going to punish them for this sin." Moses got up and quickly rushed over to their tents, warning the people to move as far away as possible so

---

[158] 2 Corinthians 12:9 (AMP)
[159] Luke 18:29–30 (NIV)
[160] James 5:16(b) (NIV, NLT)

they wouldn't be destroyed. Korah, Dathan, and Abiram heard what the Lord had said to Moses and followed him, fearing for their families. When they got to their tents, they gathered their wives and children and stood outside, wondering how to protect them from whatever was going to happen next.

I was visiting nearby in Shani's tent when we heard a loud commotion. Moses was shouting some warning, and we ran outside in time to see three men standing in front of their tents with horrified looks on their faces. Their families were standing behind them, puzzled as though they had no idea what was going on. Other people were moving back as far as they could.

Moses then addressed the crowd, which included the entire community and the leaders who had risen up against him. "Some of you have questioned whether the Lord has sent me to lead you or whether I appointed myself. If these men die a natural death, you will know that the Lord did not send me. But if the Lord does something out of the ordinary, and the ground opens up and swallows these men alive along with their families and belongings, then you will know that I am in this position because the Lord put me here."

Less than a second after Moses got the last word out of his mouth, the Lord's judgment began. The earth under the three men suddenly split apart. It opened its mouth and swallowed them alive along with their families and everything that belonged to them. Then it closed up without leaving a trace that they had ever even existed. The people who were watching heard them scream as they were snatched from amongst the living. Afraid that the earth would swallow them too, they ran away. As a grand finale, fire blazed outward from the Lord and burned up all the leaders who were offering the incense. He made it irrefutably clear that Moses and Aaron were the ones He had chosen and any attempt to overthrow them would be fatal.

Shani and I were far enough away that we were not sucked into the hole, but close enough that we felt the ground move when the others were. We looked at each other, stupefied. The last time we saw a miracle of this magnitude was the time the Red Sea opened up, and we walked through it on dry ground. The difference was that that miracle was a blessing, and this one was punishment. I only hoped that everyone else who saw it or heard about it understood that *the Lord's faithfulness is a two-sided coin. He is faithful to bless when one obeys Him and faithful to punish when one does not.*[161] *And He has no tolerance whatsoever for anyone who rises up against or tries to overthrow the leadership He has put in place.*

---

[161] Deuteronomy 30:19 (NIV)

CHAPTER 23

THE LAST ONE STANDING

During the middle of the night, the long steady trumpet sound woke me up out of a deep sleep. It had been so long since I heard it that I had to lay there for a moment and remind myself what it meant. Then it came to me. The cloud was going to be moving soon, and it was time for us to move on to the next place. We received the notice very early because there was much to do. Manna had to be gathered and prepared, and animal skins had to be filled so we would have food and water for the journey. The tents had to be taken down. All of our belongings had to be packed. And, above all else, the Tabernacle had to be dismantled with precision by the priests and made ready for travel.

After wandering in the wilderness for almost four decades, we were finally heading back to the Promised Land. A stately woman of nearly eighty, I knew that it was time. I kept track of each one of the thirty-eight years we spent in the desert after being sentenced back to it. During that period, nearly every man in the camp who was twenty years old or older died. And those who had not yet died would be dying very soon. I had lived long enough to see almost all of the old generation pass away and a whole new generation of Israelites take their place.

In fact, the only two people in my family who were left from the old generation were Shemaiah and I. We would never leave the wilderness but would both die soon. We even had a conversation about that stark reality over dinner the night before.

I knew the thought of dying concerned him. Looking into his eyes so he would know and believe what I was telling him, I said, "You have done more good in one lifetime than most people do in one hundred. You can't even count the number of lives you've changed. You taught and mentored many men, including your younger brother. They are excellent husbands, fathers, and leaders. You finished the job that you were put on this earth to do. It doesn't get any better than that does it?"

Shemaiah thought about what I said for a few moments before responding. "No, I guess it doesn't," he said, smiling. "Sometimes when I would see other men with families I wondered what it would have been like to have had one of my own. But over time the Lord gave me a peace about that and I am okay with things just the way they are. So overall, my life has been good. I'm ready to go whenever it's time. My only request is that the Lord takes me before He takes you. I couldn't handle it otherwise."

"Well if that's what you want, that's what we'll ask for," I said, hopeful that God would grant his last request. "But even if He calls me first, we won't be apart for long. I'll see you on the other side real soon." Shemaiah liked that idea. He reveled in it, convinced that the best was yet to come.

The trumpet sounded a second time around mid-morning, letting the camp know that it was time to move out. My entire family was assembled at my tent, ready to go. I led them in a prayer, asking the Lord for His protection during our journey. Then we fell in with the others and began walking.

Sometime later, we arrived in the Desert of Zin, near the Promised Land. The entire journey had been unbelievably long. Since we left Egypt, we traveled hundreds of miles south, deep into the wilderness, to Mount Sinai. It was there that the Tabernacle was built and we were given the Ten Commandments. And it was there that we stayed for a year while we were supposed to learn how to worship, trust, obey and develop an intimate relationship with God. Then we moved on, traveling hundreds of miles, with most of the camp complaining and disobeying Him the entire way. We arrived just outside of Canaan. But because we chose not to do what the Lord required and trust Him, He sent us hundreds of miles back into the desert to learn what we should have learned there before. *We found out the hard way that we had to learn lessons that could only be acquired deep in the wilderness; that until we mastered them, we could not go into the Promised Land and receive all the good things God had waiting for us. Some of the Israelites wasted valuable time wandering around in the desert, making no progress. Others were wise enough to live according to the Lord's Word and His ways.* Finally, after almost forty years, we were back at the edge of Canaan.

By the time we arrived, our water had long since run out. We felt extremely parched and light-headed, like we were dying of thirst. After being on the move for many days, we hoped to find water waiting for us, but there was none.

"We've been through this before, many times," I told my family, not even remotely concerned. "And without fail, the Lord has provided every time. This is just another opportunity for Him to prove His faithfulness. I just hope the people are wise enough to see it that way this time."

While the wilderness had been a place of tremendous spiritual growth for my loved ones, *many others never got it right. No matter how much they were told about right and wrong, and how to respond to adversity, they chose to do the wrong thing anyway – to sin, complain, and doubt God.*[162]

Without fail, some of the Israelites rose up in opposition to Moses and Aaron again. After all those years, some of the people from the old generation were still fixated on Egypt, the land of their slavery. *Their hearts were always looking back to the things they wanted to hold on to – their pet sins, fleshly gratifications, hindering habits – the things that stood between them and God. So they never learned the Lord's ways.*[163] "We wish we had died when the Lord killed all the other Israelites," they said angrily. "We hate this desert. Why did you bring us out of Egypt to this horrible place anyway? Did you bring us out here to die? There are no grapes here, no pomegranates, or figs. And there is no water!"

Moses couldn't believe his ears. *He wondered how on earth the same people could fail the same test every time.*

The Lord told Moses and Aaron to take the staff, gather the people and take us to the nearby rock. While we watched, they were to speak to it, and it would pour out water for us and our livestock to drink.

---

[162] Proverbs 15:10 (NIV, AMP); Proverbs 12:1 (NIV)
[163] Psalm 95:10–11 (TLB, NLT)

Instead of doing exactly as *he* was told, Moses, *out of anger and frustration, let his emotions get the best of him.*[164] When he and Aaron gathered the Israelites together in front of the rock, he shouted, "Listen you rebels! Do we have to bring you water from this rock?" Then, instead of speaking to the rock as he was instructed, he hit it twice with the staff. Water poured out of it, and we and our livestock drank until our thirst was satisfied.

But the Lord was not pleased. He said to Moses and Aaron, "My glory is important to me, and you took the credit for bringing the water out of the rock. Also, you did not believe me when I told you that a word alone was sufficient. So you struck the rock which showed a lack of trust in me. Therefore, neither of you will bring the Israelites into the land I have prepared for them."

Moses and Aaron looked at each other in total disbelief. After forty years of dealing with those wayward people, the only thing they had to look forward to as their earthly recompense was the Promised Land. And *they had let their anger and frustration towards those very people rob them of their reward.*[165]

Suddenly a strong, loud wind blew in amongst the people who had gathered at the rock. It was so forceful that we could barely stay on our feet. When it stopped, everyone who had complained about hating the desert and not having water was dead. The Lord was steadily getting rid of those left from the old generation. *They refused to learn the lessons of the wilderness, to obey Him and trust Him, no matter how many*

---

[164] James 1:19–20 (TLB, NIV)
[165] 2 John 1:8 (NIV, AMP)

opportunities He gave them. Therefore, their final resting place
was the desert.

The very next day, Miriam died without warning. As he did
on a daily basis, Moses went to check on his ailing sister who
was one hundred and thirty years old by this time. When he
got to her tent, she was sitting up in bed with her eyes wide
open as if she died in the middle of a thought. He buried her
in the Desert of Zin, and we moved on.

Once we arrived at our next stop, the Lord made good on
His promise that Aaron would not enter the Promised Land.
According to His instructions, Moses, Aaron and Aaron's son
Eleazar went to the top of a mountain in the sight of all the
Israelites. Moses took off Aaron's sacred garments and put
them on his son who became the high priest in his place. The
Lord put Aaron to death and brought him home to be with
his ancestors. Then Moses and Eleazar came down from the
mountain by themselves. When we were told that Aaron had
died, we mourned for him.

Many other people were also dying within a short period.
It was clear that the Lord was tying up every loose end and
closing out the Israelite's tenure in the wilderness. And it
wasn't just the rebellious Israelites that needed to meet their
end. The Lord still owed one to the Moabites for deliberately
enticing the Israelites to sin and thereby bringing a curse on
themselves.

Shemaiah came home from military practice one day with
an intriguing assignment. "Moses asked to see me today," he
told me. "He wants me to lead a group of men into Moab on
a mission from the Lord. We are to kill all the people and
a so-called prophet named Balaam, who taught the king of
Moab how to get us to curse ourselves. He said that I'm the

best military leader he has, even though I'm the oldest. The younger men may be faster physically, but even at my age I can outwit all of them. The mission shouldn't take long. It'll be over by this time tomorrow night."

Honored that my son would be leading such a mission, and confident that the Lord Himself had chosen him and would grant him success, I smiled. Then I prayed with him before he left.

Later that evening Shemaiah assembled the twelve thousand troops that would accompany him. Moses took the Ark out of the Most Holy Place, and the priests carried it to the front of the army so the Lord could lead them. They left our camp armed and ready for battle and traveled to Moab. When they arrived some of the soldiers skillfully scaled the massive wall which surrounded the city, only to find the guards already dead when they got to the top. They knew the Lord had put the Moabite soldiers to death because they had no wounds. Once inside, they went down to the ground level and opened the door to let the remaining Israelite soldiers in.

Because the entire city was caught off guard, it was easy to overtake them. By the time the Moabites realized that their enemy had invaded their city, it was too late. The Israelites slaughtered them everywhere they found them – in their homes reaching for their weapons, in the streets disorganized and separated from their fellow soldiers and neighbors, and in the king's palace, outnumbered but desperately trying to save the life of their leader.

Within no time, Shemaiah and the dozen men that were with him overpowered the king's guards. After they had been killed, the only thing standing between Shemaiah's men and the king was a large wooden door that led to his private chambers. Stepping over the guard's bodies, they stood six on one side of the door and six on the other, ready for whatever they might encounter. Shemaiah turned the knob and pushed the door open. To his surprise, the once proud, arrogant king was on his knees with his back to the door, praying. At first Shemaiah thought that if he were in Balak's shoes facing death at any moment he would be praying too. As they drew closer and surrounded him, his words became audible. "Oh Lord, God of Israel," Balak said. "Forgive me for the terrible sins that I have committed against you. I have worshiped Baal, a god that is no god at all. I hired Balaam to entice your people to sin and bring a curse on themselves, hoping to save my kingdom. I am guilty, and I deserve whatever punishment you choose. I now know that you are the only living God, and I beg you to forgive me and have mercy on me. If you do, I will serve you for the rest of my life."

When Shemaiah and the soldiers heard what he was saying they looked at each other, wondering if the king was sincere or if this was just a ruse to save his life. Their swords were drawn and ready to be driven into him at a moment's notice. Not wanting to kill a repentant man if the Lord might want to spare him, nor be tricked by a ruse, Shemaiah looked up to heaven for direction.

"Spare his life," the Lord said immediately, clearly heard by everyone present including the king. "His heart is sincere. I will use him as a testament of my mercy to draw other nations to myself. *I want everyone to know that I accept people from every nation who fear me and obey me.*" As soon as the Lord finished speaking, the soldiers put their swords back in their sheaths. Balak bowed low to the ground and thanked the Lord for His compassion. When he finished, Shemaiah extended his hand to him and helped him up. Then he hugged him, welcoming him as a brother in the faith. "You need to leave here now," Shemaiah told him. "Take the underground tunnel out of the city. From there, go wherever I Am sends you and do exactly what He tells you. He will soon reveal to you what He wants you to do for Him."

Shemaiah and his men slipped out of the palace as swiftly and undetectably as they had entered it. Back in the streets, they saw their other soldiers eliminating what remained of the Moabites. They asked a lone woman where they might find a man named Balaam. She gave them directions to a shop with several rooms that served as a brothel, located in a seedy part of town. She was sure that they would find him there since he owned it and regularly partook of its services. After taking several twists and turns down dim, narrow alleys, they finally stumbled upon his place of business. Ironically, when they found him, he was engaged in the very activity with a woman that, through his advice, the Israelites were enticed into and cursed for. Without hesitation, they ran them both through with their swords multiple times. Balaam learned *two lessons* the hard way – *when one sets out to curse another, they bring a curse on themselves.*[166]*And the person who causes another person or persons to sin can be sure to incur God's wrath.*[167]

After accomplishing their mission, Shemaiah had one of the men with him sound the trumpet to rally the rest of the soldiers. They met outside the city gate. Inside, all of the Moabites had been killed except king Balak, whom the Lord spared.

---

[166] Galatians 6:7 (NIV)
[167] Matthew 18:6–9 (NLT)

As soon as they arrived back at the camp, Shemaiah went straight to Moses to give him an update. When he arrived at his tent, he saw him sitting at the table talking to Zipporah. She saw Shemaiah first and nodded towards the door to let Moses know that he had a visitor. Seeing Shemaiah, he got up quickly and went outside, eager to know how things went.

"Well?" Moses asked Shemaiah.

"Mission accomplished," Shemaiah told him confidently. "All of the Moabites are dead, and so is Balaam. Not one of our men were killed or even wounded. We would have killed Balak but when we found him in his palace, he was confessing his sins and asking God for forgiveness and mercy. The Lord told me to spare him because He wants to use him, so I did."

"That's great news!" Moses exclaimed. "This is the third time during our journey that I've seen the leader of a foreign nation turn their heart towards the Lord. First, it was Pharaoh from Egypt. He sent me a message not long after we left there to tell me that the plagues and the destruction of his entire army convinced him that I Am is the only living God. Then it was Jethro from Midian and now Balak from Moab. *The Lord truly wants to be the God of all people in every nation.*"[168]

When Shemaiah returned home, he told me that his mission had been successful. I was happy that the Lord had given victory to the Israelites and safely returned my firstborn to me. But I also had an uneasy, foreboding feeling. An uncomfortable thought kept trying to make its way to the front of my mind, but I pushed it back just as quickly. Then finally I let myself come to terms with what I already knew

---

[168] Revelations 5:9 (NIV)

was going to happen. Shemaiah had completed his purpose for this life, and it was time for him to leave.

I called my entire family to come and have one last meal with Shemaiah. When they arrived, he already knew why they were there because the Lord had told him earlier. They laughed and talked with him just as if he were going on a trip, fully expecting to see him again one day.

When they left, Shemaiah and I sat outside enjoying the warm evening air and each other's company one last time. After a long period of comfortable silence, I looked over, and he was gone. The Lord had answered our prayer and taken him before me.

Within a short period, Moses had performed the last rites for his sister Miriam, his brother Aaron, and Shemaiah, his honored servant. Even though Moses was the youngest of his mother's children, he outlived them all. And he grieved equally as much for Shemaiah, who had contributed so much to the community. He trained multitudes of young boys to become Godly men, and he led the effort to annihilate the Lord's enemy, the Moabites. Even though death was common in the wilderness, Moses deeply felt the passing of these three.

Then it was Moses turn. After he had faithfully served the Lord and completed every task he was given, the hour of his home-going had arrived. He anointed Joshua, a young man whom the Lord had chosen, to lead the new, young generation of Israelites into the Promised Land. Finally, Moses kissed his beloved Zipporah one last time and climbed to the top of a nearby mountain as God instructed him. There the Lord ended his life and buried him in an unmarked grave. We mourned deeply for him, the only man amongst us who the Lord knew face to face.

Early one morning while I was praying, an incredible peace came over me like none I had ever felt before. The Lord spoke to me as plainly as if He were standing right next to me and said, "Put your house in order. You will be coming home today." I smiled to myself, pleased that He had given me time to properly close out my life on this earth. I could now ensure that those I left behind would live their lives committed to do and be what they were destined for.

A great-grandmother by this time, I was the matriarch of a large, close-knit family. Mychal was a married mother of three with seven grandchildren. Even Nathaniel, the baby of the family, was a father with four children of his own. Shemaiah never married and had children. But he had been a father figure to countless young boys in need, all of whom became or were becoming fine men. All of my children's lives turned out exactly like their father had foretold.

After sinning against God the first time, my husband and I were determined that we would get it right the second time around. *Instead of wasting opportunities for growth, we applied everything we learned, took advantage of every opportunity to obey, trust, and draw near to God and, as a result, our family flourished in the wilderness.*[169] Our children were healthy, thriving, and living the lives the Lord purposed for them to live. And they would all either go into the Promised Land and continue our family's legacy or, in Shemaiah's case, prepare others to go in.

So in preparation for my departure, I called my family to me, and *I did what a true matriarch should do. I spoke to them individually, imparting the priceless spiritual wisdom they*

---

[169] Ephesians 5:15–16 (NIV, AMP)

needed to remember in order to continue to walk with God and to fulfill His purpose for their lives. I prepared them to go in and take full possession of the Promised Land that the Lord had predestined for them[170] *and the faithful few.*

Then I recounted to my family how the Lord had enabled me, because of my faithfulness, to outlive almost everyone from the old generation of Israelites. Except for Joshua and Caleb, who spied out the land and trusted God in spite of the giants they saw, I was the last one standing. I told them that *I had lived a long, abundant life even though I lived most of it in the desert; that incredibly, my wilderness experience ultimately made my life rich and fulfilling.* I passionately testified, declaring to them, *"In the wilderness I suffered painful, heart-wrenching trials that drove me to the Lord. Because of those trials, I learned the necessity of spending quality time alone with Him every day, listening to His voice and cultivating a relationship with Him. It was in the wilderness that I learned to pray without ceasing, to talk to Him moment by moment about everything in my life. The dry, barren desert was the place where He taught me how to trust Him deeply even at times when things did not make sense, and I didn't know what to think or do. During the lingering struggles He taught me patience, which enabled me to keep going long after I wanted to quit. Through that same patience, I grew to be content; to want only what He wanted for me, in His perfect timing. It was in the wilderness that I learned how to obey Him even when my flesh did not want to. In the midst of agonizing hardships, He taught me how to truly worship Him out of love and devotion, in spite of my difficult circumstances, learning that genuine praise eliminates despair.*

---

[170] Proverbs 31:26 (NIV)

The hot, parched desert was the place where He prepared me to serve Him by teaching me compassion for others through my own suffering. Only then could I fulfill my purpose, which was to lead you and others to Him. It was in this same wilderness where so many lost their way that I triumphed over every circumstance and grew to become spiritually mature. Then, in that desolate, empty place, the Lord revealed Himself to me. There He taught me how to live in His Presence by becoming one with Him in thought, action, and purpose. Everything I experienced in the wilderness worked together for my good!"

So even though I never physically entered the Promised Land, I entered His rest, into a state of peace and tranquility that resulted from my heart being deeply and firmly established in my Lord. Before I closed my eyes for the last time, I praised God that the wilderness experience, which began as a bitter cup, left an amazingly sweet aftertaste.

CPSIA information can be obtained
at www.ICGtesting.com
Printed in the USA
FSHW01n1420110918
52191FS

9 781490 886794